Your Body Speaks Your Mind

**Other books by
Debbie Shapiro**

THE BODYMIND WORKBOOK

THE BREAD BOOK

THE HEALER'S HAND BOOK
Georgina Regan and Debbie Shapiro

THE METAMORPHIC TECHNIQUE
Gaston Saint Pierre and Debbie Shapiro

OUT OF YOUR MIND – THE ONLY PLACE TO BE!
Eddie and Debbie Shapiro

THE WAY AHEAD
Edited by Eddie and Debbie Shapiro

A TIME FOR HEALING
Eddie and Debbie Shapiro

Your Body Speaks Your Mind

Understand how your thoughts and emotions
affect your health

Debbie Shapiro

PIATKUS

I dedicate this book to all my teachers,
both past and present.
May all beings be free from suffering.

For the latest news and information on all our titles
visit our website at www.piatkus.co.uk

First published in 1996 by
Judy Piatkus (Publishers) Ltd
5 Windmill Street, London W1P 1HF
e-mail: info@piatkus.co.uk

Reprinted 1998 (twice)
Reissued 2000

The moral right of the author has been asserted

A catalogue record for this book is
available from the British Library
ISBN 0-7499-1595-1 pbk

Edited by Kelly Davis
Designed by Chris Warner
Illustrations by One-Eleven Line Art

Set in Sabon by Computerset, Harmondsworth
Printed & bound in Great Britain by Mackays of Chatham plc

CONTENTS

Acknowledgements

I would like to thank the many people who have contributed their stories to this book: Christine Evans, Padma O'Gara, Jenny Britton, Leela the Clown, Steve Hennessy, Karuna King, John Taylor, Cheryl and Sheila, and the many others whose stories there was just no room for. I deeply appreciate your honesty and openness.

I would also like to thank my husband, Eddie Shapiro, for his unbelievable patience, constant support and enduring love. His contribution to this book is incalculable.

──INTRODUCTION──

Human beings are extremely good at inventing unbelievably complicated pieces of technology and stunningly beautiful designs, at
understanding detailed scientific theories or producing majestic
musical compositions. As a race, we have developed, and continue
to develop, our mental and creative capacities beyond every
limitation. But there is one area where our understanding falters.
This is in relation to ourselves, and in particular to our bodies.
Although we can tour outer space and surmise how the universe
began, we are unable to agree on how the body works. A great
number of different approaches to understanding the body have
developed over the last few thousand years, each totally valid in its
own context, yet differing vastly from each other.

In the West most people believe that the body is a thing: a machine
that needs to be fuelled (with food and water) and exercised in the
hope that this will stop it going wrong. We greatly enjoy the pleasure
the body gives and work hard to keep it looking good. If something
in this machine does go wrong then it can be mechanically repaired.
Difficulties are cured with surgery, radiation therapy or drugs – the
offending part is cut out or eliminated with chemicals – and life goes
on as before.

In this context, Western medicine (allopathy) has worked
wonders. It is extraordinary when we consider the breakthroughs
that have occurred: the development of penicillin and vaccinations,
laser surgery and organ transplants, to name but a few. Medical
science has saved millions of lives and dramatically reduced
suffering. Modern understanding of the body machine and the ways
in which it can go wrong is undeniably impressive.

However, allopathy does not always work. Sometimes the side
effects of drugs cause worse complications; other difficulties may
emerge even if the original cause is cured; or the problem might go
beyond the bounds of medicine – there may simply be no available
cure. For instance, illnesses related to stress are numerous and their
incidence is rapidly rising. Maladies directly caused by stress include
migraine headaches, ulcers, irritable bowel syndrome, high blood
pressure, asthma, muscle tension, and fatigue; and those that cause

stress include cancer and multiple sclerosis. Allopathy does not have a cure for stress. Modern medical understanding does not acknowledge the influence of a patient's mental or emotional state on their physical wellbeing, so none of these stress-related ailments can be cured. Yet up to 70 per cent of patient visits to the doctor are for stress-related illnesses.

In Hippocrates' day, a physician took into account not just the physical symptoms but also the climate, race, sex, living conditions, social and political environment of the patient. Even before the Second World War, a family doctor was exactly that – someone who knew and treated the whole family, perhaps using herbs or counselling alongside more recently discovered medicines. After the war, as technology exploded the boundaries of understanding, so doctors had to start specialising in specific fields. Thus a family doctor was no longer a psychotherapist or counsellor – that was someone else's job. And, with an increase in population and demand, doctors were soon left with no time to do more than write prescriptions. Instead of a personal relationship, modern medicine encourages an impersonal transaction based on fixing the machine.

This mechanistic approach has left us with a void in our relationship with our bodies. We can apply corrective procedures to repair many of the things that go wrong. But we do not have any sense of *living* inside this machine or of the energy that makes it work.

In the East, particularly in China and Japan, we find a very different approach. Far from seeing the body as a machine, people view it as an energy system. This understanding is far older than the Western model – it dates back at least 5,000 years – and has proved to be extremely effective in curing illness and disease. Eastern medicine is based on detailed maps of energy that flow through the body. These maps chart the type of energy flow, as well as where and how to access it. Each patient is also diagnosed according to the elements: earth, water, wood, metal and air, as each is said to have a specific effect, both positive and negative. Illness is recognised as an imbalance or blockage in the flow of energy caused by poor habits, stress or negative emotions; balance is therefore sought through adjusting the energy flow.

While allopathy says the patient is a machine, acupuncture (and related healing methods) says the patient is an energy system that is alive and constantly changing. Rather than pointing the finger at outside causes when something goes wrong, we need to look at outside influences *and* the circumstances of the patient's life, mind set and feelings, and at how they interact. In *The Web That Has No Weaver*, Ted Kaptchuk highlights the difference when he explains that an allopathic doctor will ask 'What X is *causing* Y?' while the acupuncturist will ask, 'What is the *relationship* between X and Y?'

There are also cultural and religious factors which help to explain the development of the Western approach to medicine. In early Christianity the body was seen as something that threatened one's moral virtue. Lust and desire were unacceptable and had to be repressed, or released only in dark or secret moments. There are wonderful descriptions of the early missionaries who went to persuade the wild and sinful people of Hawaii that they needed to be saved. In the blistering heat of the tropics the missionaries preferred to stay dressed in layers of dark wool clothing rather than expose their bodies to the sun and run the risk of exciting their lust. Surrounded by the brown and laughing Hawaiians, happily naked or barely clothed, many of these missionaries died from the heat and bacteria generated beneath their garments.

For hundreds of years the Church was considered to own man's soul, and so physicians – rather than be judged heretics or witch-doctors – created a separation of the body and the mind. From this disassociation grew the belief that the body was simply a machine which was not subject to any psycho/emotional influence.

This is completely different from traditional Native American culture where a doctor is seen as a doctor of the soul as well as of the physical body. Here there is no separation of mind and form. Although he may have no formal medical training, the shaman or witchdoctor learns how to interpret everyday events as well as the 'other world' in order to understand the specific causes of illnesses.

In other cultures the body is revered as the vehicle through which we are able to develop beyond our personal limitations. In both Buddhism and Hinduism great value is placed on the preciousness of human life, in the belief that it is only in a human form that we can achieve true spiritual fulfilment. Sickness is seen as being both of the mind and of the body, for ultimately both mind and body are limited, impermanent, temporary. The medicine the Buddha offered is that which leads to complete freedom, beyond the bounds of the physical.

Into this picture of the body – as just a machine or as a vehicle for enlightenment – comes another dimension. The last few years have seen a growing recognition in the West of the direct relationship between the mind and the body, known as psychoneuroimmunology. This understanding does not deny the organic causes of illness – germs, bacteria and micro-organisms cause disease, as do toxic waste, radon gas or genetically inherited illness. Yet not everyone in the office falls sick when 'flu is doing the rounds, and a disease does not have the same effect in every afflicted person. It appears that our emotional or psychological state greatly influences the onset and passage of illness, as well as the ability to heal. 'Medicine is beginning to see that the origin of disease cannot be spoken of without including life-style, diet, social milieu, the environment, and, perhaps most interestingly, consciousness and the emotions,' writes Marc Ian Barasch in *The Healing Path*.

This book looks at how the mind and body affect each other, and the many ways we can work with both the mind and the body to bring about healing and personal growth. This is a new area to be explored, with more information becoming available every day – it is fascinating to see the intricacies of the bodymind relationship unfold. At last we are beginning to understand the human machine as a living, breathing, communicating, multifaceted, interrelated whole.

My fascination with the bodymind relationship began 20 years ago when I first started to work with nutrition and massage. In the beginning I felt as if I was slowly discovering different pieces that, when put together, created this extraordinary map of the physical body with another, underlying, map of the psyche and emotions. My aim in this book is to enable you to read your own bodymind map for yourself.

Part One should be read straight through as it explores the understanding behind the bodymind, particularly the myriad ways in which the mind and body inter-relate. Part Two looks at how we can use this understanding to bring healing, whether through the use of positive mind states, visualisation, meditation, art therapy, dance or expressive movement.

Part Three should be used as a healing guide. If you have an illness or particular concern, then first read the opening section of the relevant chapter. This explains the intricacies of that particular area. Next read about your specific concern. In this way, you will gain a deeper insight and a more complete picture of your bodymind relationship. There may also be other areas of the body that are connected, for no one part of our being is independent or unrelated, so cross-refer to any other chapters that are relevant.

I sincerely hope you discover the same excitement that I have found as you explore your bodymind. In understanding the interconnectedness of the many aspects of ourselves, so the interconnectedness between all beings – between all life – becomes clearer. Our world is built upon relationship and communication. May this understanding bring you health and happiness!

Debbie Shapiro
Devon, 1996

PART ONE

FINDING MEANING IN THE MIDST OF CHAOS

1

MIND OVER MATTER

NORMALLY the body and mind are seen as two separate systems, functioning, for the most part, independently. We feed and water the body, take it for walks or give it exercise, and enjoy its sensory capabilities. Likewise we feed the mind with thoughts, ideas and concepts, exercise it with intellectual pursuits, and amuse it with various sorts of entertainment.

We may be aware of simple connections between the body and mind, as when we feel nervous or excited and break out in a rash or become nauseous, or when we exercise and feel emotionally elated. But when it comes to more complex emotions or illnesses we do not usually believe this relationship to be very important. As there are obvious physical causes for illnesses, why should states of mind have anything to do with them? Emotions may influence our nerves, but how can that be relevant when faced with real illness? As Geoffrey Cowley put it, in *Newsweek* magazine:

> *People may not be surprised that they blush when they are embarrassed, that a frightening thought can set their hearts racing or a sudden piece of bad news can throw all their systems temporarily out of whack. Yet they find it hard to believe that mental abstractions like loneliness or sadness can also, somehow, have an impact on their bodies.*

The purpose of this book is to explain the enormous importance of this relationship. During the past ten years there has been a great deal of research showing how the mind and body respond to each other, demonstrating that emotional and psychological states translate into altered responses in the chemical balance of the body, particularly in the immune system. This new field of scientific inquiry is known as psychoneuroimmunology (PNI). And just as the immune system is affected by psycho/emotional states, so other parts of our bodies, such as the circulatory, digestive and nervous systems, are equally affected, thus determining our overall state of health.

─────── TRY IT YOURSELF ───────

The Effect of Thoughts

Here is a simple exercise that shows the effect thinking has on the physical body. You need a partner to do this with.

- Stand at right angles to your partner. Hold your right arm (or left arm if you are left-handed) straight out in front of you at shoulder height. Your partner than puts his or her hand on your outstretched wrist. Now put your energy into holding your arm steady and resisting while your partner tries to push your arm down. The aim is to find your natural level of resistance – there is no need for your partner to apply force. Then relax.

- Now close your eyes and, just for a moment, think of a situation or person that creates an unhappy, sad or upset feeling in you. When you get this feeling, stick your arm out and resist your partner trying to push your arm down. Then relax.

- Now think of something that makes you feel really good and that brings you joy. When you have that feeling of happiness, stick your arm out and once more resist your partner trying to push your arm down. Then relax. If you want, you can now change places and do this to your partner.

Most people notice an immediate difference between the different arm tests. They find that when they have upsetting or sad thoughts and feelings there is no ability to resist, as if all the energy has been taken out of their arm. Yet when they focus on joyful thoughts and feelings, the arm becomes very strong and easily resists. Often the arm will be stronger than when they first started the exercise. The extraordinary thing is how *quickly* the thoughts and feelings are translated into a physical response.

My own family doctor, practising in a small town, estimates that more than 50 per cent of his patients have physical problems caused by emotional difficulties. Emotions have energy. And this energy does not just disappear when it is held back or repressed. When we cannot, or do not, express what is happening on an emotional or psychological level, that feeling becomes *embodied* (we take it deeper within ourselves) until it manifests through the physical body.

Is there any real difference between one part of our being and another? Perhaps the only difference is the means of expression. H²O exists as water, steam, rain, sea, cloud or ice, yet is still H²O; in the same way our feelings are expressed through our behaviour and actions, our voices, or through different systems within our bodies but they are the same feelings. If damage to one part of our being is repressed or ignored then it can manifest as damage in another part. Having been rejected by your lover, you walk out and hit the door, bruising your arm. Isn't the pain in your arm expressing your feelings of anger or confusion at being pushed away? In his film *Manhattan*, Woody Allen brilliantly captures this intricate relationship. When his girlfriend, played by Dianne Keaton, announces that she is leaving him for another man, Allen does not respond. Keaton wants to know why he isn't angry. 'I don't get angry,' Allen replies, 'I grow a tumour instead.'

♦ THE STRESS FACTOR ♦

The most obvious way in which the mind adversely affects the body is through stress. For instance, imagine you are trying to squeeze some toothpaste out of a tube but you have forgotten to take the top off (or to flip the lid). What happens? It has to find some other way out. This usually means that the toothpaste emerges from the bottom of the tube, or perhaps forces a hole in the side – whichever is the weakest point.

Now imagine that the tube of toothpaste is you. You are under pressure and beginning to experience psychological or emotional stress. But you do not take your lid off, as it were, by recognising what is happening and making time to relax or deal with your inner conflicts. So, what happens to the mental or emotional pressure building up inside you? Eventually it has to find a way out and if it can't come out through the top (by being expressed and resolved), it will come out somewhere else. It will find the weakest point, whether through your digestive system, your nerves, your immune system or your sleep patterns. Pushed down, it becomes illness, depression, addiction or anxiety; projected outwards, it becomes hostility, crime, prejudice or aggression.

In itself, stress is neither good nor bad. It is how we respond or react to stress factors that makes the difference. For some people, stress causes elation and an increased sense of purpose; they rise to the situation assertively. For others, stress creates panic, chaos, lethargy, depression or fear. Faced with a deadline, one person may find it spurs them on to greater creativity, while another becomes frozen into inactivity. This latter response can be particularly devastating to our health.

It is everyday stress that affects us most deeply by slowly grinding away at our inner reserves. The fight-or-flight response enables us to respond to danger but it is not just major life-threatening situations that stimulate this response. Fearful or anxious thoughts do it too: the car not starting, being late for an appointment, unpaid bills, arguments with your partner, your children or your boss – all these can create a stress response. Joan Borysenko puts it well in *Guilt is the Teacher, Love is the Lesson*:

> *The fight-or-flight response is like the overdrive on a car. It comes in handy to get us out of occasional tight spots, but if we keep the car in overdrive all the time, the wear and tear on its parts will cause a variety of mechanical problems. In people, these problems are commonly called stress or anxiety-related disorders.*

Seemingly unimportant events can cause a stress reaction because the body is unable to tell the difference between real and imagined threats. When we focus on our fears about what might happen, it plays as much havoc with our hormones and chemical balance as when we confront a dangerous situation in real life. For instance, try remembering a gruesome scene from a horror movie and feel the muscles in your back, shoulders or stomach contract. Or visualise yourself on the beach on a warm, sunny day, and feel your body relax. If you imagine you are running, your nerves and muscles will produce a responsive movement. The images are just in your mind, yet they trigger an instant response in your body.

Feelings have a deeply stressful effect, especially if they are repressed. Being pushed or squeezed in the rush hour, continual bad weather, coping with an ill child, a dispute with the neighbours – our response to all these situations has to be contained, for society does not permit us to react by screaming or throwing a tantrum.

Suppressing the normal fight-or-flight response in this way means that the chemicals coursing around the body have nowhere to go. How are they to dissipate? How are they to find expression?

Some of the physical symptoms that indicate excessive stress are: headaches, high blood pressure, heart palpitations, heavy breathing, disturbed sleep, loss of appetite, nausea, dry mouth, ulcers, diarrhoea, backache, excessive sweating, rashes and hives. Alongside these, there may be psychological changes such as depression, anger, rapid mood changes and anxiety. We may also find impaired concentration, memory loss, an inability to make decisions, confusion, irrational fears, self-consciousness, or family and marital problems. Behavioural changes may include sloppy dressing, fidgeting, sudden outbreaks of tears, over-indulgence in habits such as smoking or drinking, phobias and impaired sexual performance. This is quite a list, and many of these symptoms can easily lead to more serious states of ill-health.

The link between psychological stress and physical problems is perhaps best illustrated by research, cited by Dr Larry Dossey in *Healing Breakthroughs*, which suggests that more heart attacks occur on a Monday than on any other day of the week – and not only on a Monday but most often at 9 o'clock in the morning. No other animal dies more frequently on a particular day of the week. If we believe that there is no connection between the mind and the body, then what causes so many heart attacks to take place just as the first work of the week is about to begin? Certainly there are physiological reasons why death might be more likely in the morning than in the afternoon, such as higher heartbeat rates or blood pressure, or adrenaline surging in preparation for the day ahead. But there is no reason why so many more deaths should take place on a *Monday* rather than any other day.

Job Dissatisfaction

Research conducted in 1972, by the Department of Health, Education and Welfare in Massachusetts, showed that job dissatisfaction was the leading predictor for heart disease. Further research conducted by Dr James E. Muller of Harvard Medical School showed that not just heart attacks but also strokes were most common between 8 and 9 am; while Dr Paul Ludmer examined the times of death for all people who had suddenly died in Massachusetts in 1983 and found twice as many occurring at 9 am as they did at 5 pm.

Obviously job dissatisfaction does not always result in death! But the relationship between job dissatisfaction and physical problems cannot be underestimated – millions of working days are lost each year due to the effects of stress. A study carried out in America by Dr Norman Beale found that redundancy (or the threat of it) led to a 20 per cent increase in visits to doctors and a 60 per cent rise in hospital visits.

Padma O'Gara's story shows how badly one's health can be affected by the stress of being in the wrong job:

> I had suffered from low back pain for many years with pains down my legs. Doctors told me it was wear and tear. I managed to contain it through practising yoga and was even able to teach yoga on a part-time basis, my main job being in the management sector of the Careers Service. Then in 1990 I started to have trouble with my eyes, I kept losing vision and it was quite painful. I lost my vision for three weeks and was told it was glaucoma. Leading up to all this was a feeling that I was wasting my time in my job, that I should be teaching more, rather than attending endless meetings at work. In the process of having two operations on my eyes I thought that I should give up work but I did not trust that I would manage financially. On returning to work my black flared up very badly and I was in considerable pain.
>
> A few months later I was given a proverbial push up the backside! I was driving on the motorway when something hit me very hard from behind. I never saw what it was but it knocked the car out of control and my foot seemed to jam on the accelerator. I was going faster and faster. I thought I was going to die. I found myself promising that if I lived I would give up my job and be true to my heart by teaching yoga. Immediately I felt the accelerator lift and the car come under control.
>
> The next week I gave in my notice. Since then I have built a teaching practice and have thankfully not noticed the financial change. What I have noticed is that my back problem is now non-existent and my eyes are fine. Finally I feel that I can see where I am going and it is in the right direction.

Life Changes

Stress doesn't only occur at work. It can arise at many times and in many different ways. In particular there is the stress caused by major life changes such as moving house, getting married, or losing a loved one. At these times we may experience tremendous uncertainty and fear, nervous excitement or overwhelming sadness. Emotions contract the muscles and blood vessels, heighten the release of hormones such as adrenaline, affect digestion and breathing, and weaken the immune system, leaving us vulnerable to illness and breakdown.

When I was eight years old I went to boarding school – an experience I was not too thrilled about. Within a few weeks I had developed tonsillitis. In those days having your tonsils removed meant staying in hospital for a week. After that I had a week at home, eating nothing but mashed potatoes and jelly – good comfort foods! What those two weeks really did was reconnect me with home, security and a sense of belonging. I then returned to school without further mishap. Looking back, I can see that I was finding my circumstances really hard to swallow. The nature of the illness – swollen glands and a sore throat – indicated that I was having a hard time accepting the reality of being at boarding school.

At the turn of the century, Dr Adolph Meyer asked his patients to list times when they had experienced major life changes. He then correlated this information with the dates of illnesses and physical problems in the same patients. From this came the finding that too many life changes occurring at one time can result in physical as well as emotional trauma. In the 1960s, this research was continued by Dr Thomas Holmes and US Navy psychiatrist Richard Rahe. After interviewing more than 5,000 patients they compiled a list of stressful events, allocating a rating to each one. The more events with a high rating experienced over a short period of time, the greater the likelihood of physical illness. Top of the list are death of a partner, divorce, illness, accident, moving house and loss of a job.

This research clearly indicates that illness can develop following trauma. However it does not take into account the different ways in which people may react to the same event. For instance, for some people divorce (second on the list, after death of a spouse) is a time for celebration, while for others it is a time of loneliness and depression. Likewise, while some will rejoice in moving house, others will see it as a time of loss and insecurity. Trauma does not necessarily equal illness but unexpressed fears and anxieties surrounding trauma can lead to physical problems. Obviously we cannot avoid crisis. What we *can* do is become more conscious of our feelings and try not to repress or deny them. Acknowledging and releasing our feelings as they arise, or as soon as possible afterwards, is essential.

Steve Hennessy changed almost every aspect of his life and subsequently became ill, partly because he hadn't expressed his real feelings about those changes:

> Twelve months before getting ill I had moved from the town where I had lived all my life, leaving behind family, friends, a job, and alcohol – my adult companion. I had also separated from my partner and was moving in order to set up home with a new partner. There wasn't much more I could change! Everything was different – my surroundings, work, social life, lover, and I was different, confronting myself in totally new ways. I viewed all these changes as very positive but knew that they formed a major upheaval from which I might suffer a backlash.
>
> The illness started with severe colic pains. I was incapacitated with exhaustion and energy loss. It was eventually diagnosed as irritable bowel syndrome. During the acute phase, which lasted three months, I ate very little and lost 2 stone in weight.
>
> On reflection the illness makes complete sense. Prior to moving I had spent my time looking after others (in the Social Services) and always putting others first. My move was to allow myself something good – to give to myself. I actually found it 'difficult to digest' this change, difficult to allow myself the good things. Superficially I had moved to a happier life, but on a deeper level I was still struggling to resolve all the restrictions I had lived with for so many years previously. The illness provided me with a chance to see what was going on, to look at those deeper levels. I feel I have been profoundly changed, that I am far more in touch with myself.

The Army Within

Stress has a direct effect on the immune system, lowering our ability to destroy invading viruses and bacteria. The immune system is sometimes described as an army because it fights to protect us against invasion or illness. Stress simulates the release of various hormones to provide extra coping energy but two of these hormones – adrenaline and cortisol – also inhibit the immune system.

For instance, the stress of exams can depress the immune response which in turn increases the likelihood of catching a cold or 'flu. 'Has it ever struck you as unfair that glandular fever likes to attack young people at examination time?' asked Dr Trisha Greenhalgh in *The Times* (June, 1994). 'In the past three weeks, I have seen half a dozen of the brightest and best take reluctantly to their beds with burning tonsils, swollen glands and an overwhelming miserable lethargy. They were all within a month of GCSEs or A levels.'

You may have noticed something like this yourself. Maybe at a time when you were experiencing difficulty in a relationship that was affecting your ability to relax or sleep properly, as well as influencing your diet (perhaps by increasing your intake of unhealthy foods). Then you went to work on a crowded train with people breathing germs all around you. A few hours later you felt the onset of a cold. Was this caused by so many infectious agents surrounding you on the train? Was it the lack of sleep or poor diet? Or was it an accumulation of emotional stress, resulting in a weakened physical state? When there is a 'flu bug going around, not everyone gets it. Some remain healthy, while others are confined to bed. What other factors are present in those who succumb? Is it stress, overwork, problems at home, or a depressed state of mind? If you have been ill, can you see what else was going on, weakening your immune system from the inside, reducing its ability to resist infection? Have you been feeling vulnerable, exposed, psychologically or emotionally weakened? (See Chapter 15 for more on the immune system.)

The Two-Way Communication System

Our psycho/emotional state also affects the endocrine system. Hormones flood through the body like chemical tides flowing back and forth, influencing our bodily activity, behaviour, feelings and emotions. They are secreted by the endocrine glands which make up a whole system of their own, each subtly influencing the other, all dominated by the pituitary gland which is like the director of a communications company. 'A basic emotion such as fear can be described as an abstract feeling or as a tangible molecule of the hormone adrenaline,' writes Deepak Chopra in *Ageless Body, Timeless Mind*. 'Without the feeling there is no hormone; without the hormone there is no feeling. . . The revolution we call mind-body medicine was based on this simple discovery: wherever thought goes, a chemical goes with it.'

Secreted by the brain, the immune system and the nerve cells, are neuropeptides – hormones that act as chemical messengers – carrying emotions from the mind to the body and back again. They create an intricate and elaborate two-way communication system that links the emotions with all areas of the body. Neuropeptides carry our fears, concerns, dreams and hopes into every corner of our being. 'Thoughts, coded as neural impulses, travel along nerve axons activating muscles and glands, similar to the manner in which telephone messages travel over wires in the form of electrical signals,' writes Buryl Payne, quoted in *Your Body Believes Every Word You Say* by Barbara Hoberman Levine.

Neuropeptides provide the link from perception to thought, from the brain to hormonal secretions, to the organs and cellular action in the body. The hypothalamus, a small gland in the brain, is where emotion is transformed into physical response. Clusters of neuropeptides are found there, as well as in the gut or stomach area (accounting for those moments when we have a 'gut feeling' about something). The hypothalamus is the emotional centre of the brain. It is not only a receptor for neuropeptides, it also controls the pituitary and adrenal glands, appetite, blood sugar level, body temperature, and the automatic functioning of the heart, lungs, digestive and circulatory systems. It is like a pharmacy, releasing the chemicals and hormones necessary to maintain a balanced system. As each thought or feeling creates a response, the hypothalamus comes into action. Throw in a dose of stress and the chain reaction permeates every part of the body.

There is no major section of the immune system that is not influenced by neuropeptides. 'The more we know about neuropeptides, the harder it is to think in the traditional terms of a mind and a body. It makes more and more sense to speak of a single, integrated entity, a "bodymind",' wrote Candace Pert, former Chief of Brain Chemistry at the US National Institute of Health, in an article for *Advances*, the journal of the Institute for the Advancement of Health (1986).

Far from being two separately functioning systems, the body and mind clearly function as an integrated whole, responding to both inner and outer environments. What we think and feel has an immediate effect on our physical health, just as what is experienced in the body affects our mental and emotional state. To separate the two is to miss out on a wealth of understanding and a means of deepening our relationship with our whole being.

2

ORIGINAL CAUSES

THE FOUNDER of the American Holistic Medical Association, Dr C. Norman Shealy, states that at least 85 per cent of illnesses are the result of lifestyle. The remaining 15 per cent he believes are due to environmental factors, genetic factors, and what we might call 'the mystery factor'. Although these figures are only estimates, they do underline the importance of looking at the way we choose to live our lives, and to what extent our attitudes determine our state of health.

Marc Barasch raises some of these questions in *The Healing Path*:

> *If a woman smokes to relieve the stress of an intolerable marriage, what is the 'cause' of her lung cancer? Is it a genetic predisposition? The histology of oat-cell carcinoma? The smoking itself? Her relationship? How thorough is her cure if she has a lung removed but does not change her marital circumstances, let alone inquire into the personality patterns that permitted her to cling to her longtime unhappiness?*

Such self-examination is not easy. Most of us naturally prefer to believe that any illness we experience is entirely due to something external, rather than having anything to do with our own thoughts, feelings or behaviour. We usually assume that illness is either inherited, or due to a foreign substance or pollution. Getting ill invariably feels like something over which we have no control; we are the helpless victim of the illness.

Despite living inside our bodies for so long – thirty, forty or sixty years – when something goes wrong it can seem as if we are living inside a complete stranger. We are disconnected, unable to understand how this stranger works or why it has stopped working. Not many people know where their different organs are, or how they function. This is one reason why we give doctors so much power – they know things about the body that we believe are beyond our comprehension.

The more deeply we look into the causal chain of illness the further we go beyond the more obvious, physical reasons, to ever more subtle layers of non-physical, psycho/emotional connections. However, before we explore the internal causes of illness, let us look at the external causes, those which are, to some extent, beyond our control. They may form a smaller group, but they are just as important.

♦ ENVIRONMENTAL FACTORS ♦

The environment cannot be lightly dismissed as a causal factor in illness. Pollution is rising at an alarming rate and creating long-term difficulties for which we have few solutions (for instance, the hole in the ozone layer over the Antarctic is already causing serious health problems in the Southern hemisphere). It is extraordinary to consider that we are *knowingly* ingesting poisons, in the form of chemical fertilisers, insecticides, spill-offs from factories, and car exhaust fumes. The acute rise in asthma is one example of a health problem which has been exacerbated by increased air pollution. Another example is the rise of BSE in cows, now affecting humans. The more we try to alter nature (as in feeding animal products to herbivorous animals), the more we will pay the price. Environmental issues should be considered in *every* case of illness or disease, and more research on the relationship between pollution and ill-health is urgently needed. We cannot treat our crops, animals and air with chemicals, or continue to pour chemical waste into the ecosystem, without it having detrimental effects on our own health.

However, we are not complete victims of the environment, we can introduce some limits on the amount of toxins we ingest. We can educate ourselves about the ingredients used in commercial food production, buy or grow organic food whenever possible, and help care for the planet. We need to be aware of those attitudes that stop us nurturing our health and that of the environment – feeling helpless, feeling that there's nothing we can do that will make any difference, believing that it's already too late so why bother? We have to *want* to make a difference.

National Diseases

Environmental causes also include social and cultural influences. Diseases that are predominant in a particular country, perhaps due to local customs and conditioning, can be termed 'national diseases'. For instance, breast cancer is rare in Japan and China but it affects one in nine women in America. Is this because of diet alone, or does it also reflect cultural attitudes towards women and their bodies?

Eddie and I were invited to teach in the Czech Republic. The country had only recently gained independence from communism. For many years the people had been living in a state of enormous repression (unable to express their feelings or frustration), with no decision-making powers whatsoever. We asked if there were any predominant national illnesses and were told that many Czech people suffered from throat and chest problems. These areas of the body are particularly associated with repressed feelings, especially grief and anger. It appeared that the years of withheld emotion were affecting them physically – they had so much to get off their chests. They had been unable to breathe or speak for themselves for too long. The feelings inside were so deeply buried that many were finding it hard to connect with their hearts – the core of their love and joy.

National diseases also include illnesses like malaria or those spread by man, as seen for example when missionaries first arrived on the shores of Hawaii bringing with them the measles virus. This began to kill the native Hawaiians as they had no resistant immunity. The external antigen was completely foreign to its new host. (The Hawaiians had had no opportunity to build resistance as they lived in an isolated and protected place.)

Illness is an essential part of health: the immune system needs antigens to stimulate a response and build greater immunity. Hence we have childhood diseases such as chicken pox and measles, all of which serve to increase our immunity and overall strength. In our exposure to the numerous germs and bacteria that result in colds, 'flu or short illnesses, we are actually creating a system capable of dealing more effectively with foreign substances.

♦ GENETIC INFLUENCES ♦

Inherited or genetic factors are another undisputed cause of illness. Some physical difficulties are passed between generations, so we can be born with a higher than normal chance of developing the same illnesses as our parents or other relatives. However, genes alone do not dictate destiny; other factors contribute to how genetic influences might manifest. For example, identical twins have the same genetic patterns but do not necessarily get the same illnesses.

Emotional environment and inner attitudes are equally important. These determine lifestyle – diet, exercise and personal habits – which in turn influence strength, resilience and health, and can counterbalance the effects of genetic predisposition. A body weakened by a non-caring attitude, a lack of exercise, poor nutrition, and habits such as smoking or drinking, will have less natural strength to cope with illness, genetic or otherwise. Saying to yourself 'I know I will get this illness because my mother had it and so did my grandmother' encourages a sense of fatalism and hopelessness which depletes physical resistance. The body hears and responds to these words. Developing a loving relationship with ourselves that supports an acceptance of life, no matter what happens, encourages greater resilience.

♦ THE MYSTERY FACTOR ♦

This occurs when, having eliminated all other possible explanations, we really do not know why an illness has developed. It is important to recognise this unknown factor as real, for it maintains the mysteriousness of life – not everything can be labelled, categorised or known. Nature is an enormous mystery. Where does the perfume come from in a rose? How does instinct develop? How does the brain think?

With an acceptance that we do not know comes a surrendering of the logical mind and the need for answers. But even here, attitude is of primary importance. If we surrender to a sense of hopelessness and helplessness, – a giving-up attitude – this can rapidly lead to depression, a downward spiral into victimhood. If, however, we surrender by allowing the greater forces of the universe to work through us – a letting go and letting God – then we are honouring the unknown. We can chose to stop living until we die, or we can chose to participate in the great mystery of life in as many ways as possible.

♦ AS WE THINK, SO WE BECOME ♦

If it is true that 85 per cent of illnesses – and even if it is less – are caused by attitude and lifestyle, then this needs to be considered very closely. Our chosen lifestyle reveals a great deal about us – how much exercise we take, whether we are concerned about our nutritional intake, whether we smoke or drink, how much relaxation and personal time we have, whether we treat ourselves with disregard or with respect. All these factors can substantially lower or increase our resistance to illness. Our lifestyle reflects how we feel about life: whether we want to live it as fully as we can in the most alive way, or whether we have a half-hearted attitude and simply resign ourselves to suffering or being in pain.

Our feelings about ourselves are also important. We may do everything right – jog 5 miles a day, eat a low-fat, high-fibre diet, meditate regularly – but if we do not really like ourselves, if we feel worthless, ugly, unlovable, guilty or ashamed, then over a long period of time these negative beliefs will have an effect. Our innermost feelings about how we look, about our achievements, and about our essential worth, can undermine any attempt to build good health. As we think so we become – our thoughts and words are like seeds which germinate and grow. Our state of health shows how we have been thinking – the seeds take root and begin to influence and shape our muscles, hormones, nerves and circulation.

Our own opinion about our state of health is apparently a more reliable predictor of our longevity than physical symptoms, medical examinations or laboratory tests. In *Healing Breakthroughs*, Dr Larry Dossey shows that in a twelve-month period people who smoke are twice as likely to die as people who do not, whereas, 'Those who say their health is "poor" are *seven* times more likely to die than those who say their health is "excellent".'

Patients with a fighting spirit, who want to get on with their lives, have a better chance than those who have a passive, helpless attitude. When we think of illness – or life – as being out of our control, or as an obstacle that we cannot overcome, then none of our energy will be directed towards healing, no vibrant 'living' message will reach the body. When illness – or living – is seen as a learning experience, an opportunity to deepen our relationship with ourselves, then there is greater energy for healing. 'The greatest discovery of any generation,' said Albert Schweitzer, 'is that human beings can alter their lives by altering their attitudes of mind.'

Body Images

Few of us feel loving and respectful towards our own bodies. Most of us wish we were thinner or more muscular, were taller or had fewer freckles. If you ask your friends how many can honestly say they love their bodies, just as they are – you might not find anyone. Yet those feelings do not go unheard. Thought is energy which is transmitted throughout the body.

For instance, perhaps you do not like your thighs. For the past twenty years you wished they were different – less cellulite, more lithe and slender – so every time you look in the mirror all you see are ugly fat thighs. Sound familiar? Now imagine that you *are* your thighs. Imagine that for the past twenty years you have been told that you are ugly and fat. You struggle for acceptance and love and all you get is rejection. Imagine how lost and lonely your thighs feel! This might sound flippant, but in real life this problem can be very serious.

Evy McDonald was working as a nurse when she was diagnosed with a rapid form of amytrophic lateral sclerosis (ALS) where the muscles simply waste away. Confined to a wheelchair and given only six months to live, Evy simply wanted to experience unconditional love before she died. To do this she knew she would have to start by loving herself and her own body, but when she looked in the mirror she was repulsed by what she saw. The next few months were gruelling.

> The first step was to notice and write down how many negative thoughts I had about my body in the course of each day and how many positive ones. . . Every day I singled out one aspect of my physical body that was acceptable to me. . . I couldn't pinpoint when the shift occurred, but one day I noticed that I had no negative thoughts about my body, I could look in the mirror at my naked reflection and be honestly awed by its beauty.

It was at this point that Evy's body stopped deteriorating and began reversing the ALS.

When we look at our bodies and feel repulsion, is it because we are comparing ourselves to a shape or size we have been told is beautiful? Society pressurises us to conform, to fit a particular image. In order to develop a real appreciation for ourselves we need to see without judging, touch without fear, explore like a child in a new world. It is important to be really honest about our feelings, to accept ourselves without guilt or shame. Whatever we feel is absolutely OK. The beauty of it is that the more we are able to accept ourselves as we are, the more lovely and the more lovable we become.

─── **TRY IT YOURSELF** ───

Loving Your Body

This is a difficult but honesty-testing exercise!

- Start by undressing and standing naked in front of a full-length mirror. Then, looking directly at yourself, say 'I love you.'

- Keep doing this, for at least ten minutes, every day for one week. It won't be easy at first. In fact, it will probably feel very phoney and silly. And it will undoubtedly bring up all the feelings of dislike you have for your body. If this happens, take note of the dislike but do not get sidetracked by it. Without judging, remain objective. Keep repeating the words, 'I love you', and put as much feeling into it as you can. Watch how it changes each day.

- After a week, just focus on those bits you really *do* love – even if there aren't many. You may only be able to start with a fingernail or the colour of your eyes. But each day find a different part that you love. And focus on it totally, completely loving it. Keep doing this for as many days as it takes to work through all the parts of you that you love. Then look at the parts that you *like*, that you feel are OK. And see if you can change that liking into love, simply by looking, without judging, opening your heart, and saying 'I love you.'

- After you have worked through all these parts, come back to looking at your whole body in the mirror. Are there many parts left that you still really dislike? Are you looking at these parts objectively, without judging, or are you still comparing them to what society says they are meant to look like?

- As long as there are parts of you that you find hard to love, keep standing in front of the mirror, saying 'I love you.' Watch what happens. Allow yourself to change.

Feelings Find Form

Our feelings determine whether we are tense and constricted or relaxed and open, which in turn affects our muscle formation and structure. Whether the muscles are tight or flabby, thin or over-developed, whether the joints move easily or with stiffness and pain – all reflect our emotional history. Dr Ashley Montague, author of *Touching* has shown that children who do not receive enough love – who are not touched or communicated with – can actually stop growing. X-rays provide evidence of periods of slow or minimal bone growth corresponding to times of isolation or loneliness in the child's life. Without the reassurance of love and emotional security the body simply stops growing. 'I have come to see that emotional experiences, psychological choices, and personal attitudes and images not only affect the functioning of the human organism but also strongly influence the way it is shaped and structured,' writes Ken Dytchwald in *Bodymind*.

Our self-image is usually formed in our early years through the unconscious messages we receive as children. Few people grow up in an environment that encourages free expression of feelings; instead most of us learn how to repress our feelings so as to conform to a certain norm. Repressed feelings can result in low self-esteem or an increased desire for sex, money or power, any of which can have a devastating influence on health. Caroline Myss, an American medical intuitive and healer, says 'our biography becomes our biology'.

Cardiologist Dr Dean Ornish noticed that many of his patients who had coronary bypass surgery were returning for a second or even third operation. Studies showed that up to 50 per cent of patients returned within five years – the bypassed arteries simply clogged up again. Ornish is quoted in Marc Barasch's *The Healing Path*, as saying:

> The real issue lies further back in the causal chain that leads to chronic stress and then to heart disease. . . They feel they are unlovable and the only way to get love is to somehow buy it with outward tokens (money, power, fame, posses-sions). Of course, they are left worse off than before.

How we feel about ourselves, our partner, children, parents, or other people in our lives, is an essential component of our well-being. Notice when you are angry how your heart starts beating more quickly, your stomach tenses, you get hot flushes, or your muscles tighten. If these feelings are not dealt with then, in an attempt to cover up the deeper pain, they can lead to addiction to drugs, alcohol, food, or power; to headaches, accidents, or the immune system becoming weakened; to illicit or abusive relationships, or even violence.

Karuna King's suppression of her real feelings almost destroyed her:

> My mother had four children, of which I was the eldest. There was always a sibling who needed more attention than me and although we had all our needs catered for, my enduring impression is of neglect of my emotional needs. I became more and more introverted and disconnected. When I was eighteen I joined a convent, following a desire to do something spiritual but utterly confused as to how to go about it.
>
> In the convent I began to lose touch with my own inner reality. I felt hopeless and guilty and absolutely alone. Food appeared as something I could have control over. I think deep down I was in such despair that I even wanted to die, as it seemed like a way out. I became anorexic. This created continual friction between myself and the nuns, but I was so disconnected by this time that I became locked in a dismal colourless world. No one, throughout my childhood or at the convent, had ever said 'I love you'; I felt like I had not been hugged or touched lovingly for years. I was in desperate need of being loved. In rejecting food I was confirming the rejection I was feeling inside.
>
> By the time I was persuaded to leave the convent I was desperately thin and emotionally so repressed that I no longer knew what my feelings really were. The two psychiatrists I saw simply made me clam up even more. The turning point did not come until I read about a young woman who had starved herself to death and I knew that I too could die. Finally something inside me began to stir.
>
> Getting better was excruciating. I had to break down all the phoney structures I had put up around me. I had to want to eat for my own sake, as no one else seemed to care. Falling in love eventually proved to be my healer. It brought up all my fears and anxieties, but my partner was unfazed by anything I threw at him. With his love I began to open my heart and it unleashed in me a tremendous desire to live.
>
> What I have learnt from anorexia is to stay true to my feelings and not to get distracted by shoulds and oughts; and that through eating I am loving and nourishing myself and respecting my life.

The love and support of others helps us develop the ability to cope, as well as a sense of self-appreciation and self-worth. A neglected infant may have retarded bone growth or other physical problems, while babies who are stroked or massaged grow faster. Humans are social animals. We need each other. We need to be touched. We need to be loved and wanted and cared for, just as we need to love and care for others. And we need this not just to feel better, but for our actual survival. In a study on the effect of diet on heart disease, rabbits at Ohio University were fed high-cholesterol diets. This led to an increase in clogged arteries, except in one group which displayed 60 per cent fewer symptoms. The keeper of this particular group of rabbits was holding and stroking each one before he fed them.

Margaret Bird's story further illustrates the strong link between love and health:

> It began by coughing up blood. I decided it was probably just from coughing too violently. Then two days later I began coughing up blood in earnest and was admitted to hospital where I was diagnosed with a partially collapsed lung.
>
> The previous year had been a very sad and difficult one for me. There had been a growing alienation from my younger son, and conflict with my ex who was dying. I had been made redundant and had no means of livelihood. A dear friend had moved away, a new priest at my church was making changes I found difficult to accept. My victim mentality was flourishing!
>
> Being cared for in hospital made me realise how much I needed human love, how alone and unloved I was feeling. It was as if I had emotionally collapsed. Having a collapsed lung confronted me with questions about being alive – did I want to go on, to keep breathing? As I thought and prayed the answer came as 'Yes'. Slowly I began the process of healing, accepting the joy of living and simply being in the present moment, to loving myself and developing a deeper trust in life.

Loneliness, divorce and bereavement can all lead to a quicker death, as if we were literally dying of a broken heart. According to David Gelman, writing in *Newsweek* in 1988:

> *Scores of studies. . . show higher rates of illness among people who have recently lost a spouse. The same is true of people who feel socially isolated. . . Researchers found that for all age and sex groups, mortality was three times higher among those with the fewest close relationships.*

At New York's Mount Sinai Hospital, tests showed that immune functioning in the partners of people who were sick was fine prior to their partners dying. But after the death, immune functioning dropped alarmingly and could not be raised. The immune cells, although normal in numbers, were simply not working. This continued for several months. 'There is real evidence that in the first six months after the loss of a spouse a partner is in increased danger of succumbing to fatal illness,' wrote Colin Murray Parkes, formerly consultant psychiatrist at the Royal London Hospital, in *The Times*. When Federico Fellini died his wife was devastated; she died five months later. When the television newsreader Leonard Parkin died, his wife died only four weeks later. A friend was quoted a saying, 'She just seemed to have given up on life.' It is as if the cells themselves are experiencing the grief and loneliness, conveyed from the brain to the immune system.

◆ WHO CREATES OUR REALITY? ◆

If our attitude and lifestyle are responsible for approximately 85 per cent of our illnesses, it is easy to start thinking that we are responsible for *everything* that happens to us. The logical extension of this thought is that we are, therefore, to blame for being ill – that we have brought this state upon ourselves. There is a popular belief that we create our own reality, that we are 100 per cent responsible for everything that happens in our lives, that every thought we have determines the future, both good and bad. This idea can be helpful as it enables us to see where, often without being aware of it, we are causing extra difficulties for ourselves; it can teach us to stop blaming other people or external events for our problems and instead to look at our own behaviour, to take responsibility for our actions. It also shows us that we cannot really change other people or the world, but we can work on ourselves and our attitudes.

However, the moment we start thinking we are responsible for our own reality *in its entirety* we develop an inflated sense of self, a belief that we are all-powerful. This generates egocentricity and self-centredness, which sets the stage for guilt, shame and failure. Blaming ourselves for getting ill, we then blame ourselves for not getting well. Feeling guilty for repressing our anger and subsequently developing an ulcer or a tumour, we then believe we must be a hopeless example of humankind. Saying we are totally responsible for creating our reality means we are equating physical health with spiritual or psychic development, so if we become ill it implies spiritual failure. Yet such an equation has been disproved over and over again, especially by the many spiritual teachers who have died of cancer or related illnesses.

Believing that we create our own reality – both cause and outcome – implies that 'I' am in complete control. But the individual can never be in complete control; there are always other factors present. We are not alone on the earth. Rather, each one of us is an essential component of an interwoven, interrelated whole that is constantly changing and moving. Reality is *co-created* through our mutual dependency. And it is this intimate relationship with all other things that gives life its depth and beauty.

As Treya Killam Wilber, quoted in Ken Wilber's book *Grace and Grit*, says:

> *While we can control how we respond to what happens to us, we can't control everything that happens to us. We are all too interconnected, both with each other and our environment – life is too wonderfully complex – for a statement like 'you create your own reality' to be simply true. A belief that I control or create my own reality actually attempts to rip out of me the rich, complex, mysterious, and supportive context of my life. . . to deny the web of relationships that nurtures me and each of us daily.*

We are in charge of our own attitudes and feelings, of the way we treat ourselves and our world, but we cannot determine the outcome; just as we do not make the sun rise or set, keep the earth in orbit or make the rain fall. We do not create our own reality; rather, we are responsible *to* our reality. *We cannot direct the wind but we can adjust our sails*. We are responsible for developing peace of mind but we may still need to have chemotherapy. The resolution and healing of our inner being is within our control, and this may also bring a cure to the physical body. But if it does not, we are not guilty of failure.

It is vital to remember this for, although we are intimately involved with our sickness and health, no matter what we do we are not in charge of what ultimately happens. We can affect our attitudes and behaviour; we can work on emotions and repressed fears; we can develop forgiveness and loving kindness. But the result of this goes beyond our personal dominion. We should not feel, at any time, that we are a failure if our healing falls below our expectations.

In *Healing Into Life and Death*, Stephen Levine recalls a woman

---

TRY IT YOURSELF
Body Awareness

- Over the next week, practise watching the physical effects in your body of different situations, thoughts or feelings. You may want to note these physical changes in a diary.

- For instance, be aware of times when you are irritated or frustrated and take note of where you are experiencing those feelings in your body. If you are stuck in a traffic jam, a client is late for an appointment, or the children keep interrupting your conversation, what happens to your shoulders, back or stomach?

- What happens in your body when you are worried or anxious about something, perhaps a child who is late coming home, or a presentation you have to give, or the results of your partner's blood test? Where do you hold the anxiety? What physical effect does it have? Do fears about the future create a pain in your stomach? Or in your legs?

- If your boss or your partner shouts at you, what happens to your heart, your head, your insides? Is your headache because you were shouted at, or because you feel insecure or angry? What do you do with angry feelings? Do you express them, or is there somewhere you put them? Do you swallow hard, clench your muscles, or get constipated?

- What happens if you recall past love affairs or people who were special? Do you feel warm and relaxed, or do you break out in a sweat and maybe feel nervous? Pay particular attention to what happens when you recall unhappy memories – perhaps when a parent hit you or you were bullied at school. As you follow these memories, watch whereabouts in your body there is a reaction.

- Think back to past illnesses or times when you were hurt. Note the parts of your body that were involved. Have you always held your stomach muscles in tight, have you always had recurring headaches, have you always hurt the same side of your body? Observe yourself, your reactions and your body. As you do this, you will begin to see how closely all the different parts of your being, both physical and psycho/emotional, are interwoven.

with terminal cancer who believed she had created her own illness. But she was unable to create the cure. As a result she was rapidly losing faith in herself. 'I'm not the person I thought I was. No wonder I'm sick,' she said. Levine then asked her if she was the *sole* creator of her reality. In response, 'Her mouth hung agape with confusion and helplessness, and then gradually a smile came across her face, and she said, "No, I guess not after all. But I sure am a major contributor."'

Through illness the body is giving us a message, telling us that something is out of balance. This is not a punishment for bad behaviour; rather it is nature's way of creating equilibrium. By listening to the message we have a chance to contribute to our own health, to participate with our body in bringing us back to a state of wholeness and balance. So, rather than blaming ourselves by saying 'Why did I chose to have cancer?', we can ask 'How am I choosing to *use* this cancer?' For we can use whatever difficulties we are confronted with in order to learn and grow, to release old patterns of negativity, to deepen compassion, forgiveness and insight. Our difficulties can then become stepping stones along the way rather than stumbling blocks. Instead of becoming overwhelmed by a sense of hopelessness and guilt that we are responsible for everything that is happening to us, illness can be seen as a tremendous challenge and opportunity for awakening. In this way, illness is a great gift – a chance for us to find ourselves.

3

THE LANGUAGE OF ILLNESS

THE BODY speaks to us through symptoms. Symptoms tell us something is going on, whether through the nature of the symptom, the effect it has, or the changes it demands. The word 'symptom' derives from the Greek *syn*, meaning 'together', and *piptein*, meaning 'to fall'. In other words, disturbances, difficulties or conflicting issues may have been present for days, months or even years before finally 'falling together' and creating a symptom. By paying attention to both the history of the symptom and its effect, we begin to discover deeper and more subtle causes, ones which invariably hold the key to our healing.

To do this we need to get to know our own bodymind language, for, just as we all have a unique way of speaking, so each body has its own means of expression. For instance, feeling that we are not getting the support we need, or that we are weighed down with responsibility, may manifest either as difficulties in the back or as trouble in the knees and ankles, the weight-bearing joints. It is different for each of us. Discovering our own bodymind means paying attention to such details, learning to listen to the body's communication. As Christine Evans describes:

> I try to just notice myself, without judgement. I notice that I feel sick when my ex-lover rings. I notice that I feel sad when my lower back is massaged. I notice the area between my shoulder blades that aches when I'm tired or feeling tense. I notice that the sick feeling, the retching and vomiting, is about not accepting how I really feel and not believing that I have the right to feel whatever it is.

As a physical symptom is usually the first indication that something is out of balance, the relationship to psychological or emotional issues is not always obvious. In fact, it often seems that the physical problem is causing a psycho/emotional response, rather than arising out of one. By investigating more deeply, the interwoven relationships become clearer. In *Your Body Believes Every Word You Say*, Barbara Hoberman Levine shares her story of being diagnosed with a brain tumour:

> *I wondered which came first, the thought 'I lost my nerve' or the loss of the physical nerve energy that resulted from the tumour. At first I believed that my physical disabilities led to my fearful outlook. My physical condition was literally and symbolically an unnerving experience. Today, I can see that my physical condition encouraged me to feel the unconscious emotions and fears already within me. It enabled me to realise how fearful I had always been.*

A symptom is never an isolated event. It is connected to the past because it has arisen out of previous events and conditions; it is connected to the present in the way it affects us now; and it has a tangible effect on the future, given its prognosis. It also reflects and relates to all other parts of our being.

♦ ACCUMULATED TRAUMA ♦

In exploring our symptoms, we may find that some go back a long way, while others are more recent. One of the first places to look is the two to twenty-four month period before they began. Louis Proto writes in *Self-Healing*:

> *At the Albert Einstein College of Medicine in the Bronx, it was found that children with cancer had suffered twice as many recent crises as other children. . . 31 out of 33 children with leukemia had experienced a traumatic loss or move within the two years preceding the diagnosis.*

And as Dr John Ball says in *Understanding Disease*:

> *It is certainly quite often the case that the physical aspects of disease, i.e. the pathology, can be influenced in some way by the scientific approach, but in most cases the physical*

*manifestation is only the final expression of a process which
has been continuing for a long time.*

Take some time to think about whether you have experienced an
emotional trauma: perhaps your children left home which left you
feeling lonely or useless, a parent or close relative died, or you
experienced some family strife; or the problem may be connected to
your work, such as increasing pressure or job insecurity; or perhaps
you were really longing to do something different but were scared to
change and have been feeling as if you were dying inside. You need
to consider to what extent you have really accepted or dealt with
your inner responses. It is not just a matter of seeing the event and
giving it the label 'cause of illness'. You need to focus on the deeper
feelings connected to these events.

When you look back over the past few months or years, you may
find that the issue actually goes back much further, such as into your
childhood, but something in the more immediate past may have
brought those childhood issues to the surface. Children will easily
bury confusing, frightening or unhappy feelings in their unconscious
so as not to have to deal with the reality of pain. Symptoms are one
way to help us get in touch with our buried feelings. They are
messengers from the unconscious.

Recognising past trauma alerts us to what we might have sensed
but never fully acknowledged – deep feelings that have never been
expressed, fear and anxieties kept locked inside. The symptom leads
us to the feelings. And getting in touch with our feelings opens the
door to healing. This is what happened to Cheryl:

> I was abused as a child. Constantly. My father raped me at
> least once a week. After I got away from him I got into
> drinking. I was a happy alcoholic – as soon as anything got too
> much to bear I just had another drink and all the pain went
> away. I was doing fine, the years ticking by, until I got a letter
> from my father asking me to meet with him. Two weeks later I
> went on a bender and ended up in hospital after crashing my
> car. I was paralysed, told I would probably never walk again.
>
> Being in hospital made me get sober. That was the hardest
> part. No place to hide my feelings. After that I began to think
> that I'd been given a second chance. I realised that my body
> was saying that I wasn't going anywhere in the old direction,
> that it was time to start again. And somewhere inside I knew
> my pelvis was numb because I didn't want to feel all the
> feelings that were locked in there, all the sexual memories.

And I knew that if I was to walk again I was going to have to get those memories out, and I was going to have to forgive my father. So that's what I did – day by day, week by week.

Eventually I walked out of the hospital. Now I teach dancing.

It is possible to spend years denying our feelings and convincing ourselves, as well as everyone else, that we are fine. To then begin to dig those feelings up can seem impossible. We may even have blanked out our memory of the event. In this case, it may be helpful to ask a family member or close friend if they can remember, to talk it through and see if there are events that affected us that we have since pushed away. Denial is the mind's protection mechanism, especially if the event was particularly traumatic or painful.

Giving voice to hidden feelings is an important step on the healing journey. We can cure a problem but to find our healing takes courage and honesty. It means looking objectively and clearly, not just at the outer events but at what we felt then. What feelings were ignored, denied, thought of as silly or unimportant? What had you no time for? What were all the different pieces that eventually came together to form a symptom?

♦ DECODING THE LANGUAGE ♦

An important clue in investigating symptoms is the specific *function* of the part that is not well, for the underlying psychological or emotional issues usually relate to the function of the part affected. Try exploring the part of the body you are concerned with and all the different uses it has. What does that part of your body do? What role does it play in the functioning of the whole? How does its function relate to what is happening in your life?

For instance, the knees enable us to walk, run and dance with grace and fluidity, to bend or straighten; kneeling is an act of surrendering to a higher force or power, an act of humility. The saying 'pride comes before a fall' shows how pride or a lack of humility makes us stubborn and stiff; we do not move so smoothly and, when the knees lose their flexibility, we stumble or fall. The knees also hold the weight of the body – each time we bend the knees they hold that weight without giving way. If they do give way, is it because the weight has become too much to bear, or is there a psychological pressure?

As well as the function, we need to explore the *nature* of the illness or difficulty. Is it a muscle strain or bone break, an infection or a disease, a nerve problem, a digestive problem or a blood disorder? Each one of these has a different implication. For instance, an infection means that something from outside (such as a bacteria or virus) has *affected* you, causing a fever or cold, septicaemia or inflamed area. This means that something has found its way inside you and is causing a disturbance. In response you become red, hot, inflamed – all symbols of anger, or unexpressed emotions, building up inside. Considering that there are millions of germs around all the time, what else has been going on that might have weakened your immune system? Have you been experiencing excessive stress? Are you feeling particularly vulnerable, depressed, lonely or angry? What is affecting you so deeply?

If your throat gets sore and it is difficult to swallow, ask yourself what is going on that is so hard to take in. What is making you so unhappy or is so difficult to express? If you can't bend or turn your head, can you find the place where you have become locked in your thinking so that you cannot accept another's point of view? If you have become hard of hearing, is it because you never listen to anyone, or is there something you don't want to hear?

If your eyes get cloudy or you can't see too well, is it because you are dreading what is coming next in your life? Or if you have seen too much, do you need to shut the images out? If you have a bad chest cough, is there something you need to 'get off your chest', to share and talk about? Or are you taking in something that is irritating and disturbing you? If you have broken out in an itchy rash, is something or someone annoying you so much that they have literally got under your skin? If you have cold feet, are you afraid of moving forward? If you get indigestion, is it something other than food that is really upsetting you, or eating away at your insides? Have you fully digested the meaning of something, or absorbed all its implications? If you are aching, are you aching for someone or something? Are you aching with loneliness? If you are hurting, is someone or something hurting you? Or are you hurting yourself?

Jenny Britton remembers one of her massage clients coming in with a back problem that clearly had a deeper emotional significance:

> David came for a massage complaining of a pain in his lower
> back, on the left side. As I started massaging his back, he
> began to tell me how he had just cancelled his wedding,
> scheduled for two months ahead. The church had already been
> booked, the dress made, he and his fiancée had even bought a

house together. He said he was happy to continue living with her but she wanted the wedding or nothing.

As I listened I thought of the left side, all connected to the feminine nature, and here was David talking about his fiancée and the end of their relationship. The lower back is about relationships and about finding a place in the world for ourselves. David was taking a step forward for himself and it wasn't easy; there was a great deal of emotional pain involved. His back pain was also connected to the pelvic area. The pelvis is where we stand up for ourselves. David told me that he had moved straight from living with his mother to living with his fiancée. By the end of the massage he had realised how badly he needed to get his own place and begin to look after himself, to stand on his own.

Symptoms can be subtle, elusive, indefinable. At these times, the words you use to *describe* the symptoms can give vital clues to the deeper issues. Ask yourself what the symptom feels like on the inside: is it hot, cold, hard, soft, pulling, pushing, tight or loose? If you have a cramping muscle, what does the cramp feel like? Are the words describing a tightness or restriction in your life? If you have a pounding headache, do you feel that someone is pounding you? Or are you beating yourself up? A joint is stiff and sore to move: what does the stiffness feel like? Are you being pulled or pushed around? Do you feel reluctant to move, preferring to keep things just as they are? Or are you resisting expressing your inner feelings?

What *temperature* is this part of your body? What *colour* is it? Do these represent feelings inside you? See if you can put yourself inside the part of the body that is hurting. What does it feel like to be an aching, throbbing head? What does it feel like to be a stiff joint or an ulcerated stomach? How does your nose feel when it's runny?

It helps to write down how you feel inside and then look at the words you have used. Are these words actually describing how you feel psychologically or emotionally? If arthritis is making your hand feel as if it is being pulled back from the inside, do you feel you want to pull back from what you are doing? Do you feel like a puppet, with someone else pulling the strings? How does your illness appear to you? What are its characteristics? There is an exercise at the end of this chapter to help you with this.

♦ FRINGE BENEFITS ♦

As well as observing the history and background of our symptoms, we can also explore the possible benefits the illness might be offering us. This might sound crazy – surely nobody wants to be sick or can benefit from being ill? Nonetheless, illness is not always an entirely negative experience.

Illness is very distracting. It blots out all other issues. It centres our energy firmly on ourselves. On the one hand this can be very beneficial, for it gives us a chance to let go of those things that are really trivial and unnecessary. The surplus issues blow away like chaff in the wind, and we are left with the essentials of ourselves and our morality. No longer do we take everything for granted; life becomes very precious because it seems fragile and impermanent. If we can fully enter into this state then illness will open our hearts, connecting us with what is really important, with our true priorities.

But more often we are focused on the 'poor me' aspect of illness. The word 'invalid' means both someone who is unwell, and a state of not being valid – of being void or unsound. But which comes first – the sick person in bed who feels helpless, useless and unimportant, or the person who feels unacknowledged, dismissed as incompetent and who then becomes sick? Does the illness undermine your self-worth?

Illness can give you permission to avoid a difficult situation, to offload responsibilities. Does your condition distract you from dealing with other situations? Does it provide a way of avoiding your feelings? What activities are the symptoms preventing you from undertaking? A migraine headache can get us out of having to read aloud in class or visit the in-laws, a broken leg can postpone a wedding or a holiday, having 'flu means a week in bed, while herpes keeps intimacy at a distance. How is your illness or difficulty changing your circumstances? Are there benefits to this?

Being ill can make us feel very special, different, even important. When children are unwell, their mothers will usually lavish more attention and love on them than at any other time. Is it any different for adults? Is your illness an unconscious cry for that love, a longing to be looked after and nourished? Can you tell people that you need to be cared for? Are you struggling on your own, trying to cope so as not to be a nuisance to anyone? Or are you expecting them to know what you need without having to be told?

Illness gives us something to occupy our days and is a constant conversation piece. Ask someone how they are and a long list of complaints, visits to the doctor, tests, medications and a prognosis will follow. We love to talk about our illnesses and, although this is a very natural way of finding comfort, it can also make us dependent on the illness in order to get the support we need.

Does having something wrong make you feel more important, even more lovable? Would you be as lovable without your illness? Would your friends and relatives still care about you if there was nothing wrong with you? Do you fear the changes that being well might cause in your relationships? Are you holding on to your loved ones through your illness? Or are you stopping others from getting too close?

Relationships of real honesty are not easy to maintain. Too often we pull back into our separate selves and get involved in a silent battle of wills. Was the relationship threatening to break up at the time when you got ill? Were you afraid of losing someone? Children and even the elderly sometimes use sickness to get attention. How often has your child suddenly run a high fever just as you were leaving for the theatre? What we need to do is look more closely at ourselves to see if we are also playing with guilt and blame. Perhaps you feel a slight sense of satisfaction if a previously wayward partner has to stay at home to care for you? Or maybe your illness has given you both a chance to get closer and to be more loving?

Illness can arise out of self-dislike and shame. Do you have underlying feelings of guilt that are eating away at you? Have you done something that feels overwhelmingly bad or shameful? Have you told anyone about it? Or are you holding it inside where you think no one can see it? Does being ill feel like some kind of retribution for this bad deed? Does it feel impossible for you to be well because you are somehow too dirty, too bad, and illness is all that you are worthy of?

Life can sometimes seem far too stressful to deal with. Illness can give you a respectable way out of having to meet your own high expectations or the demands of others. If illness is due to stress, then why are you pushing yourself so hard? Are you trying to prove something to someone? To your parents? Is success worth it if you are not well enough to enjoy it? Or do you actually want to get away, to avoid something? Is the illness hiding a fear of failure? Have you lost your self-esteem?

When we get ill we surrender control of the future – it has to look after itself for a while. There is a pause, a time to breathe and reconnect, a time to remember who we really are. Illness allows us to do things we would otherwise have denied ourselves, such as painting or writing. It provides space to reflect, to care for ourselves, to learn, to reassess, in a way that may not have been possible previously. It gives us the chance to get to know ourselves. These are tremendous benefits.

♦ CHILDREN'S ILLNESSES ♦

Generally, children's diseases, such as chicken pox or measles, are an essential part of building immunity for the rest of our lives. They are relatively harmless when we are children but as adults, if we do not have immunity, they can be far more serious. It is interesting to note when such illnesses occur, often at a time when the child needs extra rest, attention and love. Honouring these needs will speed recovery.

Other children's illnesses, such as problems they may be born with or develop at an early age, are not so easy to explain. One school of thought will say it is due to issues in the parents, such as smoking or drug-taking during the pregnancy, or because of emotional conflicts between the parents – perhaps about having a child. Another will say that it is due to unresolved issues in the child from a past life; or from a combination of the parents' and child's past lives, finding resolution in this life. There may be much truth in these theories, depending on the situation. Beyond them, we are confronted with the mystery factor – we need to accept that it is not always possible to find answers.

What is important is to see the illness in perspective – what benefits it offers and what can be learnt from the situation. An ill or disabled child can often be blamed for all the family's problems. But blaming the child or the condition does not resolve the issue. This is where we need to look at our own attitude, behaviour and feelings, and how these may be affecting the child or the family dynamics. It may be very important to create a chance for the child to talk about their feelings – perhaps to a counsellor or teacher.

♦ ACCIDENTS HAPPEN ♦

Some people feel there is no such thing as an accident as everything that happens has a meaning or purpose. My own feeling is that accidents *do* happen, and we can learn from the result of the accident. Accidents often happen at particular times, such as during periods of stress or chaos, or when we are going through change. At such times we tend to pay less attention to ourselves, often ignoring messages from our bodies. We are distracted and become more prone to mishap, collapse or physical disorder.

If you have had an accident in recent years explore the parts of the body that were most affected, using the questions in the exercise on p. 41. Look back to any tension there may have been before the accident happened. See if there are any connections to be made. Was the affected area already in a weakened state? Did the accident stop you from doing something? How did the accident change your life? Are there any benefits in this?

John Taylor had just such an experience:

> Breaking my back and having to lie still for six months was the best thing that ever happened to me! I actually had an excuse to stop, to get to know myself, to get to know my children. We had long conversations together, something I had never previously had time for. All my defences were down, I was vulnerable and weak, but that let them get close to me. Before, I was too well protected to show my feelings. By the time I could walk again I felt as if I had been reborn, that I had a whole new life. That accident was such a blessing!

♦ SYMPTOMS MEAN CHANGE ♦

Although we may be able to see quite clearly what our symptoms are saying, or even to intuitively guess their meaning, accepting the truth of them is not so easy. After all, a symptom often expresses an issue that we have been ignoring, denying or repressing, so acceptance means accepting this unwanted part of ourselves. Sometimes it seems easier to just keep everything the same even if we lose our health in the process. In Marc Barasch's *The Healing Path* George Melton describes how he went from one form of sexually transmitted disease to another, not wanting to look at what the message might be until:

> *One day I woke up with AIDS. . . the one disease my body manifested that couldn't be cured with a pill. It forced me to go beyond the physical and find the things inside me – the self-hatred and fear – that I had been dying of for a long time.*

A young man suffering from acute pain came to Dr Joan Borysenko's Mind/Body Group at the New England Deaconess Hospital. The pain had kept him living at his parents' house; it had also prevented him from fulfilling his career potential or having a relationship. As he became proficient at relaxation and breath control, the pain began to ease. However, he was then confronted with a far more difficult situation. 'Now I don't know what to do with myself,' he said. 'I'm twenty-seven and I've never moved out of my parents' house. I don't know how to relate to women. I should probably go back to school but I'm too scared. I don't know how to live any other way. I think I want my pain back.'

Illness gives us the chance to look at our behaviour and the pattern of our lives, at what our real feelings are and what we want to do about them. Recognising the meanings of our symptoms is the beginning of the journey, the first step towards understanding ourselves more deeply. After that has to come the commitment to releasing the old and opening up to the new. We have to really *want* to get well. The body is trying to regain wholeness, to heal. But it is going to be hindered if, beneath it all, we are holding on to the illness for more subtle motives. Making a commitment to our own healing gives us the courage to change.

TRY IT YOURSELF

Exploring Your Bodymind Messages

This is an exercise to help you understand what your body is saying:

- Find a place where you can be quiet and undisturbed for half an hour or so. You may want to play some gentle music. Have some paper and a pen with you.

- Start by sitting comfortably and closing your eyes. In your mind, work your way up from your feet to your head, part by part, letting go of tension and relaxing each part. Then take a few deep breaths. For another few minutes focus on the rise and fall of the breath as it enters and leaves your body.

- When you are ready, bring your attention to the area of the body that you want to understand more deeply. Ask yourself the following questions and allow the answers to arise spontaneously. Write your answers down, even if they seem trivial or nonsensical. (You can refer to Chapters 10-21 to help you understand the function of the part of the body, or the nature of the ailment.)

continued

1 What is the function of this part of the body? What does it do? How does it relate to the other parts of the body? What does it enable you to do?

2 On what side of the body is the difficulty, and what are all the relevant aspects of this side (see Chapter 10)?

3 What is the nature of the difficulty? Describe the condition in your own words. How does this part of your body feel? Is it sore? Hot? Stiff? Aching? Then describe the feeling *inside* your body. Can you find it? Ask your pain or hurt what *it* feels like.

4 Describe the colour of this area; the temperature; the texture. Does it change in different places? Does it remind you of anything else?

5 How does your physical condition affect your life? What can you no longer do? What do you have to do instead? Is this a loss? Or are you glad?

6 Now look at what has been happening in the past few weeks, months or years. What major events occurred and do you feel you have really dealt with your feelings about these? Are there more subtle and intangible feelings beneath the surface? Has trauma from the past resurfaced in some way? Has there been an anniversary of a divorce, death, or some other trauma? Have there been problems with your children? With your parents? A crisis at work? Anger-provoking situations that you tried to keep under control? Or feelings of loss, emotional let-down, rejection or abuse?

7 Have you had this sort of illness before? Were you experiencing similar emotions at that time? Try writing a brief synopsis of your life, noting down any physical difficulties and illnesses you have had and any traumas or emotions that occurred around the same time.

8 What does the illness mean to you? Does it mean you are a failure? Does it make you feel guilty? Are you getting enough time to yourself? Does the illness mean you do not have to work or face responsibilities? Is it distracting you from deeper issues, such as fear or insecurity? What effect is it having on your relationships? Is it getting you out of doing something? Or is it the best thing that could have happened to you?

continued

9 Are there any benefits you gain from your ill-health? Does it make you feel special? Does it make you feel loved and cared for? Is it making others feel guilty about how they treated you? Do you feel you are being punished for bad behaviour? Do you need this illness?

10 Can you imagine yourself being well again? If you are in a wheelchair, can you imagine yourself walking? If you are depressed, can you imagine feeling happy and laughing? How would you feel if someone offered you a cure right now? Be honest – this is important. Would you accept the cure? If you could be absolutely well, right now, what effect would that have on the rest of your life?

- Really take note of the ways in which you have described yourself and your body and allow the words to sink in. Do they have other meanings? Do they have implications for other aspects of your life? Are they related to other people or issues? Ask any further questions that you need to, and listen quietly for any answers.

- Consider all that you have written. Can you see what your body is trying to tell you? What is there for you to learn here? Can you see where you need to start working with yourself, what areas or issues need to be brought to the surface? Are you prepared to start this journey? Do you feel ready to let this difficulty be healed?

4

CURING A SYMPTOM OR HEALING A LIFE?

THERE IS an important distinction to be made between curing and healing. To cure is to fix a particular part. Allopathy – Western medicine – is particularly good at doing this, offering drugs and surgery so that disease, illness or physical problems can be repressed, eliminated or removed. It plays a vital role in alleviating suffering, and is superb at saving lives and applying curative aid. This is invaluable. However, the World Health Organisation defines health as *complete* physical, mental and social well-being. This is not the same as simply being without symptoms or illness. Rather, it implies a deeper state of wellness that goes beyond being cured of a particular difficulty.

This is where we enter the realm of healing. 'If you look no further than getting rid of what's wrong, you may never deal with what's brought your life to a standstill,' says a patient in Marc Barasch's *The Healing Path*. 'The thing you want to heal from may be the very thing you need to focus on in order to learn something.' Whereas a patient remains passive when cured by someone else, healing is an involved activity, less dependent on external circumstances than on the work we are prepared to do within ourselves. Many medical doctors know this. They know that allopathy is limited in what it can do. As Dr Bernie Siegel explains in *Peace, Love and Healing*: 'It is the body that heals, not the medicine.'

To be healed means to become whole. This is not possible if we are only concerned with the individual part that needs to be cured. 'The word salvation is derived from the Latin word *salvus*, which means heal and whole,' says Paul Tillich in *The Meaning of Health*. 'Salvation is basically and essentially healing, the re-establishment of a whole that was broken, disrupted, disintegrated.' Becoming whole means bringing all of ourselves into the light, leaving nothing in the dark, no matter how disturbing or painful it may be. It is an embracing of all the parts we have ignored, denied, tried to push away or eliminate. Healing brings all of this into the conscious mind, into our hearts, into our lives. As long as we reject parts of ourselves, we are not whole.

'Healing can occur even when curing doesn't,' said Bill Moyers in *USA Today* in 1993. 'It is an acceptance of the unavoidable, a grace in living that escapes us if we are simply passive in the face of trouble.' Healing comes when we make the choice to work with our vulnerabilities, to open ourselves to the challenge of change. It is a continual journey, one of embracing ourselves ever more deeply.

♦ DETERMINING OUR PRIORITIES ♦

Healing is a journey we all share, for in our own ways we are all wounded, whether the wounds are visible or not – we each have our story. A psychological wound is no different to a physical one, emotional hurts are real and often just as painful. Most of us become very good at hiding our wounds, not just from others but also from ourselves. When physical difficulties arise we invariably look for a cure while continuing to repress the inner pain. But when we want to know ourselves better, to find our wholeness, then the journey really begins.

This asks that we look at and question our priorities – the things that are really important to us, that figure most in our lives. Many people feel that their first priority is the welfare and safety of their loved ones, but beyond that our priorities can get a bit vague. For some, making money or succeeding in their career is near the top of the list, for others it is near the bottom. For some, religion and religious activities are important, while others do not mention this aspect of life at all. Beyond family, work and religion, what else is there? Ourselves?

Society has two contrasting yet equally deeply ingrained attitudes. One is that we should direct all our energy towards the care of others; that to think of ourselves first is self-centred and egotistical. Although this attitude is a very caring one it can also be very detrimental. It can lead to guilt trips, power games, blame, shame, and resentment. By putting others first and ourselves last we create a situation where we easily become exhausted, unwell and unable to give; then we pass our own dissatisfaction on to others.

The alternative attitude is that we should *always* think of ourselves first, focusing our lives on fulfilling our own needs. This would work if, after recognising our own requirements, we then turned our attention to caring for and helping others. Sadly, this is not usually the case. The 'me first' syndrome does not often include others; rather it is based on greed, selfishness, prejudice and manipulation. Invariably, this gives rise to anger, loneliness and fear.

For healing to take place, we have to put ourselves on our list of priorities – not in a self-centred way but as an act of selflessness. When we put ourselves on the list (we can share the top place with our loved ones) then we are saying that our love for others is so strong that we want to be able to *really* give by being in the most healed state possible. In this sense, healing ourselves is the most selfless thing we could do.

The following is a note written by Irene, a woman who came to a workshop Eddie and I were teaching. She couldn't talk, due to a throat operation, but her eyes spoke volumes:

> *Hello, I'm Irene. I have been extraordinarily ill and nearly dead on many occasions. I have been unkind to myself and always good to others with no thought of myself. In the last year I have felt bliss three times. I now have the complete set of pain, fear, love, bliss, life and death. I'd like to heal my life this time round. I have felt such love from others while I was ill that it has made me start to love myself.*

Looking at priorities means asking why we are really here, what our lives are about, what gives us our sense of purpose or direction. Is it just to raise a family and work, to make money, retire, play with the grandchildren and then it's over? There is nothing wrong with this and it certainly brings great joy. But it can also leave an aching emptiness inside, due to unacknowledged doubts, insecurities, fears, longings and dreams. What happened to the athletic teenager who loved to run across the fields and is now trapped inside an overweight and rarely exercised body? What happened to the paintings you never did, to the musical instrument you never learnt, to the novel you never wrote? What happened to the pain you felt when your mother died? What happened to the anger you felt towards the uncle who fondled you? Why is it so hard to spend time alone?

Illness confronts us with many of these questions. We have choices: we can take a pill and carry on as before; we can have surgery and repress our feelings. Or we can begin to become whole. If we only take a pill or have the surgery then we are ignoring a wonderful opportunity the body is providing for us to find a deeper

———— **TRY IT YOURSELF** ————

Recognising Your Purpose

Find a place where you can be quiet and undisturbed for half an hour or so. Have some paper and a pen with you.

- Start by sitting comfortably and closing your eyes. Begin to focus on your breathing, just watching the natural flow of the breath as it enters and leaves your body. Then silently repeat three times, 'I am here to connect with my purpose.'

- Allow the following questions to permeate your heart. Breathe each question into the core of your being and let it sit there before you start to write any answers. You are not looking for rational and logical answers, but the deeper ones that emerge from your heart. Try not to let your head do the talking!

1 When do I feel life is most meaningful?

2 What makes me happiest?

3 What fills me with passion?

- When you feel you have entered into these questions, received and understood the answers, continue:

4 If I could live again, what would I do differently?

5 If I could do anything I want now, what would I do?

6 What will I most regret if I leave it undone?

- Take your time answering these. There may also be other questions that arise out of them. Let your heart speak. When you are ready, continue:

7 What are my three main priorities in life?

8 Am I doing any of these now, and if not, why not?

9 What practical things can I do now, and in the next two months, to honour my priorities further?

- Respect whatever answers you have written down and commit yourself to putting these into practice. The commitment is to your own healing.

level of joy and freedom within. Are you willing to forgive yourself for a past mistake, or is it easier to stay feeling guilty and suffer the recurring backache?

Healing means letting go of resistance, of the barriers that have been constructed, of the layers of self-protection, of ingrained patterns of thinking and behaviour, of repressive control over our feelings, of all the ways we have held on and to what we have been holding on to. All our habitual ways of being: putting other's needs first, not thinking about ourselves, staying so busy there is no time in which to be alone, or focusing only on the financial and material aspects of life. Healing is releasing the holds, breathing into the space that is left behind. 'So our path becomes a letting go of that which blocks the path,' writes Stephen Levine in *Healing Into Life and Death*. 'Healing is not forcing the sun to shine but letting go of the personal separatism, the self-images, the resistance to change, the fear and anger, the confusion that forms the opaque armouring around the heart.'

♦ THE HEART'S REMISSION ♦

To be healed is to bring ourselves into a whole, it is a gathering of our lost voices and forgotten selves, an embracing of those parts of our being that have been hidden and denied. It is a journey of trust, to discover our inner strength, and it demands our total commitment.

As we gather ourselves into a whole, a beautiful thing begins to happen: we find that our lost voices have a sweet song to sing, that our forgotten selves want to dance and laugh. As we embrace the darkness and soothe our inner wounds, we come to a different purpose, one that gives rise to a new priority: that of our salvation, our freedom, a discovery of our true potential.

The original interpretation of the word 'meaning' was to recite, tell, intend, or wish. This suggests that without meaning, life is like a blank page – there is no story to tell, nothing to recite. But meaning also implies significance and purpose, without which there is no direction, no mission. No story plus no purpose equals no reason to be here. Meaninglessness can thus cause lethargy, depression, hopelessness and illness. Finding meaning gives direction and motivation, a reason for being that stimulates creativity, optimism, strength and well-being.

This is seen in the word *remission*, used to describe a period of recovery, when an illness or disease diminishes. A patient is described as being in remission when their symptoms abate. Yet the word also reads as 're-mission', to re-find or become reconnected with purpose. In other words, disease can diminish when we find a deeper meaning or purpose in our lives. Remission also means forgiveness, implying that healing can occur through accepting ourselves and our behaviour and releasing our guilt, or through accepting and forgiving another and releasing blame.

Remission arises through a blend of responsibility and passivity. It is essential that we take responsibility for our own behaviour, actions, words, thoughts and lifestyle. No one else can do this for us. Taking responsibility means acknowledging that healing comes from within. We can then work with others to find the best way to promote our health. This may involve taking medication or having surgery, but it can also involve meditation, group therapy or dance classes. The difference is that we are responding to our personal needs. To be responsible is to *be able to respond*: to hear those lost voices and remember our forgotten selves.

Action also needs to be balanced by non-action – doing by being. Many of us have completely forgotten how to simply be present and at ease with whatever is happening. Children have this capacity – to flow with each moment without holding on or trying to control. But, as we grow older, we cling to control and power; we stop being and start doing. Very often those who experience illness followed by a remission find that it occurs through releasing control and allowing whatever is to be – a return to that childlike place of trust and present-moment discovery. Perhaps we all need to stop being human doings and become more truly human beings!

This attitude towards simply being is one of letting go of resistance and entering into assurance; of releasing the logic of what appears to be right and opening to intuition and inner feeling; it is an embracing of ourselves and the universe, without the need to be in control. This is not the same as feeling we are victims of fate, that we just have to suffer our lot. Rather it is a recognition of the interdependence and intricate relationship between every aspect of the universe, including ourselves. 'Surrender means the decision to stop fighting the world and to start loving it instead,' writes Marianne Williamson in *A Return to Love*. 'It is a gentle liberation from pain. But liberation isn't about breaking out of anything; it's a gentle melting into who we really are.'

In *Grace and Grit*, Ken Wilber's wife Treya recounts her experience of dealing with cancer. In the process she came to deeply understand and balance these two aspects, doing and being, in a state of 'passionate equanimity' which she describes as being 'fully passionate about all aspects of life, about one's relationship with spirit, to care to the depth's of one's being but with no trace or clinging or holding.' Later Ken talks of how he saw this passion and equanimity in every aspect of her healing. 'Being and doing. Surrender and will. Total acceptance and fierce determination. Those two sides of her soul, the two sides she wrestled with all her life, the two sides she finally brought together into one harmonious whole.'

PART TWO

THE HEALING POWER OF THE BODYMIND

5

HEALING THROUGH THE MIND

THE POWER of the mind is enormous. The same power that can undermine or weaken our health can also bring strength and healing. In the United States, a group of healthy five-year-old-children were told about a magic microscope that showed how the cells in the body fight germs; they were also shown a film with glove puppets acting the roles of different cells in the immune system. They were then led through a relaxation exercise where they were asked to visualise the immune cells as policemen fighting the germs. Saliva was collected before and after for analysis. After the experiment it was found to be saturated with immunity substances at levels normal for fighting an infection. Through these simple techniques the children had succeeded in activating their immune systems. The 'Hot Hands' exercise on the following page will show you the power of your own mind.

If you have done the exercise and found your hand getting hot and then cold you have witnessed the autogenic power of your mind to change your body. You did this consciously, but the same thing is unconsciously happening all the time. Our thoughts and feelings are constantly influencing our bodies and, therefore, our state of health. By using our mental power we can make this unconscious process a conscious one. We can use similar techniques to quieten a racing heartbeat or help loosen congested lungs.

In Chapter 1 we saw the effects of stress: how it increases blood pressure, causes headaches, disturbed sleep, a loss of appetite, peptic ulcers, diarrhoea and disturbed moods, depression, anger and anxiety. In this chapter we will see how our minds can also help to solve these problems, by lowering blood pressure, deepening sleep patterns, reducing adrenaline surges, improving immunity and helping to create a more positive outlook on life.

TRY IT YOURSELF

Hot Hands

Find a comfortable place to sit where you will be undisturbed for a few minutes.

- Close your eyes, take a deep breath and relax. Spend a few moments just watching the flow of your breath as it enters and leaves, feeling yourself relaxing and getting quieter with each breath.

- Now begin to focus on your right hand. Do nothing and think nothing – just put all your energy into your right hand. And imagine that hand getting hotter and hotter. It may help to imagine the sun beating down on your hand, or imagine that you are holding red-hot coals. Focus all your attention on feeling this right hand getting hotter and hotter. You may even find that it begins to perspire. Keep doing this for at least four or five minutes.

- Now imagine your right hand cooling down. It is getting colder and colder, as if you are holding ice or snow in your palm. Spend a few minutes doing this. Then take a deep breath and open your eyes.

As we have seen, the major causes of stress are not the big problems we have to face but all the small, daily difficulties, such as getting stuck in traffic, a child knocking over a glass of juice, or losing a button off a coat. As we gain a sense of inner ease and relaxation, these issues become less disturbing. We learn to stop, take a deep breath, and create some space between ourselves and the situation. Is it really so desperately important? Can we not see the funny side of it? Stopping to breathe and observe creates a greater sense of the whole, so that the individual parts become lighter, looser. It matters less if we are late or if we have to clear up a mess; there is a greater ability to take it in our stride without tensing up. Because the external environment has less influence on us, there is a greater awareness of just this moment. Releasing the inner stresses creates space for ever deeper levels of healing.

There are a number of ways in which we can work with the mind to generate greater awareness and healing. By learning to pay attention and develop mindfulness we become more aware of how we affect ourselves and our world; through positive thinking and affirmations we redirect behavioural patterns; through creative visualisation we send healing images and energy to specific parts of the body; through inner conscious relaxation and meditation we release layers of inner stress and allow a deeper peace to emerge.

♦ MINDFUL ATTENTION ♦

Consciously applying awareness or mindful attention to our behaviour, actions, thoughts and feelings enables us to see the various ways we may be either sabotaging or encouraging our healing. This is a very simple process of just being aware, watching and observing. It may feel very odd at first – we may never have been aware in this way before. Indeed, many people have hardly any self-awareness. What we are doing is becoming truly present in our own being, looking at the way this being functions, where the strengths and weaknesses lie, how the energies ebb and flow, where there are resistances or limitations, and how to move through those resistances.

Watch how you treat your body, the way you move, breathe, walk, exercise, your attitude towards yourself. Do you eat very quickly? Are you aware of the food in your mouth, of the taste, the texture? If you smoke, watch when the desire arises. Is it when you feel in need of comfort? Or are there things you are fearful of saying? When you exercise, watch your response. Are you aware of your muscles moving, of the interplay of energies? When you wash the dishes, are you aware of the soap bubbles and the play of the water? If you are late for an appointment, does your mindful awareness go out of the window? Can you remember brushing your teeth? Making the toast? What you saw on television last night? At this very moment are you aware of your body and how it feels?

Paying attention means listening, watching, noticing, without comment – it doesn't mean judging, criticising or feeling guilty. We need to see ourselves just as we are, not to feel buried by everything that's wrong or to induce more bad feelings. Any judgement or criticism is based on expectations and what we think others think – all of this is relevant. Healing means accepting ourselves as we are, completely. Being self-aware is being aware of how we judge and criticise, and just noticing this – not judging our judgementalism. This is not a self-centred activity. Paying attention to ourselves does not mean becoming self-obsessed. It is simply watching, noticing.

Focus your attention on your mind by observing your thoughts. This brings you back into the present moment. 'Mindfulness is the miracle by which we can call back in a flash our dispersed mind and restore it to wholeness so that we can live each minute of life,' writes Thich Nhat Hanh in *The Miracle of Mindfulness*. Every so often during the day, perhaps once an hour, pause and note down what you are thinking about. Notice your thoughts and habits. Become aware of thinking patterns, how prejudices or judgements arise. Notice how quick you are to judge yourself or to put others down. Watch the effect your thoughts have on your body: maybe a rise in temperature, a coughing fit, or an anxiety attack. The mind is in a constant state of distraction. Watch the excuses it imposes, the fears and doubts that arise, the internal dialogue that leads nowhere. Observe, but do not judge.

You will probably notice how much you avoid yourself, particularly your weak areas. See how often you want to change the subject, start fidgeting, remember something that needs to be done, or suddenly get very tired; how easily you fill your days with things to do, so there are no empty spaces; or pass the time by socialising endlessly. If you read a daily newspaper, try going without one for a week and see what you do with the space created. Or spend a week without watching any television. Observe where and how you resist just being with yourself.

Pay attention to your feelings by watching how you respond to different situations and people. Watch your anxieties and fears. Allow them space without pushing them away or pretending they are different. Breathe into them. Notice your desires and how you manipulate events or people to get your needs fulfilled. See how your feelings influence others and stimulate different responses. Observe but do not judge.

As awareness grows you may find yourself confronting old patterns of behaviour, or lost memories that have shaped your thinking. Bringing awareness to that which is hidden, denied or ignored enables those energies to move out of the darkness and into the light – sometimes that is all that is required. Shining light on what has been hidden means acknowledging it, accepting it, bringing it into the wholeness of your being.

Becoming aware of ourselves as we are is the beginning of accepting ourselves. We can't accept something we are not aware of and we can't become aware without paying attention, watching and listening. The deeper levels are where we do the most ignoring. Becoming aware of our inner pain, and accepting it, brings warmth and softness and release. It may be very hard at times. The tendency is to run away, to cover the pain up again. But it is there to help us grow. From the garbage we get compost and compost helps flowers to grow. Illness makes us respond to what is happening now. We cannot hold on to what was, or how we used to be. Being present with what is now, and who we are now, is meeting each moment in its fullness.

♦ BREATHING THERAPY ♦

The breathing process is carried out by the automatic nervous system, meaning that we breathe without having to do anything consciously. However, the way we breathe directly corresponds to our emotions: stressful or fearful states are usually accompanied by short, shallow breathing, high in the chest; whereas peaceful and relaxed states are accompanied by longer, deeper breaths centred in the belly area. Do you find yourself gasping for breath when you feel sad or angry?

Anger makes the breath shallow and fast, while fear makes us hold our breath or breathe very quickly. Sadness will make us gulp and gasp, and breathe irregularly. When we breathe deeply the chest opens – as when we feel joy and happiness and any inner tension is released. As Kariba Ekken, a seventh-century sufi, once wrote:

> If you would foster a calm spirit, first regulate your breathing; for when that is under control, the heart will be at peace; but when breathing is spasmodic, then it will be troubled. Therefore, before anything, first regulate your breathing on which your temper will be softened, your spirit calmed.

We can deliberately induce a quieter and more relaxed state by consciously changing our breathing patterns and shifting to a deeper, 'belly breath'. This eases the nervous system and affects our entire physiological response to stress by calming both the body and the mind. Developing awareness of the breath and learning how to change breathing patterns are essential tools to aid healing, releasing stress before it is translated into physical distress. (There is a practice on the following page to help you.)

We can use the breath to release tension, to deepen concentration, and to ease pain, as seen during childbirth. Normally we tense ourselves against pain, whether physical or psychological, and

Belly Breathing

Take some time to sit quietly and observe your breathing. Either lie down, legs slightly apart, arms by your sides; or sit upright in a straight-backed chair, feet flat on the floor, hands relaxed. Close your eyes.

• Start by just watching your breath without changing it in any way or trying to control it. For a few moments just watch your breath entering and leaving your body.

• Now become aware of where your breath is normally focused. Is it your upper chest that rises and falls? Does the middle part of your chest move? Or does your belly rise and fall? Try putting one hand on your chest and one on your belly so you can feel the movement. Do this with your eyes closed.

• Belly breathing is a way of deepening your breathing. To do this, start by just breathing into the top part of your chest. Spend a few minutes breathing this way so you are fully aware of this level of breathing. Keep your hand on your upper chest, by your collar bone. Your breath will probably be quite short and quick. Notice any emotions or feelings that arise in relation to breathing here.

• Then shift your breathing and your awareness to the area of your middle chest, by your heart. Put your hand there and consciously breathe into this area. Feel as if you are breathing into your heart. Your breath will begin to slow down and deepen. Watch if your feelings or emotions change. Focus on the rise and fall of your chest. Stay here for a few minutes.

• Now bring the breath all the way into your belly. Put your hand on your belly, just below your belly button, to feel it rising and falling with each breath. At first this may feel unnatural, as if you are having to deliberately push your belly out and pull it in. Relax into the movement, breathing slowly and deeply. (The diaphragm is a strong muscle membrane which separates the lungs from the abdominal organs. The lower it moves during inhalation, the more air is taken into the lungs.) Exhale deeply and feel your hand move with the abdomen. Take a few breaths. Notice any stress or tension leaving as you breathe more deeply. How has your emotional state changed?

• Now return to your normal breathing pattern and see if it has changed. Practice this exercise often, especially if you feel your stress levels rising.

seek a way out through distraction or pills. But there is another way, and that is to breathe *into* the pain, to become more and more open to it. Breathing in this way reduces the intensity of the pain and releases the tension. It also helps separate the physical pain from the emotional tensions or fears that often accompany it, so we can work more directly with the issues involved. To do this, consciously direct your breath into the painful area, feel the pain softening and dissolving with each in-breath, and release the pain on the out-breath.

Breathing marks your entry into this world. No longer supported by your mother, it propels you into your own existence. The air is painful in the first few moments of life, as the lungs are still tender. You can use your breath to enter vulnerable and tender places within yourself. Use your breath to keep breathing into and through any resistance. Use your breath to give you courage and fearlessness, to ground you in your present reality. Your breath is your greatest friend, always present, always there to help you.

Remember the phrase 'soft belly' and repeat it to yourself whenever you need to: you can't get tense or nervous if you have a soft belly, and as soon as you repeat the words it will remind you to relax and breathe. Softening the belly softens your resistance, limitations and inner tension. Do this any time, anywhere; eyes open or closed. Sitting on the train feeling tired and stressed – soft belly and breathe. Standing at the sink surrounded by dirty dishes and a screaming baby – soft belly and breathe. About to go into surgery – soft belly and breathe. On your way to an important meeting – soft belly and breathe.

The breath has a rhythm and it is the rhythm of the universe – of the tides, the seasons, the sun and moon. Every living organism breathes. It is this that connects us together for we breathe the same air, we share each breath with every form of life. Watching the breath, as in the Breath Awareness Meditation exercise at the end of this chapter, enables us to connect with this universal rhythm. Breath is life. Through our awareness of it we can find a renewed life, a renewed rhythm.

♦ AFFIRMATIONS ♦

Affirmations are a good way of shifting hidden or fixed thinking patterns. They are not a way of making everything appear wonderful, or of trying to achieve unrealistic goals. Rather, affirmations can help you move from feeling like a helpless or hopeless victim, to gaining inner strength and a more accepting and loving attitude.

Our normal use of affirmations tends to be negative and unconscious – affirming our lack of love or money, our weaknesses or stupidity, saying things like, 'I can't do this' or 'I never seem to have enough energy' or 'I always get the wrong end of the stick'. Even by saying 'I will not get angry' we are affirming that there is anger. In this way a thinking or behavioural pattern is created that maintains the original thought.

Conscious affirmations help us to re-program our thinking because they channel the energy in a different direction. Instead of maintaining the 'I feel unloved' state of mind, we can turn that around and create an 'I am surrounded by all the love I need' state. Doing this may feel very superficial at first, as if you are just repeating platitudes in order to keep reality at bay (especially if you are not well and the pain continues, no matter what you do). Just trust that it does work, but it may take time. It is all too easy to give in to the old thought patterns, to slide into a mire of self-pity and depression. Affirmations are like the rungs of a ladder that enable you to climb upwards, towards sanity, self-acceptance and good health. You are taking action, you are no longer a victim. It is very empowering to say, 'I will make a difference. I care enough about myself to make this effort.'

Affirmations not only create a positive alternative but also enable us to see ourselves more clearly. For instance, if you want to lose weight you may create an affirmation such as, 'With each day, my slim and slender body is emerging.' If you repeat this as you go through your day, then you will be far more aware each time you reach for a biscuit or chocolate – the action will be highlighted because it is no longer in accordance with the behaviour you are affirming. You will also notice that you feel better about yourself because you are affirming and supporting your desire to change.

To create an affirmation, chose a single subject to focus on (it gets too complicated if you try to work on more than one issue at once). The affirmation needs to be a positive statement such as 'I am full of love and acceptance for John,' rather than the negative, 'I am no longer getting angry with John.' Keep the statement short and to the point. It should be repeated silently, as often as you want. It can be done spontaneously whenever you become aware of a negative thought pattern.

We may need to start by becoming *ready* to let go of our problems, for many of us unconsciously want to hold on to them, even though we consciously say we want to let go. This is due to deeper levels of negativity about ourselves which are not so easy to identify. In this case, you can start by affirming, 'I am ready to change my behaviour', or 'I am ready to let go of the need for . . . (alcohol/food/self-destructive mind states)'. Then you can move on to 'I am clear and free of all . . . (intoxicants/self-destruction)'.

♦ CREATIVE VISUALISATION ♦

Creative visualisation is an extremely effective way to use the power of the mind to bring about change in the body. In the same way that we can change the temperature in our hands, we can use visualisation to strengthen the body, bring healing to specific areas, communicate with the body itself, or induce a calm and peaceful state of mind. As Herbert Benson writes in *The Wellness Book*:

> *All thoughts and images created by the mind affect the body. When you dream you are being chased or assaulted, or that you are falling, for example, your heartbeat quickens, you tremble, you may even perspire. While the dream is not a reality but only a series of mental images, the physiological response is real and measurable. The challenge is to use imagery to promote health and well-being.*

It is important to remember that visualisation is not a medical cure. It creates images for the body to respond to, but if we do not fully believe those images then another part of the mind will be undermining the effect of the visualisation. We have to put wholehearted effort into it and trust the process, not doubt it. Doing the visualisation for half an hour a day, while spending the rest of the time worrying that our illness is worsening, will mean that the visualisation has no chance of working – it will be overshadowed by the worry.

To use visualisation to affect the state of your body, it helps to understand the structure and function of the parts involved. Very different images may be used to build the immune system or to help mend a broken bone – one is working with rebellious cells, the other with joining tissue. Before you start, spend some time getting to know what is actually happening in that part of your body and what action is needed.

It is also very important to find images that work for you, not ones that make you feel uncomfortable in any way. For instance, when using imagery to help heal cancer it has been found that the warrior or knight in shining armour type image seems to be stronger than using ferocious or killer animals such as sharks or alligators. One of the drawbacks of using a 'hunter and the hunted' image is that it makes the hunted into an 'alien thing' that must be eliminated or killed. Yet each part of the body is a part of our whole being, even cancer cells. One of the patients quoted in Stephen Levine's *Healing Into Life and Death* came up against this problem:

> *As my immune system became more ferocious and I saw it attacking the tumours, it only seemed to intensify the tightness in my gut. Rather than using aggression to encourage the immune system, visualising white alligators (lymphocytes) ravaging rotten hamburger (cancer tumours), I began instead to image sending love. What a relief not to stimulate hate in my gut, nor to fear myself there anymore.*

Imagery that worked particularly well for another patient was seeing her immune cells as white hearts that filled each cancer cell with a pure white love liquid. In this way she was acknowledging the cancer cells as simply being wayward cells who had forgotten about love, rather than as the enemy. In *Peace, Love and Healing* Dr. Bernie Siegel suggests visualisations in which the disease cells are ingested as a source of growth and nourishment. This encourages us to see the disease as a part of ourselves that needs integrating, that is actually beneficial.

Recently, an abscess in a tooth made me tune into my immune system. When I focused on my immune cells the image that came was of a host of really big women – big mammas – of all races and all dressed in flowing white robes. I saw the invading bacteria as a group of superficially tough young men. At the sight of the advancing wave of large, white-robed women, the men cowered, trembled, and fell to their knees. Teenage girls, in training, came around afterwards to lead the quaking men away. This imagery said a great deal about my own energy at the time. I was going through a phase of thinking I could do everything, of acting all tough and capable. What I really needed was to be able to ask for help, to let more of my feminine qualities come through. The abscess was showing me where the request for help was getting stuck.

Imagery can help to mend broken bones, open blockages in arteries, heal wounds, or calm stomach ulcers. In each case you can visualise the particular area and focus on what form of healing is required. For instance, you can visualise yourself cleaning a wound with cotton swabs, followed by stitching it together. Imagine the wound closed and the skin healing without a scar. Or focus on an inflamed area and visualise yourself rubbing in some cooling balm that contains herbs and healing ingredients, easing the area, releasing the anger. If you have severe muscle tension visualise the tense muscles, feel the stress and aching stiffness and see it relaxing. Perhaps see yourself rubbing in some warming and softening ointment, or soothing the muscles in a hot, steamy bath. Visualise them being nourished and stroked so that the tension begins to dissolve. Through visualising movement in paralysed limbs, physical movement may even become possible.

We can use visualisation to communicate with different parts of the body to find out what is happening and what is needed (this practice is available on cassette tape from the address on page 247). Sometimes the images are obvious, sometimes more obscure, yet they always offer a clue to healing. During a visualisation exercise, a woman who was very addicted to sweets went to check on her pancreas. She saw a big dump truck offloading pure white sugar, burying the organ beneath it. This alerted her to the seriousness of her addiction. A man suffering from overwork and stress went to check his brain. He saw electrical sparks shooting off in all directions and realised that he was very close to a power failure (a nervous breakdown). Steve, whose story of irritable bowel syndrome was shared in Chapter 1, went to his intestines:

> I saw the inside of my intestines encrusted with crystals. These were very beautiful, but they caused me much discomfort. However, there was an enormous amount of energy stored in the crystals. I knew that they represented all my old hurts and angers, but then I found I could tap into their energy, I could convert it for present use.

Creative Visualisation

Start by finding a comfortable position, either lying down with your legs slightly apart and your arms by your side, or sitting in a chair with your hands on your lap. Close your eyes. Take a deep breath and let it go.

- Start by becoming aware of your feet, then slowly become aware of each part of your body. Relax and breathe into each area. Your legs. . .hips. . .back. . .abdomen. . . midriff. . .chest. . .hands. . .arms. . .shoulders. . .neck. . . head. Then spend a few minutes watching your breath entering and leaving your body. With each breath feel yourself relaxing, becoming quieter and softer.

- Begin to imagine you are in a beautiful place where it is very peaceful. This may be a place you already know, or you can let your imagination create the details. What is this place like? Are you walking on the earth, on grass, or on sand? What does the ground feel like? Is there water breaking at your feet, or flowers and trees around you? What qualities fill this special place? What colours are around you? Are there sweet smells, perhaps of flowers or of incense? Is there birdsong or the sound of water on sweet music? Can you feel sunshine on your body or a soft breeze? Explore this beautiful place and let the wonder of it fill your being.

- Now relax by either sitting or lying. You may want to sit in an old tree or amongst the grass; you may want to lie on the warm sand or in an old boat floating on the water. Find your place and relax there for a few minutes, absorbing the serenity and peace that is all around you. Visualise yourself here as you would like to be – perfectly healed, perfectly peaceful, full of radiance and joy. Let this image fill you. Feel yourself being filled with light and love and stay with this for a few minutes.

- Then gently take a deep breath and begin to let the images dissolve. You can come back any time you want to. Become aware of the seat or ground beneath you and the room around you, begin to stretch your body and slowly open your eyes.

Some people find that they do not respond to visual imagery but they do respond to sensations, such as feeling touch like warm sunlight, or listening to different sounds. One man listened to the sound of running water to help him pass a kidney stone lodged in his urethra. Any of the senses can be used to stimulate change.

Visualisation can also create psychological states of peace and equanimity. Imagining a beautiful or peaceful scene triggers the release of endorphins and increases feelings of tranquility. At the same time it lowers blood pressure and releases tension while stimulating the immune system. In this state, we can connect with our deeper qualities such as compassion, forgiveness, inner strength or fearlessness. Making contact in this way brings these energies into the conscious mind.

As with relaxation and meditation, the effectiveness of creative visualisation depends on doing it regularly – preferably once a day for about half an hour, longer and more often if you wish. You may want to play soft music. Make sure you will be undisturbed. You can lie down or sit up – whichever is most comfortable. Spend a few minutes relaxing by watching your breath entering and leaving the body, feeling each part of your being relax. Then begin to create whatever visualisation works for you, depending on where you want to bring healing. Or try the visualisation opposite to generate a sense of inner peace and balance.

♦ INNER CONSCIOUS RELAXATION ♦

Deep relaxation is essential to healing, whether our wounds are internal or external. If we are in a state of tension and feel nervous, edgy, irritable, worried, fearful, pressured, unsupported or unable to cope, then it is very hard for the body or the mind to heal itself. We need to create a space for relaxation, where we don't just put our feet up, watch television and relax the superficial layers, but where we consciously relax the inner layers of stress. As long as there is any psychological tension then there will be muscle tension. Having a drink or watching a movie might lessen stress momentarily, but long-term relief needs more effort.

Practising deep relaxation slowly loosens and releases the inner knots and enables us to go deeper into ourselves to connect with our sanity and peace. It puts everything back in perspective. Relaxation slows down nervous palpitations, deepens sleep patterns, lowers blood pressure, balances the appetite, strengthens the immune system, releases muscle tension, lowers cholesterol levels and

────────── **TRY IT YOURSELF** ──────────

Inner Conscious Relaxation

You can practise this for just a few minutes anywhere – at work, sitting on a park bench, at home, even on a train. Just don't do it while driving a car or operating machinery!

- Start by finding a comfortable place to either sit or lie down. You may want to play some very gentle and quiet music while you are doing this, and make sure you will not be disturbed. If you are sitting then try to find a straight-backed chair and sit upright, with your feet flat on the floor (not crossed) and your hands on your thighs, palms facing upwards. If you are lying down, then have your feet slightly apart and your arms by your sides, palms facing upwards. You may want a light blanket to cover you. Close your eyes.

- Begin by becoming aware of the rhythm of your breathing. Just watch the movement of the breath, as it enters and leaves your body for a few moments.

- Now bring your awareness to your right foot. Tighten the muscles, hold, then completely relax your foot. Do the same with your right calf – becoming aware of that part of your leg, tightening, holding and then releasing. Move systematically and slowly throughout your body from the calf to the right thigh . . . then the left foot . . . left calf. . .and left thigh. Then the right buttock and the left buttock – tensing, holding and releasing. Work your way up the whole of your back. Then the lower abdomen . . . the midriff . . . the chest. Then your right hand . . . lower arm and upper arm . . . then the right shoulder. Then the left hand. . . lower arm . . . upper arm and left shoulder – tensing, holding and releasing. Then do the same with your neck . . . with all the muscles on your face . . . and with the whole of your head. Feel your whole body relaxing.

- Now go through each part of your body again, this time simply bringing your awareness to that area. As before, start with your right foot . . . right leg . . . left foot . . . left leg . . . buttocks . . . back . . . abdomen . . . chest . . . right hand, arm

continued

and shoulder. . . left hand, arm and shoulder. . . neck and head.

- Repeat silently to yourself: 'My body is heavy and relaxed, sinking into the ground; my heartbeat is normal; I am breathing easily; my mind is calm and peaceful; my heart is open.' Watch the flow of your breath for a few minutes. Let yourself sink into the natural rhythm of the breath as it enters and leaves your body. When you are ready, take a deep breath and let it out. Then gently open your eyes and have a good stretch.

increases the blood supply to the heart. It also eases mental and emotional stress, depression and anxiety, thus increasing your inner resources and resilience. Every part of your being benefits. This is the *relaxation response*, as opposed to the *stress response* described earlier.

The technique that is most recommended is called inner conscious relaxation. It is based on ancient systems of yoga and has been tried and tested over hundreds of years. It induces an inner relaxed state that, when practised regularly, affects our whole life. If we are not at ease with ourselves then we will impose that stressful state – our irritation, frustration or annoyance – on those around us, creating more pain, confusion and emotional chaos. When we enter a relaxed state then even a life-threatening illness becomes easier to deal with because we are not tensing up against it. Blame and guilt recede and there is a deeper acceptance of ourselves as we are.

You can practise for just a few minutes, perhaps a few times a day. Or you can practise for up to half an hour at a time, once a day or every few days. Accumulation, and therefore consistency, is important. The more often you can sink into the deeper levels of ease, the more this practice will become an integral part of your being and the less you will succumb to stress. Opposite is a mini inner conscious relaxation (ICR) practice, or you can use one of the various ICR tapes, available from the address on page 247.

You may want to do this exercise alone or you may find it beneficial to do it with a partner or friend. If you are doing it once a day, work out when you feel most awake and make sure that you will be undisturbed. Some people are morning people, others prefer the evening. Experiment with different times until you find the one that feels best for you. It may mean getting up a little earlier in order to have some quiet time to yourself, but it is well worth it. The benefits will soon show.

Whatever you do, do not judge your relaxation progress. It does not matter if, during a session, you are unable to relax, if you just lie there with thoughts going through your mind, or even if you fall asleep. All good things take time to develop. Give yourself that time; be gentle and patient. This technique is not intended to create more tension!

♦ MEDITATION ♦

Meditation is an experience of complete inner silence and peace where the individual 'I' dissolves into the universal whole; and it is the technique or practice that helps to achieve this state. Many of us experience meditation quite naturally when we are very focused or concentrated, usually on a creative project, or when we are sitting quietly surrounded by nature. It is that moment when the thinking subsides and we are totally and completely in the present, when all sense of separation dissolves and there is a complete unity with all beings and all things – the bird flying above, the earth beneath, the flower in our hand. There is no sense of ourselves as separate in any way from any thing. We may have had this experience and not realised what was happening. Now, through the practice of meditation, we can begin to re-experience this, but with full awareness.

Meditation is an invaluable tool for healing – traditional yogis who use relaxation and meditation techniques are known to reduce their risk of cardiovascular and nervous diseases by up to 80 per cent. Dr James Gordon, a clinical professor at the Georgetown School of Medicine, says, 'I'll almost always "prescribe" some form of meditation to them [his patients] along with any medicine I might give them. *Meditation* and *medicine* come from the same root: "to care" and "to cure".'

There are many different meditation techniques but they all have the same basis. Each is a means to quieten and calm the mind by focusing attention inwards on a particular object or thought. This may be breath, a candle, a mantra or sound, a visualisation, or the development of a particular emotion like loving kindness or forgiveness. This gives the mind something to do so that the constant turmoil of thoughts, scenarios or concerns begins to settle. Beneath those thoughts are ever deeper layers of inner quiet, creative energy and clarity.

The object of meditation is just to see but without attachment, to be a witness to ourselves. At times it may feel as if we are witnessing an enormous and eventful drama; at other times it may get very quiet and we hear a different silence that comes from inside. Simply witnessing brings all our energies into the present moment. Nothing else is going on, nothing else exists. In this space, it is very joyful. There is a surrendering of resistance, a letting go of chaos.

During meditation we meet ourselves in an entirely new way, for there is nowhere to hide. This leads to an increase in self-awareness and self-respect, a release of fear and self-judgement, and a greater ability to deal with issues such as guilt or grief. Through the development of the subtler energies of love, compassion and forgiveness, we are able to confront those places within that are holding on to past trauma and to release the pain. Meditation creates the space for us to see how our minds work, how thoughts and dramas come and go. But instead of getting lost in the story and then feeling bad about it, we can develop greater objectivity. We no longer need to identify with the story. We are free to find out who we really are.

However, as with relaxation, meditation doesn't always come easily at first so perseverance and practice are important. It helps to spend a few minutes relaxing before you meditate, as any stress or tension can cause a disturbance when you begin to draw your focus inwards. The mind is very good at finding all sorts of reasons why you should not be doing this; if that doesn't work then the body starts aching or getting pins and needles. Move your body if you need to, but stay firm with your mind: you are here – and it is only for a short time – to be quiet and to focus within.

There is no right or wrong way to practise, and therefore no reason to berate yourself for not having a 'good' meditation, for thinking too much, for not being able to keep still, or for getting distracted. All these things happen to everyone at different times. Treat whatever you are experiencing as a part of the session – simply observe the shopping lists or conversations going on in your head and then let them go. It's no big deal. Just come back to the practice again. This is what finding the quiet space within is all about – we have to work through the noise first. Trying to make the mind become quiet is impossible; that would be like trying to catch the wind. The mind becomes quiet on its own when we stop struggling.

It is also important to choose a place where you will be undisturbed and where you feel comfortable. Many people create a special place for meditation because this helps them focus their energy. Having a meditation space means that you respect meditation as an important activity. Each time you are there it will remind you of feeling peaceful and in touch with your inner self.

Find a sitting position that feels right for you, whether in a straight-backed chair or cross-legged on a cushion on the floor. Sitting with a straight back is important as it maintains alertness and focus. However, if you cannot sit upright, then it is better to do it lying down than not at all. Find a time that works for you. For many people this is early in the morning (before the family wakes up), later in the morning if you have the day to yourself, or in the early evening. Some prefer late in the evening while others find they are too tired to concentrate then. It is important to practise every day if you can. This is your special time to be with yourself.

It is advisable to start by meditating for just 10 or 15 minutes. As you get more accustomed to the position and the technique, then you can stay longer, up to 20 or 30 minutes. Many people like to meditate in a group at least occasionally – it can really intensify the experience. Various meditations are available on cassette tape from the address on page 247. Below is a short one to get you started.

Breath Awareness Meditation

Find a comfortable and upright seated posture, in a chair or on the floor. Your back is straight and your eyes closed.

• Take a deep breath and let it out through your mouth. Spend a few minutes relaxing your body – if there is any tension anywhere then breathe into that tension and feel it release.

• Now become aware of the natural in- and out-breath. Do not force or change your breathing in any way – simply watch the natural breath. Bring your attention to the space in the centre of your chest – the heart space – and focus your attention on the movement of that place with each in- and out-breath. Just watch.

• Silently repeat the word 'in' with each in-breath and 'out' with each out-breath. In. . . out. . . in. . . out. Just watch the breath, focused at the heart space in the centre of the chest and follow its in and out movement. If any thoughts arise, just see them as thoughts, label them *thinking*, and let them go. If you find you are getting distracted, label it *distraction*, and let it go, always coming back to the breath. In. . . out. . . in. . . out. As you become more focused, your mind will quieten and the space between your thoughts will lengthen.

• Continue for as long as feels comfortable – ten to thirty minutes. Then take a deep breath and let it out through your mouth. Slowly open your eyes and stretch your legs. Be aware of how you feel. Have a smile on your face.

6

HEALING THROUGH THE HEART

WE SPEND many years building a wall around the heart in order to protect it from being hurt. In so doing we wall ourselves off from our own feelings of pain and passion. Eventually we become isolated, locked into separation, unable to experience our own aliveness, to feel our heart's desire. Healing the heart means opening it up to both our wounds and our love.

Emotional pain is just as real as physical pain, and can be even more invasive. Long-held resentments, anger, bitterness, fear, guilt, shame – all play their role in affecting health, limiting the free flow of energy. We feel shame or guilt for something we did or didn't do, long-held resentment or revenge for something that was done to us; we feel unworthy or lacking in confidence, overcome by fear or panic, helpless, depressed, or full of grief. These feelings lie heavy in the heart. We are unable to love for fear of being hurt, unable to forgive due to past resentment, unable to achieve success for dread of failure. All these feelings have their effect in the body and on our health.

But they are there to help us to grow stronger and wiser by acknowledging, accepting and embracing ourselves. This does not mean being immersed in or obsessed with our pain – we do not need to use emotional issues as a cross to bear – but we do need to listen to the messages so we can heal the pain and transform it into freedom. Sheila's experience shows the consequences of ignoring one's heart:

> A four-year relationship ended abruptly. I believed I should stay outwardly calm and balanced no matter what I was feeling inside. As during my childhood, I kept my inner thoughts and feelings in check and my outer persona become

one of being in control. My whole life became a hive of activity as I took on more and more work in an effort to avoid looking at the mental and emotional inner turmoil. Yet my heart was weeping.

The bleeding began after the relationship ended. I kept thinking that each month it would get better. Then I was diagnosed as having fibroids in my womb that were causing heavy and sustained haemorrhaging.

I knew immediately why this had developed. My psychological and emotional states were in total confusion as I continued to present the 'I'm OK' facade. For years I had chosen not to express my inner feelings but to resort to the 'insignificant child' who had learnt to keep quiet in order not to upset anyone. Because the tears were denied, my body was weeping through its feminine heart, the uterus. The blood was the tears of my inner being.

When I finally talked to my ex-lover and expressed my feelings, when I shared the contents of my heart, the bleeding stopped. It was as if my body knew my tears were being acknowledged.

♦ ACCEPTING OURSELVES ♦

To heal ourselves through the heart we have to start by accepting ourselves, just as we are. If we are not at ease with ourselves then we will be sending unlovable, unacceptable, ugly, don't bother messages to our own bodies, as well as to other people. If we are to 'love thy neighbour as thy self,' then we first have to discover what it is to love ourselves.

After trying every form of treatment for cancer, Carl came to a spiritual teacher for advice. 'And you know what she told me?' he asks in Stephen Levine's *Healing Into Life and Death*:

> *'Just love yourself.' It knocked me off my feet. . . She had hit the nail on the head, and the nail was driven right through my heart. . . Those words were the most difficult words I have ever heard, but it was the healing I came for. . . I saw that only by examining and letting go of that fear of loving would I ever get healthy again.*

The process of accepting and making friends with ourselves is not necessarily an easy one. Many of us grow up feeling inadequate, not good enough or pretty enough, not tall enough or clever enough. And it is not just the physical body we have to accept – it is the whole of ourselves, inside and out. Even now you may be wanting to turn the page and move on from this subject, for it can feel quite uncomfortable! Yet we have to start here, by opening our hearts to ourselves.

This means opening up to the guilt, shame, inadequacy and doubt. Feelings like these arise from judging ourselves as bad or wrong. And the feelings get bound up with each other. For instance, guilt proves we are bad, which proves we deserve to suffer, which proves we are unlovable. We get attached to the pain, to regrets, mistakes, shame, or helplessness; we spend our lives disliking ourselves which only creates further pain. We can indulge in guilt or we can develop self-respect. This is the challenge. It is about having an intimate and caring relationship with every part of ourselves, not just with the bits we like. To do this we have to stop judging and criticising, just see each part of ourselves for what it is, without prejudice. The point is not to repress or deny our feelings – by accepting ourselves we grow stronger.

Our bodies need to be appreciated, our long-buried memories need to be tenderly embraced, our past sins need to be forgiven; every part of our being needs to be loved and it needs to be loved by us. Without that love we are lost, alone, discarded, unwanted. With that love we are embraced, vital, alive, connected. 'I guess that is the most important point of healing, whether or not I heal physically – to soften around my heart, to open my heart. This is always the issue, isn't it?' wrote Treya Wilber in a journal chronicling her final experiences with cancer, in *Grace and Grit*.

When we take away the judgement and the shame and the embarrassment, we discover an inherent loveliness within. We do not have to look perfect to be beautiful; we do not have to be acceptable to others to be acceptable to ourselves. Getting angry does not make us bad; doing something we are ashamed of does not make us unlovable. Within us lies a deeper loveliness and this is where our healing is.

♦ ACKNOWLEDGING ANGER ♦

Accepting ourselves means not repressing any of our feelings. They need to be brought out into the light. It helps to recognise that our feelings are not the whole of us, they are only a part. For instance, imagine a scene where your children have been particularly irritating. You get angry with them and tell them to go to their rooms. Afterwards you feel awful – guilty and shamed by such a display. In that moment it can feel as if you are nothing but a hopeless, angry person. But you are not. Yes, there is anger, but it is not the *whole* of you. There are other aspects to you that are not angry ones, that are very loving and caring. It is important to remember these so you can see your anger in perspective.

Then, shifting into a different mode, as the mediator, you can recognise where the feelings came from and why you lashed out like that. Was it something that your parents did to you? Did your children push a button of insecurity or guilt inside you? Did you feel threatened? See what really happened, what actual feelings manifested as anger. Then take a few minutes to completely forgive yourself for reacting that way and, if you can, ask for forgiveness from your children. You are not denying you were angry, simply having a deep appreciation and respect for your own humanness.

Anger, in itself, is not necessarily bad. It is a strong and powerful energy that cuts through confusion and hopelessness, a force that rises up to protect us from being used or abused, like a serpent guarding the entrance to a cave. Patients who are angry and have a fighting spirit are known to get better quicker than those who are passive and ready to submit without an argument. Recognising long-held anger or resentment is vital for healing – anger against being ill, against the injustice, against the doctors. Discovering our capacity for anger can be a moment of pure revelation the discovery of a long-lost voice – without which we are weak and defenceless.

But are you using anger or is anger using you? For anger can also be a vicious weapon that destroys all in its path – a single match that starts a forest fire. Watch as anger arises. Observe the effects on your body, your mind, your heart, your family and friends. See if it creates separation, fear, loneliness, loss. In acknowledging our own feelings, we need to ensure that we are not causing harm or hurt to someone else. Having a loud and angry outburst can leave us feeling great but can leave others feeling as if they have been run over by a truck. In this way anger can be very harmful. And we are here to heal, not to cause more pain. If you need to be angry, then try not to continue the anger beyond its natural expression. There is no need to alienate your partner for three days because he or she did something you don't like. Accept that you are angry, talk it out, and then let it go.

Experience what you are feeling but do not get attached to the feeling. *It is not the whole of you.* See if you can find a way of working with that energy so that it does not become destructive.

Anger is power and it can power you into going for a walk or a run. Write your anger, dance your anger, sing your anger. See what it is saying, what it is really wanting to say. It is a source of tremendous passion. Let the feelings move and flow. Remember to breathe – being angry causes tension which is instantly released through deep breathing.

Anger is about how we feel, not about anyone else. No one *makes* us angry – the anger is our response to what they have done. So it's better to express our feelings by saying, 'I feel angry because. . .' rather than blaming the other person. Making friends with ourselves is about taking responsibility for our anger and being willing to look at it and let it go, rather than repress it or blame the world for it. This means that, instead of being a victim of our anger, we are responding to it. 'To take responsibility for our anger means to relate *to* it instead of *from* it,' writes Stephen Levine in *Healing Into Life and Death*. 'To be responsible to our anger is to bring it within the realm of the voluntary. To react to it leaves life frozen in the mechanical action of old mind.'

Having acknowledged our anger, we can start to look deeper for anger often acts as a mask. Beneath it we may find more tender feelings of loss or abuse, of insecurity or fear, of intense grief or shame. Find these feelings, give them a voice, and see what happens to the anger. And keep going deeper. Further in, you will find your heart. The strength needed to heal the heart is found in the heart itself. There is not just pain there, or past wounding. The heart is a storehouse of compassion, fearlessness, forgiveness and unconditional love.

♦ FEAR AND FEARLESSNESS ♦

Fear is an instinctive response that is released when our survival is threatened; when what we believe in is undermined, or the ground we are standing on becomes shaky and there is nothing to hold on to that feels secure or safe. Healthy fear is an important part of our defence mechanism: it maintains our alertness to danger; it keeps us on our toes. But unhealthy fear is neurotic anxiety which creates worry, panic and non-specific tension the 'what if. . .' syndrome. Physical signs include trembling, sweating, sleeplessness, exhaustion, heart palpitations, short breath and dizziness. If they continue for any length of time these symptoms have a detrimental effect on our health.

Unhealthy fear paralyses us. Every movement forward is undermined by doubt, not being good enough, the fear of what has happened or of what might happen, fear that we are not good enough to be loved, fear of the pain in our heart and fear that we are not strong enough to deal with it. We fear being healed, that we will no longer be sustained or supported. We fear that if we give something up – even bad memories – we will no longer be worthy of love. 'If I give up a bad relationship, maybe no one better will come along. If I look for a new job, maybe I will get a worse one,' writes Joan Borysenko in *Minding the Body, Mending the Mind*. 'If I let go of my suspicion, maybe I will be hurt and disappointed by people. It is fear that masquerades as the need to control, a fear that deprives us of the chance to be free.' Fear is the ego's hold on us, the control button that keeps us prisoners of our own minds.

Find your unhealthy fear – find out where it is in your body, where it is in your past, where it is in your present, where it is in your future. Get to know it. Feel it. Breathe into it. Do not hide from it. Every time it arises, see it, smell it, hear it, touch it, taste it. How does it affect you? What does it stop you from doing? What does it make you do? Follow it and ask it questions. Where does it come from? What does it want? Find its source and give it a name. Fear maintains control by being nameless. How often have you felt fear but not been able to identify what you are fearful of? Define it. And remember to breathe – soft belly.

Allowing unhealthy fear to have power over us means we are resisting change, yet change is the very essence of life itself. Fearlessness is not a fear-less state. Fear is a natural part of being alive and to be completely fear-less would mean being without love and joy. It would mean being emotion-less, without any feelings at all. Fearlessness means being able to feel fear to acknowledge and accept it but not to let it have any hold or influence. We do not have to invite fear in. We become empowered when we stop giving fear our power. This is an opening of the heart to courage and inner strength – to feel fear and yet be fearless. Then love, compassion and gentleness arise – we do not have to fight fear but rather to embrace it.

Fear makes the breath short and shallow; it creates an inner tension that stops us being able to breathe fully. So when you take deep belly breaths and relax into your breathing, the fear is released. And once it is outside you can see it and deal with it.

We can meditate with fear – sitting quietly, watching if fear arises, breathing into it, and simply observing how it affects us, witnessing without being attached or emotionally involved, without judgement. This way we get to see fear objectively, see that it has no foothold in reality but is made up of mental projections and assumptions. Breathing into it we find our ground and fear has less control – we can taste freedom. A fresh taste of flowing and moving and allowing things to happen without expectations or resistance.

'The more you practise [meditation], the more comfortable you become in your own skin,' writes Jon Kabat-Zinn in *Full Catastrophe Living*. 'The more comfortable you feel, the closer you come to perceiving that your anxiety and fears are not you and that they do not have to rule your life.' We are more than just our fear – it is something we experience but it is not the whole of us. By focusing our attention on fear we forget and ignore all the other aspects of ourselves. Remembering this, fear gets put in perspective. We start to see that it is just another emotional state that needs to be accepted and transformed. It does not have to control every part of our lives.

Recently, Eddie asked a 28-year-old Buddhist monk what he found hardest to deal with in his life and he replied, 'uncertainty'. A few weeks later we were with a 71-year-old woman who had few possessions and no home of her own. The same subject arose, about how life contains so much uncertainty. 'I *love* the uncertainty!' she laughed. 'It makes life so much more interesting.' If uncertainty is resisted it brings fear; if it is embraced it brings security in the knowledge that everything changes. The unknown can make us fearful or it can be a challenge. We don't know how long we will live – life itself is an uncertainty – but we can live in fear or we can live with joy, openly meeting each moment. The more we try to control life, the greater the fear. When we let go and jump into the unknown we reclaim our power.

♦ FINDING FORGIVENESS ♦

Forgiveness is the releasing of negativity towards ourselves or others. It sounds simple but it's not easy to do. You may not feel ready to forgive – perhaps the wound is still too painful or the anger too strong. Or you may believe that you could never forgive because the act committed goes beyond the realms of mercy. You may think that forgiveness is a way of abdicating responsibility for what was done, or that it ignores the intensity of the emotions involved. These feelings are justified – they need to be heard and felt.

Yet forgiveness is essential to healing. Earlier we explored the word 'remission'. It means becoming free of symptoms but it also means forgiveness, a pardoning of sins or crimes. In other words, healing and forgiveness are interdependent – without forgiveness we cannot become whole, for some part of us will be held in the past. 'One of the first steps on the path of healing is the deepening of forgiveness,' writes Stephen Levine in *Healing Into Life and Death*. 'Indeed, after awareness has brought us to the path of healing, it is forgiveness that softens the path and allows a continued progress.'

Holding on to pain strengthens and maintains anger and resentment. But we are hurting ourselves, no one else. A lack of forgiveness keeps the guilt, hurt and rage eating away inside us, creating walls around the heart. It locks us into the past, limiting our ability to change. A lack of forgiveness shuts us out of our heart – whereas forgiveness opens the door. It liberates the past, like flood-gates being opened; there is a wave of released energy and we are lighter, freer as a result. It releases us from our attachment to the pain. Forgiveness is saying 'I care enough about myself not to want to keep hurting, to keep carrying this pain around.' In a television programme about forgiveness, Bill related the story of his grand-mother's brutal murder. He was justifiably distraught and had become quite depressed. However, he spent time getting to know the murderer, Paula, visiting her in prison so he could understand her and why this terrible thing had happened. A year later he was able to say that, 'Forgiving Paula did more for me than it did for her.' It freed him of his hate.

Forgiveness does not mean forgiving what happened. Forgiveness does not rationalise or explain away; it does not erase what was done or dismiss its severity – nothing will change what happened. But we can forgive the person who did the act, accepting that they acted out of ignorance or pain, and that what was done was wrong. Forgiveness is not about denying the hurt or suffering – it is very important to acknowledge the pain and the anger, to really know it and feel it, for only then is true forgiveness possible.

However, it is often the experience of pain that creates a resistance to forgiveness. For when we forgive we are not only releasing the story but also all the excuses for our suffering. There is no longer anyone to blame, no reason for the pain. And it is much easier to blame someone else than to take responsibility for our own state of mind. By not forgiving we have the perfect excuse not to change, not to let go. So we hold on to being wounded, to the 'poor me', to the victim. Yet by holding on to the pain we are staying locked into a relationship with the other person, the thought of them controlling our moods and emotions. In this way the hurt from the past is constantly re-created. It is for own benefit to move beyond the hate – holding on to it simply keeps us in the role of victim.

Forgiveness defuses the situation; it releases the emotional charge. When we really forgive someone they no longer have any power over us. It removes the barriers, the walls constructed in defence and anger that keep us separate. Forgiving someone takes away all the potency, there is no more fear, they can no longer hurt. Forgiveness involves seeing the other person just as they are – not as we might want them to be, think they should be, or thought they were, but just as they are.

Forgiving others completes the past so that we can move on. There is a spaciousness in which we can breathe and feel and let love come in. With it may come great grief, sadness, and a sense of emptiness or loss. Let these feelings pour through you; do not deny them expression. Beneath the grief lies your love, compassion and tenderheartedness.

Forgiving others is important, but we also need to forgive ourselves. If we really want to be healed we have to work with the inside stuff – the layers around the heart. Forgiving ourselves does not mean absolving ourselves of responsibility for our actions, nor does it deny guilt. It is simply a recognition of our humanness and a complete acceptance of our vulnerability. To forgive ourselves for past deeds, past words, things we did or didn't do. To forgive ourselves in the present each time we don't get it right. To say, 'I forgive myself', again and again.

Forgiving ourselves means accepting ourselves just as we are, accepting all our weaknesses, mistakes and helplessness. We have to strip ourselves naked emotionally and start from there: bringing forgiveness to every part of our being, into our pain, into our fear, into our illness, into our shame; forgiving our childhood, forgiving ourselves for being abused, for thinking we deserved to be punished or hurt, for the way we have treated others, for the guilt we feel, for all the mistakes we have made and the hopelessness we have felt. The more we forgive ourselves and release our own pain, the more we can forgive others.

It can be very hard to accept forgiveness. We are used to paying for our sins. Forgiving ourselves can feel like skipping class and getting away without punishment. But we are no longer the person who committed the offence. We are forgiving the person we were then – even if it was only a minute ago – the one who acted in ignorance, perhaps to the best of our ability at the time, or even acted in malice, creating pain. We can forgive this person and, in so doing, release the holds of the past. This does not diminish the consequences, but it releases the pain.

Forgiveness does not necessarily come easily – it takes practice

---

TRY IT YOURSELF

Opening to Forgiveness

Start by deciding who you want to focus on – yourself or another person. These instructions assume that you wish to forgive yourself. If you want to direct your forgiveness to another person, simply alter the instructions accordingly. As you do the practice, allow any issues that need forgiving to arise spontaneously.

- Find a quiet and comfortable place to sit, cross-legged on the floor or in a straight-backed chair. Make sure you will not be disturbed. Straighten your back and close your eyes.

- Take a deep breath and blow it out. Feel yourself relaxing through your whole body and mind. Bring your awareness to your breathing and for a few minutes just watch the breath entering and leaving your body. Sink into the rhythm of the breath as your mind becomes quieter.

- Now begin to focus on the heart space in the centre of your chest. Watch your breathing from this place for a few moments. When you feel ready, bring forgiveness into this heart space. Silently repeat the words 'I forgive myself, I forgive myself, I forgive myself for. . .' and let all the things that you forgive yourself for arise in your heart space. Take your time, be gentle. Let yourself go back in time, forgiving and releasing. Do not hold on to any one incident – forgive and let go and move on. Remember to keep breathing – soft belly. Breathe into any pain or guilt or shame that arises and keep releasing, 'I forgive myself, I forgive myself.'

- Let each issue arise, see it without judgement, without attachment, acknowledge it fully and then bring forgiveness to it. Some things will be easier to forgive than others. Keep chipping away at the hard ones and in time they will soften and release. When you feel you have done as much as you can, then take a deep breath and let it out.

- Watch your breath for a few minutes, feeling the forgiveness pouring through your being, washing through you and releasing you. When you are ready, stretch your legs and slowly open your eyes.

commitment and sincerity. It is something we all need to do every day, slowly softening resistance, opening the heart, letting the love in. It means being willing to look at whatever feelings arise as we delve deeper and to accept those feelings as they are, without judgement. But eventually forgiveness removes the walls and we are free to dance and feel love again. Forgiveness is the greatest gift we can give ourselves. Forgiveness meditation is described on page 81 and is also available on cassette tape from the address on page 247.

♦ UNCONDITIONAL LOVE ♦

Our normal approach to love is rather self-centred. We give love in order to receive love, we suffer when there is a lack of love, we put conditions on the form love should take. Healing requires us to go beyond such conditions and limitations, beyond self-centred needs, to awaken into the heart – into fearlessness, forgiveness, mercy, compassion and unconditional love. Loving unconditionally means not holding on to past grievances, not giving fear any power; it means accepting any weakness or insensitivity that causes pain, and putting love in its place. 'Healing occurs in the present, not the past. We are not held back by the love we didn't receive in the past, but by the love we're not extending in the present,' writes Marianne Williamson in *A Return to Love*. 'As we love, we shall be released from pain, and as we deny love we shall remain in pain.'

We need to bring love alive: to think love, talk love, read love, act love, walk love, breathe love, sing love, touch love, eat love and sleep love. We spend so much time focusing on difficulties and pain. This needs to be balanced by dwelling in and experiencing the positive things. They are there. We need only look. We can look at rain and feel depressed, or we can see it watering the plants and feeding the rivers that in turn give us water to drink. Seeing this, we can thank the rain for nourishment. The choice is ours.

In the moment of facing death many people's deepest desire is to say 'I love you' to their loved ones before they die. But we don't have to wait until we are dying to say this. Say 'I love you' at least once a day – even once an hour – to yourself or to someone else. Don't just think it but say it out loud. Giving love a voice makes it come alive, brings warmth, gratitude, security, comfort, healing. If you can't talk, you can write love. Write to those you love and tell them how you feel. Write words of love to yourself. Write poems or songs of love. Fill your head with words of love.

Touch with love. Let love shine through as you reach out a hand to hold, to caress, to soothe. Without touch babies can die and adults go insane. Touch everything with love, being aware of your actions, treating all things with respect. Walk with love, feeling the beauty of your body as it moves, feeling the love that the breath, bones, muscles, blood, nerves, organs, joints, and even the toes have for you, as they support and care for you throughout your life. Love your body – thank each part for its service.

This is opening the heart. Letting love into every crack and crevice of our lives enables us to take risks and embrace the unknown. We do not need to turn our backs on our neighbours because they are a different colour or practise a different religion – we can accept the differences while recognising our shared humanity. In place of fear, see a challenge that can be met with creative awareness. Fear contracts and pushes away; it holds tight and denies change or movement. Love is expansive and all-embracing; it welcomes change as an expression of all life.

Opening the heart to ourselves and others is a coming home, a rejoicing in the love we have always longed for. Through the open heart we find a healing of our whole being. In *The Healing Path*, Marc Ian Barasch describes one woman's journey:

> *Beneath the tears. . . she discovered love, tenderness, and a fullness of being – feelings her inner defences against early, unsustainable suffering had never fully permitted. For many journeyers, this is the inner work of healing: to uncover the heart layer by painful layer.*

At the core of all life is unconditional love. What is the force, the energy, that maintains life if it is not unconditional love? See how the sun shines equally on us all, whoever we are. When we experience the unconditional nature of love we open to a vista of unlimited healing power.

7

PASSION AND CREATIVITY

WHAT FILLS YOU with excitement, purpose and delight? Finding your passion means finding a way of expressing your innermost yearnings and desires, that which makes you feel most alive. It may be as simple as basket-weaving or flower-arranging, it may be amateur dramatics or hospital visiting. Challenge yourself. Go trekking, climb a mountain, work in a soup kitchen. Meet people and have experiences that encourage you to grow. Become a clown. Do something you thought you would never do. Then experience the freedom and delight that comes from going beyond your conditioning and limitations.

Whatever our passion may be, it is an important part of our healing to give it expression. In so doing we are tending the creative and expressive part of our being that, invariably, has been buried beneath years of having to fulfil the demands of parents, society or family. In *Peace, Love and Healing* Dr. Bernie Siegel tells the story of a cancer patient who, as a child, had always wanted to play the violin. Pressure from his parents led to him putting the instrument away and becoming a solicitor. Now in his fifties and facing an uncertain future, Bernie asked him what he would *really* like to do. In response the man gave up his legal practice and started to play the violin for the first time since he was a child. His inner being awoke after so many years of being ignored and the cancer went into remission. Bernie asks: 'Do we have to wait until we have cancer to do what we really want to do?'

Liz was feeling there must be more to life than just sitting alone, night after night. She was recently divorced, her children grown and gone. There was an aching emptiness inside her. One evening, as she walked past her neighbourhood church hall, she was intrigued to see lights shining. When she investigated she found a group of women playing lawn bowls on mats. Amused, she watched for a while and then continued with her walk. The next evening one of the women Liz had seen bowling knocked on her door. She asked if Liz would like to join them. It seemed ridiculous but something inside her said yes. That was 12 years ago. Liz is now a member of one of the best bowling teams in her county and president of her club. She has found her passion.

Below are some suggestions for activities to try for yourself. Don't be shy! Healing comes to those who are willing to let go of their limitations and self-consciousness by stepping into the unknown.

♦ ART THERAPY ♦

This involves exploring the whole realm of form and shape, texture and colour, as a means of expressing deeper psychological issues. It is a way of reaching into ourselves to gain an understanding of our real feelings, especially those that are beyond our conscious grasp. 'There are some states of feeling that are far beyond the reach of words,' writes art therapist Patsy Howell Hall, in *The Seeker's Guide* (by J. Button and W. Bloom). 'How can one penetrate the core of loneliness and speak to that – or out of it?' Painting or sculpting gives form to these feelings, a means of seeing what they are saying, so we can find resolution.

Art therapy usually involves joining a class where we have the benefit of a trained teacher and the support of others on a similar journey. But we can also do it in our own way at home with a simple watercolour set or crayons and a pad of paper. Who cares what it looks like? It's how it feels that is important. And the only way to do it is to start. Paint anything and everything and do it without thinking about it – let your feelings do the painting, without your control. You may find yourself creating symbols and dream-like images rather than clear pictures. That's fine. The unconscious shares itself in many different ways. Whatever you create is an expression of you, whether it be swirling lines or a page of dots.

Try not to paint a particular object, for this will distract your feelings from finding their own form. Paint freely, simply letting the brushes or pencils play on the paper, letting the colours and forms speak to you. And slowly begin to paint your feelings – your inside feelings. Spend some time each day painting your anger or fear and watch how the paintings change as the feelings begins to emerge. Try using other media for different expressions, such as wood, clay, sand or fabric.

Try painting yourself. Use a large piece of paper. (You may want to have an anatomy book nearby to help you put the various bits in the right places.) What does your picture look like? Are all the different pieces in proportion? Are some of them missing? If so, where are they? What does your face look like? Is it smiling or frowning? Are your eyes opened or closed? Do you have a heart in this picture? Is it happy or sad? Do you have a liver? Is it full of anger? Do you have kidneys? Are they full of fear? What do your stomach and intestines look like? What shape are your legs or arms? Are the muscles relaxed or tense? What do your hands look like? Is your back straight or bent over? Is it leaning against something? Is there anything or anyone else in your picture?

Draw any illness you have or areas of discomfort. Does your illness look dark all over or are there bright and colourful areas? Are there different images in different parts of your body? Paint whichever part of your body is under stress. What images come to mind? What do these tell you about your feelings? Paint your treatment. Does it look like poison or a healing balm? If it is poison, then perhaps you should consider changing to a treatment that makes you feel good – we don't get well by taking poison. Draw you healers. What does your doctor or therapist look like? An angel or a devil? Someone who will save you or someone who is going to harm you? Paint or draw your parents, your siblings, your children or your spouse, or even your job. See what images arise, what forms and feelings. Let them speak to you.

Drawing spontaneously gives you a valuable insight into what is happening inside and what action is needed. In *Peace, Love and Healing*, Bernie Siegel recounts the story of a little girl who came to him with enlarged lymph nodes in her neck and jaw. As lymphoma was prevalent in both her parents' families, there was natural concern that she might also have it. Bernie asked her to do some drawing. She drew herself, but she also drew a picture of her cat with very long claws:

> As I stared at her drawing, wondering why this cat was such a vivid presence to her at a time when she was so sick, it suddenly dawned on me that she had cat scratch fever. Tests confirmed the diagnosis, and the diagnosis itself confirmed, yet again, the bodily wisdom we all possess.

♦ CLOWNING ♦

Clowning means allowing ourselves to play, to become like children and rediscover the magic in all things. It is so easy to forget about magic, to become jaded or think we know it all, but in the process the awe and wonder of life are lost. Clowning gives us permission to rediscover awe. More than that, it brings laughter, and laughter heals. In the twelfth century, Dr. Thomas Sydenham said, 'The arrival of a good clown exercises more beneficial influence upon the health of a town than do twenty asses laden with drugs.'

A dear friend of mine, Leela, previously a medical doctor for twelve years, is now a fully fledged, official clown. Leela was born with a hole in her heart. She has experienced, and healed, numerous medical problems in herself and others. She says:

> Changing from being a headstrong, bossy, frustrated GP to a gentle, heart-centred, understanding and emotionally aware clown, who along the way had to suffer to gain compassion for other people's pain, has been the most challenging journey of my life. Clowning has allowed me to be totally human again, complete with my awkwardness, frustration and shyness. The intense joy, excitement and spontaneity inspire me to discover the long forgotten, neglected treasures within. I'm learning to walk beyond the edge of my own imagination.
>
> My accordion teacher regularly plays at an old people's luncheon club and knew my newly born shy clown would be safe with them. She played 'Pack Up Your Troubles In Your Old Kit Bag' while I danced around making faces and coaxing the audience to put their troubles in my bag. The difficulty was that most of them knew me as a doctor and found it hard to now respond to me as a clown!
>
> Except for one old man who had had a stroke. Very slowly, using his strong arm, he lifted his paralysed arm up to his brain. His fingers moved like a crane's claw, grabbing at the contents, until he took an imaginary something out of his head. Our eyes met, and in that second there was complete understanding. The tears began to roll down both our faces. He carefully and accurately let go of this something into my kit bag which I then went to put outside. When I came back he wanted to dance. His stroke had left him semi-paralysed and yet, somehow, we danced. As a doctor I had never before watched tears change into the radiance of a dance.

♦ DRAMA ♦

Acting out different scenes and playing various roles is a favourite game for most children. As they explore the world, they try on different personalities, dress up and pretend to be adults, create fantasies or stories with various characters. Many domestic dramas are enacted, the child playing out the role of angry or even abusive parents, the loss of a loved relation, the death of a pet, or the jealousy of a sibling. The acting enables the child to externalise their deeper feelings, to gain a distance from the inner intensity and to accept and heal what has happened.

As adults, we can also play out our dramas. In a group setting we can enact past events or repressed feelings, such as anger towards our parents. In this way we not only release the feelings, we also see the situation in its entirety. Or we can create scenes that confront a character with various situations or feelings in order to help expand our understanding of how to deal with such issues in our lives. Drama therapy is used in many different social settings, such as hospitals or schools, with youth groups, or as a part of psychotherapy.

Although not as confrontational, you can also do this at home by yourself. Use pillows to represent other people or roles and play out your dramas. Play different characters and enact the same drama from different perspectives. Or write a script and invite some friends to act it with you. Be brave enough to ad lib, so that your feelings have a chance to speak. Try not to script too much – let the contents unfold as your feelings find form.

♦ MUSIC AND SONG ♦

Sound is one of the most essential of our senses, giving us the means to communicate, to balance and uplift energies, and to release feelings. 'Everything in the universe is in a state of vibration,' writes Jonathan Goldman in *Healing Sounds*. 'This includes the human body. Every organ, bone, tissue and other part of the body has a healthy resonant frequency. When that frequency alters, that part of the body vibrates out of harmony and this is what is termed disease.'

The effect of music is striking. We can be moved to tears by a violin, feel our hearts leap with joy at the sound of a melodious harp, or find our bodies wanting to dance to the rhythm of African drums. Other music may make our nerves jangle and muscles tense

– obviously such sounds do not bring healing. Soothing music played during surgery has been shown to speed recovery; inspirational music has been used to help release emotional blocks. Seek out music that brings balance to your body and makes you resonate in harmony or feel energetic and alive. As you play this music, give it your full attention, letting it wash over and through you, letting it sink into every cell of your being. This is music therapy of your own making. If it inspires your body to move then let yourself respond freely.

Another way to use music for healing is to learn a musical instrument. It's never too late! And it can bring such joy to hear music flowing as you strum a guitar or breathe into a flute. Find that long-lost desire to play the piano or violin and follow wherever it leads you. It may take time to become accomplished but reaching the goal is not the point – there is so much healing to be gained on the journey.

We can all sing. We don't have to rival Kiri Te Kanawa, but we can find our own voice, a voice that is unique and expressive. We may have stopped singing when we were at school (perhaps we were told we couldn't sing in tune) but we can re-find our voice and rediscover the release gained through singing.

Start by just singing simple songs. Do this in groups or on your own. Sing along with a favourite song and feel your voice stretch and expand. Let it soar. Sing your feelings, sing your body, sing your heart. Sing your illness, sing your healing. Let your inner voice come out through song. Sing in the bath, in the kitchen, or in the car.

Chanting or incantation is another way to use the voice. This is the recitation of sacred sounds which has been used throughout the ages and in all religions. Listen to Gregorian incantations, Hindu bhajans, or Tibetan overtone chanting. These sacred sounds resonate within, balancing and healing, leading to ecstatic and meditative states. Try chanting 'OM' (the Sanskrit sound of the absolute). Take a deep breath, open your mouth and start with a long 'AU' sound and then close your mouth and feel the vibration of the 'M' as you complete your breath. 'How do we create a sense of balance with a resonant universe?' Jill Purce asks in *The Way Ahead*. 'One of the best ways is by resonating with it, by re-enchanting our lives, for the heart and the voice are one and if we open the voice, we open the heart.'

◆ SACRED RITUAL ◆

Rituals are moments when we stop and acknowledge the importance of life's milestones. They provide landmarks to move towards and away from. In honouring various rites of passage we connect with the movement of the seasons, the relationship of the earth to heaven, of the spirit to its highest fulfilment. There are many rituals we normally participate in: social rituals such as prayers before meals, birthdays, weddings, anniversaries, graduation, funerals; those of the earth such as harvest festivals, the equinox and solstice celebrations; and those belonging to religions such as Christmas, Easter and Passover. But many of these rituals have lost their emotional meaning and become commercialised, leaving us with a longing to celebrate the sacred.

We can create our own rituals, specific celebrations to mark the beginning or the completion of a life-changing event. In this way we are acknowledging the transition from one state to another, rather than letting it slide by without recognising its full importance. *Beginning rituals* mark times when we embark on a new venture or stage of life, such as moving home or starting a new relationship, the birth of a child, or a new business venture. Symbolic objects can be used to represent this new beginning and signify the power of the arising energy. *Completing rituals* mark times of passing or finishing, such as the end of a relationship, the death of a family pet, or a child leaving home. Objects, photos or letters that represent what is being released help focus the energy on the fulfilment and conclusion of this time.

You may want to light a candle, have some flowers, read some poetry or meaningful passages to uplift and inspire, sing a special song, play some appropriate music, or sit in silence. Perhaps invite special friends or family members to participate. Let your imagination create a ritual that is meaningful to you, that fully acknowledges the moment.

Sitting each day to meditate, or writing a journal of your feelings, are both rituals that bring healing. Or you can create a ritual for health by forming a healing circle with friends or family to give and receive love and blessings – it is important not only to give help but also to be able to ask for and receive help. A massage can be a ritual, a way of acknowledging and honouring your body by bringing love to it, as can any form of loving care such as a bubble bath or specially cooked meal. Making your home beautiful – perhaps filling it with flowers or colourful rugs – is also a ritual, one that respects the environment and honours the role it plays in your well-being.

◆ CREATIVE WRITING ◆

Writing down feelings, thoughts, ideas, insights, experiences – all these are very powerful ways of connecting with our healing. This sort of writing enables us to externalise our innermost being and, therefore, to see ourselves more clearly. When a feeling is locked away inside it can easily stay there – untouched and unacknowledged. As we begin to write, those deeper issues have a chance to come to the surface and be released.

Try writing your autobiography. Take your time over this, entering into your memory objectively and honestly. Look at the whole of your life, and write your thoughts and feelings. See the threads that connect each part of your life, that connect events with feelings, feelings with experiences. Tell your own tale. Try writing for at least 20 minutes at a time. As you think back you may find unexpected insights emerging, ones that deepen your understanding of who you are now.

Or you may want to keep a journal – writing each day or each week. Write about what happens and your response; write about your feelings, your inner world, your health. Write about any treatment you are receiving and about your doctors. How do you feel about your prognosis? How has this affected your life goals or priorities? How has it affected the other people in your life? Write about your parents, your spouse, your children, your work, your home. You may want to focus on a particular issue – a feeling, a relationship, a conflict, or a part of you that needs healing – and write about how you feel, what you want to do about it, how you would feel without it. Write your anger, hurt or resentment; write your forgiveness, love and concern. And, as you write, just let the words come. They may surprise you. Be as candid and open as you can – this is just for you, not for anyone else. It is a way of becoming your own best friend, of letting the voice within you speak.

Try writing a dialogue with your illness or with a specific part of your body. You can even do this in the form of a letter. Write to this part of you and let it know how you feel. 'Dear Cancer, This is how I feel about you. . .' Tell it everything. But then let it write back to you – communicate with it. To do this, breathe into your heart and let the answer come on its own, in its own words. You may be surprised to hear what your illness has to say. This process helps you see the illness or affected area of your body as a part of you. Rather than being something you must get rid of, you can recognise that it needs to be claimed, loved and even embraced.

Or you can start each page with a specific question. Write a statement at the top of the page and then let your responses flow freely. If you repeat this each week with the same issue, you will see how your responses change and evolve. For instance:

How I see myself is . . .
How I feel about my body is . . .
How I see my illness is . . .
How I see my healing is . . .
I am ready to release . . .
I am ready to accept . . .

Writing opens the door to communication. Without communication we live in isolation and fear. When you communicate with yourself you discover a new friend, a playmate, with whom you can explore your inner world.

8

BALANCING THE BODY

THE BODY is a living, breathing organism in which every cell is aware of every other cell: hundreds of hormones and neuropeptides – chemical messengers – constantly convey information through numerous communication pathways. Some of that information accumulates in the structural body (in the muscles or joints), hindering the free flow of energy or limiting movement. Communication can break down, perhaps due to too much pressure or because of conflicting messages, and the body needs assistance to regain its strength and balance. When physical tension is released there is a corresponding psychological or emotional release. Deep levels of stress and fear, or layers of blocked emotion and buried memories may be accessed.

This chapter and the next one explore some of the ways we can work with the body, whether through different forms of complementary therapy or through expression and movement. However, this does not mean that we can just go to an acupuncturist or massage therapist, lie back and come away healed. The different techniques are there to support and assist our healing; they cannot do it for us but they can give us the strength, balance and energy we need to help us access our own healing ability.

There are numerous different forms of body healing. Follow your intuition as to what feels most appropriate – the technique that worked for your friend may not work for you. You will hear many stories about particular cures, diets or therapies that have brought miraculous results. But it is essential to trust yourself and your gut feeling, to listen to your own wisdom. Perhaps more important than the technique is the faith that it will work, for doubt can cause resistance. Trust yourself and do what feels right.

Always make sure that any practitioner or therapist you go to is fully qualified. Don't be afraid to ask.

♦ BALANCING CHI ♦

Vital to Eastern systems of medicine, such as acupuncture, is the concept of energy. This is known as *chi* or *prana*, the life force that flows through every cell of the body and throughout every living thing. When chi becomes unbalanced or weakened, whether because of psychological, emotional or lifestyle factors, illness or disease can develop. Chi is balanced through stimulation or pressure, and strengthened through diet, exercise, meditation and attitude.

Acupuncture

Acupuncture has been used for well over 5,000 years. It recognises fourteen meridians or channels of energy within the body, with numerous access points along each channel. Meridians are like rivers. They get blocked, or the water backs up and floods elsewhere. One part might get too little water, another too much. Each meridian is connected to a particular organ and certain states of mind. Stimulation of the main points, usually achieved with very fine needles, propels energy along the meridians to bring balance where it is needed.

Apart from the physical benefits, the energetic changes that occur through acupuncture greatly enhance psychological well-being, especially if we are feeling depressed, low in energy, out of harmony within ourselves, or in some way emotionally blocked. Acupuncture addresses the inner balance, particularly of the *yin* and *yang* energies – the feminine and masculine aspects in each of us. *Yin* is intuitive, receptive, soft, gentle and expansive; *yang* is active, rational, assertive, hard and contractive. An imbalance in these can lead to both psychological and physical ailments.

Shiatsu

Instead of needles, shiatsu uses finger pressure and gentle manipulation of the points on the meridians. It works with the meridians as a whole, stretching, stimulating and loosening areas of resistance. This releases blockages in the flow of chi, thereby increasing overall balance and harmony. It can help with numerous different complaints, particularly those related to stress, circulatory or digestive disorders. There is also a form of water shiatsu, known as watsu, where the treatment is done in a warm pool. The water not only supports the body, enabling a deeper release of tension, but it can also connect us with buried memories of birth or pre-birth.

Reflexology

Through specific finger pressure and manipulation of the feet, and, to some extent the hands, energy can be released to benefit the whole body. If energy becomes congested or blocked, causing illness or disorder, then tensions and crystalline deposits are found in the related part of the feet. By gently working on these areas, the pathway is cleared. The manipulation also improves circulation, releases tension and encourages an elimination of toxins.

The left and right foot correspond to the left and right sides of the body. For instance, the heart is found on the left foot and the liver on the right. The spine runs down the inside of both feet, from the big toe to the heel. Specific areas that relate to physical problems will feel more painful. As energy is unblocked, that pain begins to diminish and there is a sense of relief or release. There may also be feelings of sadness or of emotional upset as energy in the physical body is opened and blocks in the psychological or emotional centres are also released.

♦ POSTURE AND MOVEMENT ♦

Experiences and feelings get locked into the musculature of the body, creating ingrained habits of posture, movement and behaviour. Tight shoulders or a hunched back are examples of how we may have had to repress feelings from childhood, locking memory or attitude into the physical body. Learning to recognise and open these positions not only improves posture and frees movement, but also enables the release of associated unconscious feelings.

Massage

Massage is one of the oldest forms of touch therapy. It is used to release all forms of physical tension and inner stress. It stimulates the circulation, calms the nervous system, eases pain and realigns structural problems. By working with the muscular system we can shift energy blocks, allowing the life force to flow more freely and our whole body to function more fully. There are numerous forms of massage therapy, from remedial and neuromuscular, to stress reduction and deep relaxation techniques.

Massage is also something we can do for each other at home. Through the nerve endings and tactile quality of the skin we can experience the loving touch of another as the immediate reassurance that we are safe and loved. This alone helps to create inner harmony and balance. Without touch we easily feel unloved and unwanted, and may develop mental difficulties. Taking time just to rub someone's shoulders or to massage their feet brings many healing benefits.

Rolfing

Developed by Ida Rolf, rolfing involves very deep tissue manipulation. Ida Rolf recognised that posture and structure were held in place by connective tissue, formed through years of habit and conditioning. Trauma gets locked into the muscles, distorting them from their proper alignment. Rolfers talk about these distortions as the limitations we have imposed, or that have been imposed upon us, as we grow. These limitations create habits – ways of being, moving and behaving that get built into our psychological being. Releasing the physical resistances puts us in touch with the related emotions, such as anger, fear or grief, that were frozen into the body. Wilhelm Reich called these blockages our 'body armour'. When traumas and tensions are loosened the body is realigned and finds its natural form, posture is balanced, the energies throughout the body are freed to function more fully, and we experience feelings of aliveness and joy. Rolfing is usually done over a period of ten sessions.

Alexander Technique

This is a gentle corrective technique that works on improving posture so that the body is aligned and in harmony. It was developed in the 1880s by F. M. Alexander, an actor who lost his voice. Through close observation he noticed that every time he tried to speak he also contracted his neck, which in turn pulled his head back and down. Retraining his movements enabled him to speak again. Alexander went on to explore further instances of how the position of the body affects behavioural and psychological functioning, particularly in the head, neck and spine. The advantage of this work is the awareness brought to the areas where tension is being held, and how this influences the rest of the body. The practice is gentle and directive, not strenuous or invasive. During Alexander lesson, the focus is on the relationship between thoughts and movement. When learning with an Alexander teacher you will be given lessons to practise at home.

Feldenkrais

After damaging his own knee, Moshe Feldenkrais used the understanding he had of both physics and martial arts to learn how to walk again. This led him to discover a series of exercises aimed at undoing harmful patterns of movement. This gentle, non-invasive technique works directly with the nervous system, seeing how messages from the nerves influence the movement of the muscles. The physical body can be re-educated at the same time as releasing old blockages or thought patterns. The focus is on awareness through movement and functional integration. You can learn this technique with a qualified practitioner and practise at home by yourself.

♦ SPINAL SYSTEMS: OSTEOPATHY ♦ AND CHIROPRACTIC

The spine is not just the backbone of the body, it is the central core of our whole being. The spine connects and communicates with every part of the structural body, as well as containing the spinal fluid, central nervous system and blood supply, so any disruption in any part of the body will also be found in the spine. In the same way, if the spine is disrupted or put out of alignment, the rest of the body is affected.

The spine enables us to stand upright and to function as a full human being. Yet we constantly abuse it, whether through bad posture, lack of exercise, or dumping in it unwanted and ignored emotions. Many illnesses and physical disorders, such as headaches, constipation, menstrual problems or breathing difficulties, can be treated by correcting the spine.

The rest of the skeleton is equally important, particularly the joints. They *join up* thoughts with actions – through them we are able to express our feelings and ideas, to bring life to our inner world. Imagine how stiff and unresponsive we would be without joints! Treatments that focus on the spine and joints release physical constraints at the same times as freeing related psychological constraints.

...ns that focus on the spine are osteopathy and ...systems differ in technique but are similar in ...ring balance to the nervous system and blood ...g proper functioning of the organs, as well as ...get in touch with and release energy-blocking patterns w... ...e long ignored – ways of holding our muscles or posture. Oste... ...ay involves manipulation of the joints and spine as well as massage of the soft tissues to release blocked energy and realign the structural body. The chiropractic approach is more focused on manipulation of the spine and whole body energy balancing. These systems are especially valuable for any form of muscular or skeletal disorder, from scoliosis to sports injuries, or for back problems.

♦ WORKING WITH ENERGY ♦

Within each of us is the life force, that power that enables a plant to grow through concrete or the skin to heal over a wound. Energy is not tangible, yet it can be sensed, perceived and experienced. The systems outlined in this category each deal with energy in different ways, seeing how it is constantly moving, expanding and contracting, and how this movement influences our state of health.

Hands-on Healing

'Healing' is a term applied to the practice of channelling energy, where the hands of the practitioner either touch the body or are held a few inches away. The practitioner helps increase the amount of energy in the body so that the patient is stimulated to release any energy weaknesses or blocks that may be causing physical distress. This is done by the practitioner letting energy move through his or her hands, unimpeded. In a sense, the word 'healer' is not quite appropriate, as it is the life force within the patient that does the healing – the practitioner is more of a catalyst or agent for change. Whenever we put our hands on another, such as a sore knee or upset stomach, we are giving energy that will stimulate a relaxed and healed state.

Receiving healing feels wonderful; there is a sense of being filled with light, vibrancy and softness. It can have very beneficial results through releasing physical restrictions and blocks, and it has an immediate calming effect on the mind, helping to put emotional or psychological concerns in a clearer perspective.

┌─────────────── TRY IT YOURSELF ───────────────┐

Hands-on Healing

- If a friend or relative is hurting, lightly place your hands over the area of pain and close your eyes.

- Become quiet within yourself and just focus on your hands and the image of light pouring through you. See that light go from your hands into the body beneath them.

- Stay like this for as long as feels comfortable, usually about 5-10 minutes.

- Then let the image fade and gently open your eyes.

└──┘

Metamorphic Technique

This technique focuses on the relationship between matter and energy. It uses the spinal reflexes found on the feet, hands and head, and the spine itself, to access the nine months before our birth, the time when the potential for our present life is established. By bringing this period of gestation into focus, any limitations or blockages created can be loosened and our full potential can be released. The practitioner does not try to bring about a change in the client, for we each have within us an innate knowledge of any change that is needed. Rather, the practitioner stimulates the life force within the client to access their own knowledge, encouraging a releasing of old patterns of thinking and behaviour. This technique is easily learnt and practised, or you can go to a practitioner.

Kinesiology

This system of gentle muscle testing clearly demonstrates the intelligence of the body. Through channels of energy – the meridians – and the interconnectedness of each cell with the whole, we can 'ask' the body questions and receive answers through the strength or weakness of a muscle's response. In this way we can gain information about health problems and the treatment needed; information can also be 'put in to' the body to help restore balance and health. In Chapter 1, I suggested a simple exercise to show how thoughts directly and instantaneously affect the body, by testing the resistance of your partner's arm. This is a kinesiology technique. It works because the heart meridian runs along the arm. When we have an emotional response to something it is felt in the heart where there is a cluster of neuropeptides. The feeling is then transmitted along the meridian and the response is felt in the muscle of the arm.

Developed in 1965 by a chiropractor, George Goodheart, kinesiology is now used by many different practitioners in order to gain otherwise unobtainable information. It is particularly helpful in testing for food allergies, nutritional deficiencies, or learning difficulties. Simple kinesiology techniques can be learnt by yourself; for a fuller treatment it is advisable to go to a practitioner.

◆ NATURE'S WAY ◆

Just as nature provides each form of life with the food and nourishment it needs to develop and maintain itself, so it also provides remedies for illness. Plant medicine is as ancient as mankind.

Ayurveda

Ayurveda is a Sanskrit word meaning 'the science of life'. Just as acupuncture is the traditional medicine of China, so ayurveda is the traditional medicine of India. It is equally ancient, records dating back beyond 4,000 BC. 'Ayurveda is the healing gift to us from the ancient enlightened Vedic culture,' writes David Frawley in *Ayurvedic Healing*. 'The medicine of India has much in common with both the Chinese and European, and often represents a point of integration between them.'

Ayurveda recognises the subtle energies of both organic and inorganic matter – in the body as much as in thoughts and feelings. The body is seen as consisting of constantly changing processes but with a stable, underlying energy or constitution, unique to each individual, that includes psychological and emotional states as well as physical ones.

A specific relationship between three fundamental energies or *doshas* determines body shape, size, differing personality or psychological characteristics, health and individuality. Once we understand our own dosha or type, then we can attune our diet, lifestyle and activities to support it. Ayurveda focuses on diet and nutrition, exercise such as yoga, and stress release through deep relaxation and meditation, to correct imbalance, each dosha having specific needs.

This can all be practised at home. For more complex treatment, such as specific herbal or nutritional remedies, it is advisable to go to an ayurvedic practitioner.

Homeopathy

First developed in 1796 by Samuel Hahnemann, a German doctor, homeopathy is based on the principle of like curing like. This is very different to allopathy which is based on the principle of curing through opposites. Where allopathy will try to stop symptoms by applying a medicine that has an opposing effect, homeopathy argues that the symptom is the body's way of healing itself and should be supported. Natural substances are given that, in large doses, produce the same effects as the symptoms, so as to assist the body, but they are given in such small doses that no ill-effects are felt. In fact, remedies are given in very minute doses for they work energetically as a signal to stimulate mental, emotional and physical healing.

By recognising that symptoms reflect the inner processes of the body and using remedies that support this, homeopathy brings a profound balancing of energies. In homeopathy we come to appreciate the subtle levels of energy at play, that life is not just black and white but there are many shades of grey. When making a diagnosis, our physical, emotional and psychological states are all taken into consideration. It is not easy, therefore, to correctly diagnose ourselves. Some homeopathic remedies are commercially available, but for more effective treatment it is advisable to go to a trained practitioner. Remedies are prescribed for the whole person, not for the illness; each prescription is attuned to the individual's body type and energetic needs.

Herbalism

The roots, stems, leaves, seeds and flowers of specific plants assist the healing of both internal and external wounds and diseases through teas, tinctures or tablets, or with poultices, oils and ointments. Many modern medicines are derived from plants, although herbs in their natural state are gentler than their medical derivatives and may take longer to work. As the herbs bring a physical easing and balancing so energy is released into the system, assisting us to work with deeper issues. Using herbs also enables us to listen and respond to our own needs because we can administer them ourselves, encouraging us to take responsibility for our own healing. We can go to a herbalist for treatment, or we can learn the various herbs and their potencies to treat ourselves at home.

Aromatherapy

This 'therapy of smell' is based on the healing properties of herbs. Throughout the ages the sense of smell has been known to bring relief: incense or perfume made from plants, trees and flowers were used to purify, balance and stimulate energy. Aromatherapy uses essential oils – oils imbued with the extracted essence of the plant – that are absorbed into the body through massage, bathing or inhaling. Each oil has its own benefits. For instance, lavender will ease a tension headache or help lift depression, tea tree is antiseptic, while chamomile is excellent for insomnia and indigestion.

Essential oils have either a stimulating or relaxing effect; some are antiseptic, others are antifungal, toning or purifying. Receiving an aromatherapy message or putting specific oils in a bath are ways of working with deeper issues we may have been unconsciously holding on to. It is not uncommon to feel either sad or uplifted after an aromatherapy session, as a connection is made with our inner feelings.

Flower Essences

First developed by Dr Edward Bach, a physician in the 1930s, the Bach Flower Remedies are the most well known of flower essences, but there are also others available, including tree essences. They are a direct bodymind remedy because they are taken for emotional and psychological issues, not for physical problems. They are used to help ease and balance states such as worry, apprehension, nervousness, fear, irritability, resentment or lethargy, that in turn have a detrimental effect on the body. This does not mean that all we have to do is take a flower essence and we will stop being fearful or anxious. Rather, the essence is there to support us in our inner work by providing a respite from debilitating emotions. We can go to a practitioner for these remedies, or we can learn to treat ourselves as they are available in most health food shops.

9

EXPRESSIVE MOVEMENT

MOVEMENT and emotion arise from the same Latin root: *e movere*. To be moved by something is to be physically affected by it, so our emotions influence the way we move. If we are sad or depressed, then our movements will be heavy and slow; if we are angry they become jerky and dramatic. Moving the body beyond its habitual limitations loosens energy on both the physical and psycho/emotional levels. In other words, releasing tensions in the body also releases them in the mind.

Feelings and memories get locked in the joints, muscles and ligaments, often from as far back as childhood. The joints enable us to move with grace and fluidity; they also join up thought or feeling with action. If that connection is restricted or blocked then the energy cannot flow freely and there is a lack of grace or ease. Expressive movement, therefore, helps to open up the communication between feelings and actions. It also stimulates a positive attitude and greater inner strength. For instance, when we exercise, various hormones are released into the body, particularly endorphins. These produce an uplifted, positive feeling that can have a very beneficial effect on depression or fear.

If you have not moved your body in a creative or expressive way before, you may find it difficult at first – joints seem to need oiling as they creak open; muscles ache from stretching, only to be stretched again. But slowly you will see your body come alive as inhibitions are released and new dimensions explored. Simultaneously you will find yourself letting go of mental limitations – *I can't* becomes *I can*. Through moving the body, freedom comes to the mind, our overall health is improved, we have more stamina and a greater resistance to illness.

♦ THE MARTIAL ARTS ♦

The martial arts originally developed in ancient China and were refined by Japanese warriors. The more external forms include *karate*, while the more informal forms include *chi kung* and *tai chi*. The basis of martial arts is the development of inner strength and balance, through practising specific movements again and again until they become completely natural to the body. The more external forms can be used in combat, although they are mainly used as an expression of discipline and commitment. The true contest is seen to be with oneself and one's own limitations, rather than with an opponent.

Chi Kung

Literally translated, chi kung means 'the cultivation of energy or *chi*.' There are many different forms of chi kung, most of them handed down through the ages by word of mouth, but all are based on the ancient Chinese understanding of energy and movement. Simple exercises that can be practised at home encourage a process of inner balancing and strengthening, developing stamina, clarity and relaxation. Specific movement and breathing techniques are used, stimulating chi to flow along the meridians (or channels of energy that flow throughout the body), clearing blockages. Chi kung focuses on three parts of the body, known as lower, middle and upper; on internal or static development; and on external or dynamic movement. It involves movements done lying down, sitting or standing, incorporated with the breath. This helps harmonise the exchange of energy between inside and outside.

Chi kung is practised daily by thousands of Chinese – they regard it as a means of curing ill-health and preventing disease, as well as prolonging life. Through cultivating chi, personal problems and limitations are recognised, become more fluid and less of a restriction. As the body and breath move so does the mind, clearing the energetic blocks that normally lock us into fixed emotional and psychological patterns.

Tai Chi

Tai chi is one of the most spiritual forms of the martial arts, as well as one of the most gentle and meditative. It is a series of slow, graceful and connected movements, like a dance in a slow motion, that is done with a completely focused yet relaxed attitude. Energy is focused at the *hara*, an area that lies just below the navel, and each movement flows from that place. It is a kind of meditation in action, yet can be just as demanding as any exercise done at a faster speed. The late Professor Cheng Man-ch'ing writes, in *Chop Wood, Carry Water*, compiled by Rick Fields, that tai chi is intended to 'Throw every bone and muscle of the entire body wide open without hindrance or obstruction anywhere.'

Watching hundreds of Chinese practise tai chi is an awesome sight, especially in the city parks in the early morning sunrise, or in the evenings at sunset. In silence, the forms move in rhythm and flow, each posture telling a part of a great story. The movements don't just improve the physical body, they also develop concentration, purpose and sensitivity, releasing old patterns of physical behaviour and opening the mind and body to the peace within. Tai chi is ideal for all forms of stress as it promotes deep relaxation of the whole system. It has a calming yet energising effect on the nervous system, digestion, metabolism, and circulation. The Chinese consider it to be so important that it is practised both as preventive medicine and as a cure for many physical problems. In calming and balancing the body, the mind is also calmed and inner pressures are released.

◆ DANCE ◆

Dance is a powerful means of communication which can be used to express tribal rites of passage, religious beliefs, and ethnic or national traditions. To dance is to feel the gift of life in our veins, to directly experience the joy of each breath. This is particularly true of free dance, where the body moves of its own volition, self-consciousness dissolves and in its place comes self-awareness – an awareness of each part of the body and its relation to the whole.

We can all dance – even those who say they can't – but it does involve a willingness to let go of the restrictive mental patterns that limit freedom. There are numerous dance groups available, from formal dance classes through to free dance and dance therapy. In the latter, movement is used to stimulate a release of inner pain or emotional restriction in an environment of gentle guidance and support.

Or you can dance at home. See how therapeutic it can be to put on some fast and uplifting music and just dance. Let yourself go – no one is watching! Feel the music in every part of you and let it move you. See what it feels like to open your chest, to lift your arms, to spin or bend, to move quickly or slowly. Keep breathing throughout. Let your emotions ebb and flow with the music. Dance your anger, dance your fear, and then dance your joy! Dance your feelings, your relationships, your parents. Dance your illness or your treatment. Dance who you really are.

♦ YOGA ♦

The word *yoga* literally means 'yoke' – that which unites. It is the uniting of the body, mind and spirit, encouraging a full understanding of the intricate relationship between the mind and body and how to bring this relationship into balance and harmony. Developed thousands of years ago, there are many aspects to yoga: relaxation, meditation, discipline, devotion, knowledge, ethics, the recognition of the true self, and movement.

Hatha yoga is so well known in the West that many people do not even know that other forms of yoga exist. Hatha uses movement through different postures or *asanas* to stretch, invigorate, balance and tone the body. As the body finds greater equilibrium and harmony, so does the mind. The word asana means 'seat' because the movement enables us to find our seat or centre, the place in our being that is always still, around which the world flows. The system of asanas was developed so that each posture relates to a different attitude which is expressed both physically and mentally. As we move into the posture it opens us to releasing these attitudes and to ever higher levels of awareness.

Although some forms of hatha yoga are taught in an energetic fashion, generally it is done slowly, with awareness. The effect develops over a period of time, subtly changing the way we move, walk and behave, as well as the way we think, react and feel. It is ideally suited to relieving stress, and indeed it is taught in many stress reduction clinics; it also offers considerable benefit for those with multiple sclerosis or other physically debilitating illnesses – ME, migraines, asthma and insomnia, to name but a few.

But it is especially important as a means of helping us to recognise our limitations and to go beyond them. Without pushing or straining, we breathe and move through our resistance to a posture, simultaneously watching the mind going beyond its limitations. Gradually we find ourselves in a different position, where the boundaries have shifted and the body has opened in a new way. At the same time the mind opens and shifts into an expanded understanding.

Standing Pose

Although this is a very simple pose, it can have powerful results.

- Wearing loose clothing, and with bare feet, stand with your feet just a couple of inches apart. Have your arms hanging by your side, and your head upright. Very gently begin to straighten, as if a string is slowly pulling you upwards from the top of your head. As you lift upwards, let your belly come in and your shoulders drop back. Slowly feel your spine lifting up, and each vertebra opening. Feel your chest opening and your neck lengthening. Now feel your whole spine lengthening as if space is coming between each vertebra. Remember to keep breathing – this is not a tense pose, just a natural opening. Feel the lengthening from the top of your head to the bottom of your feet. Stay like this for a few minutes.

- Now, very slowly, begin to feel the string unwinding. Let your body gently come to a normal upright position, with your back straight. Feel the dignity and inner strength there is in this position, where you are upright yet completely relaxed. Try to maintain this uprightness, without falling back into a bent or collapsed posture.

PART THREE

THE BODYMIND
REVEALED

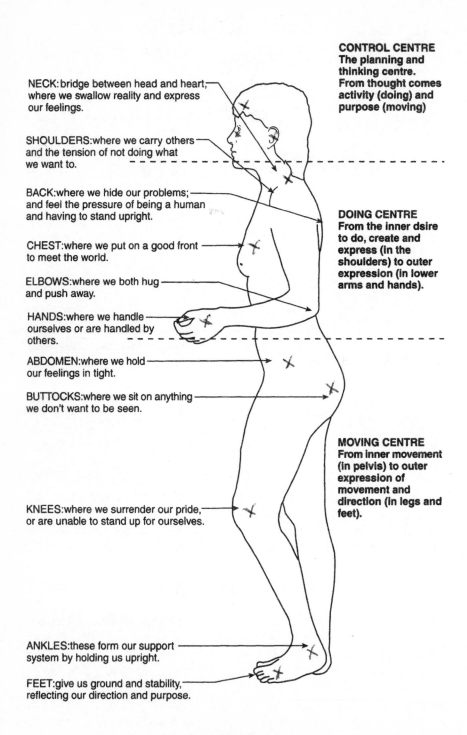

NECK: bridge between head and heart; where we swallow reality and express our feelings.

SHOULDERS: where we carry others and the tension of not doing what we want to.

BACK: where we hide our problems; and feel the pressure of being a human and having to stand upright.

CHEST: where we put on a good front to meet the world.

ELBOWS: where we both hug and push away.

HANDS: where we handle ourselves or are handled by others.

ABDOMEN: where we hold our feelings in tight.

BUTTOCKS: where we sit on anything we don't want to be seen.

KNEES: where we surrender our pride, or are unable to stand up for ourselves.

ANKLES: these form our support system by holding us upright.

FEET: give us ground and stability, reflecting our direction and purpose.

CONTROL CENTRE
The planning and thinking centre. From thought comes activity (doing) and purpose (moving)

DOING CENTRE
From the inner dsire to do, create and express (in the shoulders) to outer expression (in lower arms and hands).

MOVING CENTRE
From inner movement (in pelvis) to outer expression of movement and direction (in legs and feet).

The Structural Bodymind

10

THE BODY BEAUTIFUL
From Top to Bottom

IN THIS CHAPTER we explore the structural body from the head to the toes. By observing the function and nature of each part we gain tremendous insight into the bodymind relationship and the underlying significance of problems in a particular area of the body.

The body operates as a whole, each part connected to the other, communication flowing throughout. A pain in a toe may emanate from a pain in the back; a pain in the shoulder may be due to a problem in the pelvis. To understand each part we need to recognise its relationship to every other part. For instance, a difficulty with the knees is related to the function of the knees as well as to that of the thighs, the calf muscles, the legs as a whole, the pelvis and back, and to the functions of standing or moving. Our body is where we spend our whole life – it is our home – so it is vital to get to know and make friends with our whole physical form.

♦ THE HEAD ♦

The head is the control centre: from here come all the orders for action, the intelligence that governs those actions, the responses to information received, and the maintenance of all our physical and psycho/emotional systems. Through this centre we reach upwards into the heavens to discover vistas of abstract wisdom and spiritual awakening, and we reach outwards and downwards into the world to explore the realms of individual, relative communication and creativity.

The skull is the container for this meeting of the abstract and the relative. **A crack or accident to the skull** can indicate a great longing to expand and grow from within that is being restricted by external circumstances; it is like a shell breaking to let a new being emerge. Or it may be due to a conflict between the physical demands or reality of the world, and a deeper spiritual desire or motivation, both pulling in different directions.

We tend to think of the head as the centre of our being while the body is there to provide a vehicle for the head and to give some pleasurable diversion. We cover the body with clothes and put it out of sight, while the head is left bare, open to communication and contact. But the body contains the heart and our deepest feelings. The result is a separation between head and heart, thoughts and emotions. Below the neck becomes private and hidden; it is where we keep those feelings we want to remain secret. The body, therefore, contains all the repressed issues that are too unpleasant to be shown in public while the head shows the stress of separation from the heart.

♦ THE NECK ♦ ⚕

Through the neck and throat we take in that which gives physical life – water, food and air – and we share outwardly our feelings about that life. From the head come thoughts and experiences that go down into the body to be translated into action. From the body, the responses come up into the head to be expressed – the neck acts as a mediator between these two, a bridge between the absolute and the relative. This is, therefore, a natural cut-off point, a place where a mind-body split is often found, especially if the two-way communication between the intellectual mind and the feeling heart is in any way conflicting.

Most of us have more energy in our heads (we can spend hours thinking or talking) but often at the expense of our hearts. This can create tension or even rigidity in the neck – a battle between the two. If the head and heart can communicate with each other, and respect each other, then they may not feel so throttled or denied. Find out what constriction your neck needs to be released from. Do you need to listen to your feelings? Do you need to put less energy into thinking and more into action? Conflict here may also indicate a repulsion of our bodies, perhaps due to past abuse or because of a disability. There is a lack of energy moving through the neck into the body, a lack of relationship with who we are as physical beings. Do you feel your body as vibrant and energetic? Or does it feel like a stranger – unfamiliar, even unknown?

The neck holds the head upright so we can look forward, maintaining dignity and courage. A **drooping head** implies a hopeless, giving-up attitude, an inability to face what lies ahead. The neck also allows the head to move so we can see all sides, embracing a larger reality than just the one in front of us. This implies an openness of mind and acceptance of others' views.

If you have a **stiff or painful neck**, are you only seeing your own point of view? Are you feeling prejudiced or resistant towards someone? Are you becoming narrow-minded in your attitudes? Or is someone being a 'pain in the neck', perhaps by asking you to look beyond yourself? A stiff neck also limits the amount of feeling that can be expressed from within. Are you holding back your feelings? Are they too strong to express? When you cannot move your neck freely, this implies stubbornness and rigidity. What is needed to ease your neck? Is something strangling you, do you feel unable to move? A stiff neck may also indicate an inability to make a decision – not knowing which way to turn.

◆ THE SHOULDERS ◆

The shoulders are traditionally where we 'shoulder our responsibilities'. When we carry other people's problems, or take on burdens that aren't ours, that responsibility may start to weigh very heavy. This can be a way of avoiding our own issues: being so busy dealing with our obligations to others we have little time for ourselves. **Tense shoulders** may mean that you are carrying too many burdens. Are you responding to your own needs? Do you really want to say, 'Please look after me, please give me some caring and nurturing.' Have you been carrying other people's problems for too long? Is there something or someone you need to put down?

This area of the body is our doing centre. From the shoulders, our doing and creative energy flows down the arms and into the hands where it emerges in what we do in the world. This applies to the work we do as well as the way we live our lives – what we do with our time, do with our relationships, or do with our feelings. The shoulders get tense and rigid when we aren't expressing our real needs, when we are doing something we would rather not be doing, when we feel we have too much to do, or when we feel scared of reaching out and prefer to pull back into the safety of doing nothing. Tension restricts the flow of energy and feeling. Not many of us are doing what we really want to. In the process of putting others' feelings first, our own activity may be stifled. The shoulders are where that doing energy becomes blocked. See what small changes you can make in order to start doing what you really want to do.

The heart energy comes up to the shoulders and then out to manifest in our arms – in hugging and touching. It should be a smooth expression but often there are blocks along the way which cause pain and stiffness. Conflict can arise in the shoulders if we are hugging the wrong person, or feel our advances are being rejected, or we are fearful of intimacy. This can manifest in a **frozen shoulder** ✗ where we are giving or receiving coldness.

Shoulders get raised in fear. If this continues over a period of time the shoulder muscles begin to lock into that position. As the posture develops, so does the attitude that goes with it. **Hunched shoulders** indicate a desire to protect the heart or chest by closing in; whereas **shoulders that are pulled back,** pushing the chest outwards, indicate false strength, often hiding feelings of fear. Pulling the shoulders back is also a way of holding back feelings, especially ones that want to reach out to touch and caress.

♦ THE ARMS ♦

The arms express the energy coming from the heart out to the world through hugging, touching, expressing and caressing. Open arms are saying 'Here is my heart, come and share it', they are an expression of fearlessness and acceptance. When we fold our arms we are closing them across the heart, putting a protective barrier between ourselves and others; the message is 'Stay clear, keep your distance, intimacy not wanted'. Each time you notice yourself crossing your arms, try opening them instead and watch how it feels. Try spending time each day with your arms open and relaxed.

Arms express the active, doing energy which moves from the shoulders, down the arms and through the hands into the world. They manifest all our inner desires and longings. Are you doing what you want to do? Are you doing something you should not be doing? Are you extending yourself too far, or holding yourself back? Arms are also weapons. We can use them to attack, deny, reject or repel; we can push away or we can pull towards us; we can hold and embrace. Is there something or someone you need to let go of? Arms are for lifting and carrying, but sometimes the load gets too heavy and they ache or feel sore. Are you carrying too much?

Weak or tired arms imply an inability to let feelings or energy flow outwards. There may be a sense of being unable to take control or make decisions, an inability to grasp hold of life or a timidity about expressing real feelings. **Stiff or painful arms** indicate a resistance to activity or expression. What are you holding back from sharing? What feelings are in your arms? **A bruised arm** indicates that you are hitting some form of resistance – or that you are feeling beaten up by something. **A broken arm** indicates a deep level of conflict with your activity. What does the broken arm stop you from doing and what does it enable you to do? Does it stop you from hugging someone? From going to work? From being the care-giver? Do you need a break from what you are doing?

♦ THE ELBOWS ♦

Joints give movement and flexibility. If we did not have movement in the middle of the arms we could not reach the mouth in order to eat, we could not hold someone close, we could not play the violin, or express ourselves when we talk. They enable us to open our arms to embrace our world. Elbows give us grace in our movements but they can also be a weapon, as when we 'elbow someone out of the way'. Or perhaps you are being elbowed out of the way by someone else?

The elbows enable us to respond with energy and vigour (as in 'elbow grease') but can also express conflict about what we are doing. Do you feel capable or competent enough? Are you asserting yourself enough? Are you becoming too inflexible in your attitude? Or are you fearful of expressing your heart energy? **Tennis elbow** is an inflammation of the joint, implying that something is making us irritated, hot and angry about what we are doing. Are you holding on too tight? Are you feeling resentful that you are working harder than someone else? Or is there a fear of opening to the future, embracing that which is ahead of you?

♦ THE WRISTS ♦

These joints connect thought with the impulse for activity. **Stiff or painful wrists** limit a whole range of activities – driving a car, eating, writing or expressing your feelings. If your wrist hurts, is there an activity you are resisting, avoiding, wish you weren't doing, or perhaps feel restricted from doing? Are there feelings you don't want to express? A **sprained wrist** implies a mental conflict with your activity. Do you feel pressured, or under strain? Do you feel unable to do what is being asked of you? Are you being pulled in different directions? **A broken wrist** indicates a very deep level of conflict over what you are doing, or what is being done to you. What is broken inside you? How does the break affect your activity? Do you want to stop what you are doing? Are you being stopped?

♦ THE HANDS ♦

Children develop their mental capacities by working with their hands and when brain activity diminishes, as with a stroke, so does dexterity. The hands are where we create, so represent all the ways we do things and all the feelings we have about what we are doing.

The hands go ahead of us to meet the world, they symbolise how we are handling life or are being handled. They are the most outward expression of the heart energy, where we touch, caress, show love, or form a fist and express dislike. Are you touching the right person? In the right way? Do you really want to punch someone? Are you feeling resentful at giving someone else a hand and then not getting the help you need?

Hands are wrung in anguish, gripped in desperation or clenched in anger, perhaps enacting the movement we would like to make towards someone. We can let things slip through our hands or we can grasp them – perhaps too tightly. Are you fearful of letting go? Are you holding on to someone too tightly for fear they will leave? How strong a grasp do you have on your world?

We touch each other with our hands. Touching is fundamental to life; without it we feel unwanted and insecure. We bring healing through touch, releasing loneliness and pain. Are you longing to touch or be touched? Conflict in our hands may be showing that we want to reach out and touch but fear or insecurity is holding us back.

Stiff hands indicate a stiff or resistant attitude towards our activity or expression of feelings. **Painful hands** imply that what we are doing is causing discomfort, or something being done is hurting us. Is someone cramping your style? **Arthritic joint pain in the hands** often implies an overly critical attitude about what we are doing or what is being done to us. **Excessively sweaty hands** indicate that we are feeling nervous, anxious, even scared, about what we are doing. **Very cold hands** may show that we are withdrawing feelings from our activity – perhaps withdrawing love or emotional involvement – or are feeling fearful of being involved or participating.

Fingers stretch out into the world and often get damaged before other parts of our bodies. Are you extending too far? Reaching out inappropriately? Are you moving too quickly and in the process not being aware of the details along the way? The fingers show us where we are being insensitive to subtler or smaller issues. The thumb is to do with control and power, as well as anxiety and fear; whereas the index finger is pointed when we blame someone else without recognising our own involvement.

If the **fingers are becoming bent or crooked**, follow that movement and see where it wants to go. What is the movement trying to tell you? Does it make a fist and, if so, does the fist want to hit out at someone or something? Or do the fingers point away as if reaching out to new areas of experience? Or are they going off in different directions, as if unity of purpose has been lost?

♦ THE BACK ♦

This is the pillar of our being, giving us support and strength, uprightness and dignity. Yet approximately five million people suffer from chronic back pain in the UK, while over 30 billion dollars are spent in the USA each year on medical treatment and lost productivity resulting from back trouble. Many cases of back pain begin with an injury or weight-lifting problem, but, if we look carefully, we may also find psycho/emotional issues that have caused tension, weakness or contraction in the back prior to the accident.

The back represents the unconscious because it is where we dump issues or feelings that we don't want to deal with – they are kept well out of sight there. And if we can't see them, how can anyone else? If you have a **painful back**, is it something you have pushed away that is trying to get your attention? We talk about having a 'bad' back, as if it has done something wrong, but is it the back that is bad or the stuff we have dumped there? What would it have to do to be a 'good' back? If something is 'holding us back' from moving forward, or we 'push back' feelings inside us, then they will often be found in the back itself.

Issues of survival are connected to the back: the responsibility of earning a living, carrying our own weight, being the 'backbone' of the family, or standing on our own. Thoughts like 'I'm not being supported' or 'I'm being let down' can translate into back pain or weakness. We can stand up for ourselves and walk tall, or become bowed and bent over by the weight of our burdens. Is there someone or something putting pressure on you? Is someone being a pain in the back? Do you feel overloaded?

The upper back reflects the reverse side of the heart so this is ⋎
where we find the reverse side of love: fear, irritation or anger, pain
from the past, long-lost memories; feelings of guilt, shame or
emotional confusion. Is there anger or resentment you are not
expressing? A deep frustration? Do you want to turn your back on
someone or something? The upper back is also connected with
expression through activity (energy moves up from the heart to the
shoulders and down the arms) and with any obstacles to that
expression. If you have lost touch with your real desires you may
have buried them in your back. Are you compromising so much that
you feel spineless or powerless? Unexpressed feelings, such as long-
held but unfulfilled ambitions, can contort the muscles or bones.
Tight muscles may be loaded with rage or longing. Or you may feel
overly pressured. Do you feel as if you have your back against the
wall? Are you up against difficulties?

Like the pivot of a seesaw, the middle back holds the balance in
the centre of the body. It is, therefore, about decision-making.
Problems here can indicate that you are locked in indecision, caught
between your own needs and demands from others. Do you want to
assert yourself more and make your needs known? Resentment is
also found in the middle back. How many times have you 'bent over
backwards' to help someone, or 'put your back into' something,
only to find that when you need help it isn't there? Do you tend to
let people walk all over you?

When we stand up straight it can feel as if the abdomen is exposed
and unprotected, so there may be a tendency to bend over to protect
this delicate area. Are you feeling particularly vulnerable? Do you
want to curl up and hide? When animals evolved from being on all
fours to standing up, all the weight of the upper half of the body, no
longer supported by the arms and the hands, came to rest on the
lower back and pelvis. Try bending forward at the waist and then
slowly lift yourself back up. In this movement you are 'becoming a
human'. The lower back, therefore, can express all the weight and
responsibility of being human. If there is no one to help with the load
– no sense of being supported – this part of the back may give way.

This area is also to do with survival, security and self-support. If
you are feeling insecure – perhaps unable to meet other people's
expectations of you – then the pressure may be felt in the lower
back. Do you doubt your ability to support yourself? Or are you
feeling isolated? Are you able to ask for help? Are you trying to do
too much? As the nerves that flow down the legs issue from the
lower spine, pressure here can affect your movement forward,
sometimes creating pain or numbing sensations in the feet and legs.

What happens when you feel you're carrying the weight of the world? Is there someone you want to get away from?

Interestingly, **pain in the lower back** often arises at times when we are reminded of our advancing age, such as anniversaries, children leaving home, or retirement. These occasions confront us with our own mortality and can bring up deep layers of fear and insecurity, especially about what lies ahead, or about our standing in life.

Muscular back problems, such as stiffness and pain, show inflexibility in attitudes; perhaps there is a resistance to what is coming next in life, or you feel you cannot continue doing everything without more support. If it is a **posture problem**, then you need to look at your standing in the world. Are you standing upright, or are you bent over? Do you feel weighed down by psychological or emotional burdens?

A **slipped disc** is primarily to do with feeling pressured, as the weight of the spine puts pressure on the jelly-like substance around the disc and causes a **prolapse**. Discs are like shock absorbers. With inappropriate pressure they get squeezed out of line. Do you feel pressured to live up to someone's expectations? Or are you putting undue pressure on yourself, perhaps trying to keep yourself strong and upright, while not showing your real feelings? Is the weight of responsibility too much to bear? Do you feel unsupported?

A **broken back** indicates a very deep conflict with your purpose or place in life. Are you trying to go in two different directions at once? Do you feel unsupported, alone, even abandoned? Do you feel unable to stand up for yourself? What burden was so great that it finally broke your back? What does a broken back enable you to do, or not do?

To help you understand any difficulty you may be experiencing, close your eyes and let your back talk to you. Let it tell you what the difficulty is associated with, what it needs, and how you can help.

♦ THE BUTTOCKS ♦

The buttock muscles have developed in response to our humanness; they add balance, enabling us to stand and walk on two legs, rather than having to rest on our hands. This is also where we sit on things that no one else can see. Just for a moment, right now, check your buttock muscles. Are they relaxed? Or are they clenched tight? If so, consciously relax them and notice the difference in your attitude. What feelings are you sitting on? What energy is being held in your backside? Are you sitting on feelings of insecurity? Or a need for support and comfort?

This area is also to do with elimination and release. The experience of being potty-trained as a child can have a marked effect on the rest of a person's life, especially on their ability to feel relaxed and spontaneous, as opposed to tight and constrained, fearful of the unknown or the unexpected. Tension here is related to our parents and their expectations. Do you feel you have to do what your parents want? Do they interfere with your decision-making? (See also Chapter 12.)

♦ THE CHEST ♦

When saying 'I' we always point to the centre of the chest. We don't point to the head or to the belly and say this is me – we point to the heart. The chest represents our public image, strong and powerful or weak and retracted. Buried in the chest are all our deepest feelings and conflicts – our passion, anger, fear, grief, forgiveness and love. So difficulties here tend to indicate issues to do with our feelings towards ourselves – perhaps issues of self-worth and introversion, or of self-centredness and false grandeur.

A **puffed-up chest**, which is pushed out to make it look bigger and more powerful than it really is, often hides a deeper doubt or insecurity, as seen in the 'military chest' where soldiers are taught to lift their shoulders back and push their chests out in a posture of false bravado. This puffed-up chest creates an image of strength and power, a protective armour that hides an inner vulnerability.

A **weak or concave chest** indicates a lack of self-identity, as if we have not really found ourselves yet. The 'I' inside is still unformed. There may be an emotional timidity, a shyness of expression and need for reassurance. This posture indicates a depressed, sad or helpless attitude, which can be uplifted by deep breathing. ✗

♦ THE RIBCAGE ♦

The ribs protect our most vulnerable organs – the heart and the lungs – and represent our sense of protection. If you have **bruised or broken ribs** you may have been letting your guard down at the wrong times, or perhaps you are feeling vulnerable or exposed. As they surround the heart, sadness can be found here. The ribs are also to do with boundaries and limitations. Are you clear about your

─────── TRY IT YOURSELF───────

Opening Your Chest

Stand upright with your shoulders relaxed.

- Pull your shoulders back and puff out your chest, as if you were a proud soldier. Hold this posture for a moment.

- Now release your shoulders, letting them fall forward slightly, until you come into an open-hearted position, where the chest is open but not rigid.

- Now pull your chest inwards, bowing the shoulders and folding your arms as if protecting your heart.

- Keep moving between these three postures and let yourself experience the different feelings in each position.

boundaries, about how far you want to go, and how much you can give? Or do you try to please everyone and fail to look after yourself in the process, thus going beyond your capabilities? Recognising our limitations is very important in establishing balance – our inner and outer worlds need to be at ease with each other. It may be necessary to be clear with others about how far they can go before we reach our limit.

♦ THE DIAPHRAGM ♦

A large flat muscle in the chest, positioned below the lungs, the diaphragm is essential for the breathing process. It enables us to breathe in deeply and take life into ourselves and, in releasing that breath, to let go of tension or stress. **A stiff diaphragm**, seen in shallow or restricted breathing, creates a block between the upper realms of abstract thought and the lower realms of emotion, sexual energy, communication and intuition.

Difficulties here indicate a resistance or fear of sharing our deepest feelings. By drawing a line here, we can keep our more intimate self separate from the world. Control and power issues are focused in this area, especially control over others. Deep belly breathing relaxes the diaphragm, relinquishes the need for control and releases any feelings that were being held back.

✦ THE ABDOMEN ✦

This strong muscular area, stretching from the ribs to the pubic bone, protects the front of the body. If we do not trust our world but believe it is hurtful, then we will protect this area by becoming closed off, even rigid. This stops any flow of feeling.

Tightly held abdominal muscles show a sense of vulnerability or fear of intimacy; they are a way of warding anyone off who may be getting too close. They indicate a fear of feeling, for the gut is a centre of emotions. By pulling in the muscles we are able to hold back the feelings that lie behind them. Conversely, **flabby abdominal muscles** imply a lack of care or self-respect. There is a sloppy letting go, a 'who cares' attitude that often masks a deeper unhappiness or lack of satisfaction, a real longing to be cared for.

About two inches below the navel is an area the Japanese call the *hara*. This is known in the East as the energetic core of our being, or the centre of chi; in the West we connect this area with having guts or courage. If the hara is strong and balanced you cannot be pushed over; whereas a weak hara leads to despair and helplessness. The hara is strengthened through belly breathing, tai chi, yoga and similar practices.

✦ THE PELVIS ✦

The pelvis is a ring of bone that forms a pivot between the upper and lower halves of the body, balancing the realm of action and creation above with the world of direction and movement below. Within this area an enormous amount of activity takes place: here we make love, give birth, digest food and eliminate that which is finished with – all actions connected to security, survival, communication and relationship.

The pelvis is also the centre of movement: from here the legs take that movement out into the world, enabling us to stand on our own and walk our own path. Through the moving centre we find our groundedness and purpose.

Where there is any fear of movement – perhaps a fear that there is nothing to move towards (felt most by the elderly), or a fear of where we are going – then the hips will reflect this. A problem here indicates a very deep fear of change, an inability to let go of the past or a feeling of being unable to stand on our own. **Stiffness in the hips** is a sign of resistance to change, perhaps in your work or living situation. Are you due for retirement and feeling fearful about how you will find a purpose to life without work, or how you will be able to manage financially? Does the ground you are standing on feel shaky and uncertain? When we feel useless, our hips prove that uselessness by preventing us from moving. The fear of survival makes us hold on tight to what we have, until eventually we become immobile.

This area also contains our sexuality, which is about intimacy and trust in a relationship. Intimacy can give rise to enormous doubts and uncertainties, leading to a breakdown in communication. Are you fearful of letting someone get too close? Has past hurt caused a withdrawal of energy from this area? Or do you want to go in your own direction, to move away from the relationship? **Layers of excess fat over the hips** often indicate a covering up of feelings to do with sexuality and intimacy, as if by hiding the area we can also hide our feelings.

The pelvis is involved with our relationships with our parents, particularly with our mothers, as this is the area of birth. There may be unresolved issues concerning our own birth held here, or towards our mother and her feelings about her pregnancy. This will influence our ability to be creative or enter into new situations, rather than holding on to the past. As we make our journey through life by moving away from our parents, so in the pelvis we can carry unresolved issues to do with our independence. Are you taking on the role of mother too much, carrying the weight of others, just as a mother carries a child on her hips? Are you carrying your own mother here? Is it hard to put her down and stand on your own?

♦ THE LEGS ♦

The legs carry us forward in life, moving us through the world. They ground us, give us our sense of place, our purpose and direction. They enable us to walk, run, dance and jump. The way in which we stand or move is indicative of our feelings about the direction we are going in. Are you stumbling and tripping your way forward, or do you take giant confident strides?

Strong legs give stability and the power to stand up for ourselves, but **over-developed or very muscular legs** can be so firmly grounded that it is hard to be spontaneous or to move with lightness and ease. Are you holding on to something too tightly? Are you fearful of change? Has the rug been pulled from under you once too often? **Under-developed or weak legs** represent insecurity. Do you feel unsure of your place in the world? Are you holding tight to the ground? Do you feel overwhelmed by worldly issues? Do you find it hard to be alone?

Locked into the thighs we find issues to do with the past, such as parental problems, traumatic childhood memories, anger or resentment. This area is closely associated with sexuality, which we initially learn from our parents' attitudes. By holding the legs together we protect our sexual organs, while opening the thighs means we are conceding, willingly or not, to sex. If there is any fear or resistance then it is often found in tight muscles or layers of excess fatty tissue, like a protective wall hiding our real feelings. Women often develop excess weight in this area after having children. Have your sexual relationships changed? Has parenting brought up painful issues from your own childhood?

The shin bone and calf muscle are connected to the movement we are about to take and any resistance or fear we may be feeling. This area is also related to our standing and position in life.

Difficulties in the legs are associated with a fear of moving forward, or a conflict with the ground we are standing on. Is there something you want to run away from? Would you rather be moving in a different direction? Is the ground beneath you getting a bit rough? **Bruising a leg** indicates that you are knocking into something, or you are going in the wrong direction and need to re-route. What are the obstacles standing in your way? Are you fearful of what lies ahead? **Tight or tense muscles** indicate an inner fear or tightness, a clinging to things as they are and a resistance to movement, perhaps due to feeling let down by someone, or because the future appears scary.

A broken leg signifies conflict on the deepest level – about where you are going or if it would be better to go in a different direction. Do you feel unable to stand up for yourself? Have you lost your standing? Do you feel unsupported? What is happening to your movement in the world?

♦ THE KNEES ♦

Through the knees we are able to move with grace and ease, to dance and run. Try walking without bending your knees and see the arrogant, stiff attitude it represents. By bending the knees we can release and express our feelings.

The act of kneeling gives us a clue to the importance of the knees. This is a position of surrender, usually to some form of higher authority. The knees allow us to bend, to concede, to give, especially to give way, to be humble. In kneeling we relinquish the ego and embrace humility; without this ability we become stubborn, proud, inflexible, self-righteous. Remember: pride comes before a fall! Too much pride and inflexibility puts a strain on the knees. But when the knees give way *too* quickly, knocking and trembling with fear or an inability to stand up for ourselves, we need to rise up and claim our place in the world, developing greater pride, self-esteem and confidence.

The knees are like shock absorbers, taking the strain between the weight of the body above and the ups and downs of the terrain below. When we can't bear the load any more, the knees may start to react. They are telling us to relax, to find our flow again, to let go of the pressure.

Water on the knee indicates a holding of emotional energy, particularly a resistance to surrender; or there may be too much emotion to cope with and the weight is being carried in the knees. **An inflamed knee** indicates that something or someone is making us feel irritated or angry, and we will not give in! Or we are feeling inflamed about how much we have to deal with. **A dislocated knee** shows a resistance to giving way; the knee can no longer take the pressure so it collapses, and we are unable to maintain our standing. To dislocate is to lose. What do you need to do to regain your ground? To refind your balance and dignity? ✳

♦ THE ANKLES ♦

These thin little parts of the body support our entire weight – if an ankle slips the whole body falls to the ground. Support is the key word here, as the ankles reflect the support we depend on, not just from others around us, but from the inner support system we have built for ourselves. This inner system consists of the psychological and emotional beliefs that give our lives meaning and purpose; the emotional support of our loved ones and religious or spiritual convictions. If any of this is taken away, doubted or questioned, then there is nothing to hold us upright. This can happen when we experience extreme shock or trauma, or when we feel rejected, betrayed, or unable to stand alone. As the ankles are essential to our uprightness they tend to collapse when we can no longer stand it, or when the weight from above is too much to bear. Are your beliefs being questioned? Is your support system letting you down?

The ankles also enable us to be more flexible in our movement. **A sprained or twisted ankle** indicates a lack of flexibility for the direction we are going in. The strain is too great, causing the energy to buckle or twist, to go in all directions at once. Are you being pulled in different directions? Do you need to change direction? What needs to be untwisted, unravelled, redirected? Or is there a stiffness in your movement, a lack of going with the flow? **Swollen ankles** indicate a holding of emotional energy, a frustration or resistance to letting go, to do with the issues mentioned above.

A broken ankle indicates a very deep conflict about the ground we are standing on and support for where we are going. Perhaps you need to go in a new direction but you are resisting making the change? Are you questioning your underlying beliefs? What has damaged your ability to stand up for yourself? What does the broken ankle enable you to do and what does it stop you doing?

♦ THE FEET ♦

Our feet connect us to the earth, to the reality of the physical world. We extend them forwards as we make our journey through life. It is a sign of growing up when we can 'stand on our own two feet' and not be dependent on someone else. 'Putting your foot down' means not letting someone take advantage of you. We 'put our best foot forward' as we step into the world with courage and confidence. If our direction is unclear then we may walk with our feet turned inwards because we do not know which way to go, or outwards because all directions appear possible. The former is the more introverted expression, the latter the more extroverted (the 'I'll try anything' approach).

Our feet also indicate how we feel about where we are going. If, for instance, there is fear of what lies ahead – perhaps due to old age, illness, or insecurity – then the toes may curl or the feet become sore so that we cannot walk easily. This stops us moving forward, as if we are trying to stop the future from happening. Or it may feel as if there is nowhere to go, so why bother? **Cold feet** are due to a withdrawal of blood from the area, implying an emotional uncertainty, withdrawal or resistance to what lies ahead. **Very sweaty feet** indicate a nervousness about the direction we are going in, an excess of emotion. **Swollen feet** mean we are holding on to fearful or frustrated feelings about our direction; or the weight of our emotional burdens is too much to bear. **Peeling skin on the feet** implies that we need to let go of old mental patterns, so that new directions can emerge.

If we 'dig our heels in' it implies we are holding on tight to reality

– a stubbornness indicating a fear of change. The heels may also reflect conflicts connected to your mother or to being a mother. **Flat feet** tend to imply that we have no roots, that we are moving over the surface of life without being grounded; or that there is a lack of boundaries between our private, more personal life and our public activities. **High arches** tend to indicate the opposite – our boundaries are so firm that our private and public worlds hardly meet. We may appear quite aloof and separate from others.

The toes go forward furthest of all, so they are most likely to get knocked or trodden on when we are pushing forward too quickly or in the wrong direction. They indicate the small, subtle issues that easily get overlooked. So if the toes keep getting hurt, we need to make sure we are not pushing forward too fast and in the process missing the details. Those who tiptoe through life may be fearful of making their presence known or of coming down to earth.

Bunions on the side of the big toe are usually caused by wearing the wrong shoes. However, this may also indicate that we allow others to make decisions for us, rather than taking responsibility for ourselves – such as when buying shoes! A bunion can develop if we find ourselves in a relationship where we have surrendered decision-making to someone else, as the big toe is connected to issues of authority and personal power.

◆ LEFT AND RIGHT SIDES ◆ OF THE BODY

The right side of the brain controls the left side of the body and vice versa – the nerves cross over between the head and the body. The left side of the brain is the logical, rational side, involved with daily work, assertiveness and decision-making, whereas the right brain is the creative and intuitive side, involved with home life, relationships, feeling and insight. This applies to the body, and particularly if one side of the body tends to get hurt more than the other side.

The right side of the body represents the masculine principle in both men and women. It is to do with the ability to give and to be dominant or assertive; it is the authoritative and intellectual part of our being; involved with the world and work, our job or function in society, finance and business, politics and power. It reflects the feelings you may have about being a man and functioning in a competitive world or maintaining the breadwinning role; or about being a woman and having to work or be assertive at the same time as being a nurturing mother. This side reflects your feelings towards your own masculinity or masculine qualities, as well as your relationships with men such as father, brother, husband or son, and any conflicts you may be experiencing in those relationships, or towards men in general.

The left side of the body represents the feminine principle in both men and women. It indicates the ability to ask for help, to receive, or to surrender; to nourish and care for others; to be tender and caring; to be creative and artistic; to listen to and trust our own wisdom. It is the inner world of the home and family, of healing, gentleness and nurturing. This includes how you feel about being a woman, or expressing your feminine energy, especially in a male-dominated environment; or how you feel as a man connecting with the ability to be tender and loving, able to show more caring qualities. It also reflects your feelings about the females in your life, such as mother, sister, wife or daughter. Any conflict in these relationships, or towards women in general, may manifest on the left side.

── TRY IT YOURSELF ──

Finding Your Balance

- Over the next few weeks, become aware of which side of your body is most dominant. Does one side get hurt more than another? Is one side stronger, or more well-developed?

- Think back to past accidents or illnesses. Was one side most often affected? Which part of your personality is more developed – the feminine or masculine?

- Are there conflicts with the feminine or masculine energies in your life? In your relationships? What is needed to bring greater balance?

Finding the right balance between these two energies is not easy. In the last fifty years we have seen a shift from women being the principal care-givers and men being the principal money-makers to women making up a major part of the workforce and men spending more time at home. A woman making the change from mother to careerperson may feel that she is going against her essential nature – having to work late when her child is coming home early from school, or dealing with hormonal changes while giving a presentation at a business meeting. The resulting stress isn't just due to overwork. The same applies to men. As their role is changing they are confronting the problem of how to get in touch with their inner feelings. How can men find the tender, caring, nurturing part of their nature when society says they are meant to be assertive and aggressive? These issues touch on deep questions of how to define our essential nature, and how to develop differing sides of our personalities.

♦ THE OVERALL PICTURE ♦

Take a good long look in the mirror – naked! Are you standing straight and upright, or are you bent over or lopsided? If so, were you taught not to be straight with people? How does it feel to straighten up? Which side of your body is most dominant? Is your head held high or slightly to one side, as if to avoid a confrontation? Can you meet the world head on? What happens when you move your neck? Are you stiff and unbending or do you move with fluidity and ease? Do your joints move freely? Look at the way you hold your muscles or joints. Are they locked into position, holding back your feelings? What do you need to do to release them?

Is the top half of your body bigger or smaller than the bottom half? The top half of the body is the part that meets the world (it is the social and thoughtful side of us) while the bottom half deals with practical and worldly issues. A strong or heavy top with thin or weak legs tends to indicate someone who is very sociable and friendly, even self-confident, but who may be somewhat ungrounded, unsure of dealing with physical or worldly issues. Big or strong legs combined with a small or weak top can indicate someone who is very grounded and practical, sometimes too much so, with less energy going into communication or self-confidence; they are likely to lack playfulness and spontaneity. Take note of where you have most physical difficulties and see how this part relates to the rest of you. Is it smaller and less energetic? Is it more rigid or tense? Is it more over-developed and puffed up?

If your body is aching, what is it aching for? To be held? To be comforted? If your body wants to move, where does it want to go? Follow the movement and see what happens. Where are the areas that hurt or don't function properly? How do they feel inside? Draw a picture of yourself or write down what your body is feeling.

Look carefully but without judgement – simply observe and get to know and make friends with your body.

11

MOVING PARTS
The Bones, Joints and Muscles

THE MOVING PARTS – the muscles, joints and bones – together create the framework within which we live. This structure enables us to move, and allows our thoughts, ideas, beliefs and feelings to find expression, determining whether we walk with a confident, joyful step or drag our feet behind us. Just as our emotions affect our physical state, so physical movement elevates our emotional state: exercise creates a positive and vibrant feeling about ourselves, while a lack of exercise soon depletes energy, leading to lethargy and depression.

Figuratively speaking, there are three main types of tissue in the human body: hard tissue, as in the bones and teeth; soft tissue, as in the flesh, fat, skin, organs, muscles, ligaments and nerves; and fluid, as in the blood, urine, water and lymph. These correspond to three inner states of being.

The hard tissue corresponds to our core beliefs: the skeleton forms the supportive inner framework of the body, fundamental to the health of the whole, just as our deepest beliefs support and give meaning to every aspect of our lives. The soft tissue corresponds to our psychological attitudes and thinking patterns: our thoughts and experiences directly affect the state of our nerves and organs, and are visible in the condition of our muscles, skin and flesh. The fluids correspond to our emotions and feelings – we boil with anger or overflow with love – and to the distribution of those feelings throughout our being.

♦ THE BONES ♦

Bone marrow nourishes us with minerals, salts and nutrients and produces vital immune cells, while the hard outer tissue forms a strong and resilient framework upon which our whole being is built. Bones are the densest form of energy in the physical body; like the rocks in the earth, they support and sustain. They enable the muscles to move, and the muscles in turn help to move the fluids.

In the same way that we cannot live without bone, so we are not truly alive without being in touch with the deepest part of our psycho/spiritual being, with the inspiration and impulse that gives life meaning. Just as the bones support our physical being and give life to the muscles and fluids, so our core beliefs give us constant inner strength and support while finding expression in our lifestyle, behaviour and relationships. Problems with our bones, therefore, represent conflict within the deepest parts of our being.

Broken Bones

If our beliefs become stiff and limited, our physical movement will reflect this. A broken bone is a sign of being too inflexible; there is a resistance to going with the flow. When there is a resistance to movement, we break. A broken bone indicates a deep split or conflict at the very centre of our being. Do you feel fractured, split or broken into pieces? Are you going in one direction yet inside longing to go in a different one? Are your loyalties being divided? Are you getting the support you need? Can you no longer stand the pressure on your own? Is there a need to reassess what you are doing and why you are doing it? Are your deepest beliefs being questioned?

Take time to see the effect of the broken bone. What is it stopping you from doing? What is it making you do? Are there benefits to this? A broken bone usually forces us to rest and ask for help – two things many of us are not very good at. But perhaps this is what we really need: to be cared for and given extra attention. Having a rest provides an opportunity to look at where we need more strength and flexibility. (See also Chapter 10 for the part of the body broken.)

Osteoporosis

Due to changes in the hormones, this condition causes a loss of bone mass, common in women after the menopause, making the bones brittle and liable to fracture. Osteoporosis implies a thinning of the life force flowing through the bones, perhaps due to a sense of giving up, of feeling helpless or hopeless. After menopause, a woman can believe her reason for being has gone and there is no impulse to create a new direction, to find a new purpose. Do you feel a loss of purpose now that the potential for motherhood is over? Do you feel you have lost your womanhood or femininity? Have you found a direction for yourself that is just for you, and not related to being a mother or wife? Have you lost the support or attention of your partner?

The strength of the bones is at stake, as is the strength of our core feelings, our inner purpose for being. The bones are connected to spirit, so we need to raise our spirit, to bring it into action, rather than let it fade away. What can you do to bring more vibrancy and spirit into your life? (See also Chapter 18 for more on the menopause.)

♦ JOINTS ♦

The joints *join up* thoughts and feelings with movement and action. They give freedom of expression: the ability to dance, jump, hug and hold. They allow us to move with grace and ease, or with a jerky and disjointed action, depending upon our psycho/emotional attitude. They give stability and balance to the whole body.

Inflammation of the Joints
The most common difficulty with joints is inflammation. This is connected to movement and communication and indicates a fear of the future, or a resistance to what is happening; a build up of angry or irritable emotions, or an inability to say what we are really feeling. What is making you feel so hot or fired up inside? What is so irritating that it is restricting your expression? When the joints are sore or inflamed then the feelings being expressed are often critical, irritated, or inflexible ones, so we need to release the cause of those feelings. What is needed to loosen the joints? More forgiveness? Acceptance? Love for yourself? (See also Chapter 10 for the part affected.)

Joint Stiffness
If the joints become stiff or unable to move, then where has our thinking become rigid or unbending, critical or dismissive? Rigid joints become useless – they lose their purpose which is freedom of movement – and the relationship between thought or emotion and expression is lost. Stiff joints imply that we are not expressing our

deeper feelings, there is lack of freedom, a holding on to old ways of being. (See also Chapter 10 for the part affected.)

Bursitis

Bursitis is an inflammation of the bursa or fluid-filled sacs in the joints that normally prevent friction. Bursitis often develops through excessive use, as in tennis elbow. As the bursa are filled with fluid, this indicates an emotional irritation or inflammation – our feelings are building up inside and this is restricting our ability to express ourselves. There may be inner sadness, anger, or unresolved guilt. Are you feeling resentful at all the work you are doing? Do you feel you are not being appreciated? Is a particular activity causing you intense conflict? What action is needed to release the pressure? Rest is essential but, in taking rest, what happens? Does it shift the weight of responsibility to others?

Dislocation

To dislocate is to lose our place. Having lost our place, we cannot move forward easily; there is pain and uncertainty as to how to proceed. Putting a bone out of joint indicates that we are feeling deeply put out, have lost contact with our centre, or perhaps have lost our standing or place in the world. It also signifies difficulty in expressing our feelings. Do you feel put out about something? Is the direction you are going in causing confusion or uncertainty? Is your activity contradicting your inner feelings? Do you feel pushed out of place? What do you need to do to get realigned? To reconnect with the flow? (See also Chapter 10 for the part affected.)

Gout

This is caused by an accumulation of uric acid in the joints, often in the big toe. Uric acid is normally removed by the urine, which is the body's way of releasing emotions that are finished with, no longer needed, or poisoning our system. If we do not release these old emotions they begin to get stuck, to solidify and crystallise, causing rigidity and inflexibility. Gout is an expression of being stuck. Do you feel stuck in your present direction? There is also anger involved, as the toe gets very red and swollen, full of hot emotion. Can you find the emotion, what it is that is unmoving? If we cling to the past, we are unable to move forward. Are there past issues that are very important to you? As gout is more common in the elderly, holding on to past memories is often a contributing factor.

Osteoarthritis

This is an inflammation and slow degeneration of the joints, a wearing away, creating stiffness and pain especially in the weight-bearing joints. As the main function of the joints is to move with ease and fluidity, such a condition implies a deep resistance or fear of movement. The inflammation implies a build up of toxic thoughts or attitudes, such as anger, irritation or frustration, either with ourselves or someone else. Arthritis is often associated with an overly critical attitude (uptight and unrelenting) and with bitterness or resentment (which brings stiffness and pain) as if these attitudes are wearing away our joy and appreciation. The lack of movement implies a hardening of our attitude towards life.

Are you getting so deeply frustrated or irritated that these feelings are limiting your ability to be gracious or loving? Do you dislike spontaneity and find it hard to relax? Is it difficult to receive? Arthritis brings up issues of control, as we slowly lose control over our joints. Do you find it hard not to dominate or demand attention? Or do you feel you are being controlled by someone or something and this is making you angry or resentful? What is wearing you down so much? What can you do to release some of the tightness in your life? (See also Chapter 10 for the part affected.)

Rheumatoid arthritis

This is an auto-immune disease where our own immune system attacks the membrane of the joints due to an abnormal rheumatoid factor in the blood. The illness means that movement or change becomes very limited, and the joints become rigid and painful. Many people with this condition have previously been very active, such as athletes. Perhaps the over-activity was hiding an internal rigidity, or a tendency to be overly disciplined and self-critical. There may be an inclination always to give to others but not to give to ourselves, leading to repressed anger. Anger needs expression – athletes can channel that energy into sport, but this does not necessarily resolve the underlying issue. When they retire they have nowhere to put those feelings.

The auto-immune aspect of this affliction implies an overly self-critical or judgemental attitude, perhaps combined with low self-esteem. Do you feel stuck in a negative or criticising mode? Are you feeling resentful or bitter about something or someone? Do you lack assertiveness and, feeling inhibited, find yourself unable to act in the way you really want to? Are you destroying yourself with guilt or shame? Do you have a tendency to undermine yourself through criticism or a lack of self-respect? Due to the condition, arthritics often have clenched fists – is the fist really indicating a desire to hit out at someone or something?

Movement is essential, especially going with the flow and allowing change to happen. Life is movement, so the more stuck we are, the more lifeless we may become. There can be a feeling of having lost our sense of purpose, a self-dislike eating away at us so that there seems no point in doing anything. No longer able to do what we did before, we need to find a new way of being, a softer, more self-appreciative way. (See also Chapter 10 for the part affected and Chapter 15 for more on the immune system.)

♦ MUSCLES ♦

The soft tissue in the body is found in the muscles, flesh, fat, skin, nerves and organs. While the hard tissue in our bones is most closely associated with our core beliefs, the soft tissue reflects those core beliefs in mental activity and thought patterns. As we think so we become; as we have become, so we can see how we have been thinking. Past memories, conflicts, experiences and feelings are all found in the soft tissue. The nerves reach out to every cell of the body, carrying the chemical impulses of our attitudes and experiences – prejudices, repressed anxieties, fear, guilt, levels of self-worth or self-esteem, joy, vibrancy – all reflected in the condition of the organs, flesh and muscles. As we change within ourselves, so the soft tissue reflects this change, whether through tight or floppy muscles, gaining or losing flesh, fatty deposits, nerve disorders, skin eruptions or organ deterioration.

Muscles work with the bones to provide movement, at the same time as stimulating circulation, digestion and the breathing process, and providing warmth. They absorb and respond to tensions and feelings. If they do not relax sufficiently following stress, then the tension accumulates and causes deeper, longer-lasting damage. The muscles reflect past experiences, traumas and conflicts that colour our present behaviour. For instance, frozen anger, fear or grief create a kind of body armour which further blocks and holds back feelings, locking the musculature into fixed positions. As the body becomes affected by this, the physical posture reinforces the psychological patterns. You can see this for yourself by simply tightening the muscles in any part of your body, and then watching how your feelings change as a result of the tightening.

If this continues over a long period of time, the muscles become set and fixed in this restricted form. In this way, a depressive or fearful attitude becomes built into the physical structure, which in turn maintains the mental attitude. To bring change we need to work from both sides – to release the physical structure *and* the psychological patterning.

Cramp

Cramp occurs when the muscle tightens and goes into a spasm. This indicates a psychological cramping or holding, perhaps holding back anguish, fear or inner pain. Something is making you want to hold on tight. Are you fearful of what would happen if you let go? Fearful of moving forward, of what is coming next? Perhaps you want to shrink back from it? Are you anxious about what you are doing? Find the place that is feeling cramped or tight and breathe into it to release the pressure. What do you really need to let go of?

Hernia

A hernia is a weakening in the muscle wall that allows an organ or fatty tissue to move out of position. *Hiatus hernias* occur when a part of the stomach becomes trapped above the diaphragm (the flat muscle that separates the chest from the abdomen). They can be caused by exertion or injury. *Inguinal hernias* occur in the groin and are the commonest of hernias, most often in men, where a section of the intestine protrudes through a gap in the abdominal muscle wall and forms a sac. This can be caused by heavy lifting or straining, or excessive coughing.

A hernia indicates a weakening or collapse of psycho/emotional energy, often because we try to cope with too much at once and collapse under the weight, or we strain to do everything right and therefore push ourselves too far (perhaps motivated by guilt or anger); or we feel weakened by inner fears and anxieties so there are no reserves of personal strength – this is connected to over-anxious thinking patterns and fearful mental states. In the process the guts spill out – we lose our psychological control, strength or courage. A hernia may indicate an inner longing to explode that is being restrained. This puts a strain on the muscle – and it implodes rather than explodes. Do you need to be contained in some way? Or are you resisting someone else's control? A hernia can also imply that you are pushing away a part of yourself. What is that part? What do you need to do to reclaim that part of your being?

Some boys are born with a hernia, due to the descending of the testicles. Very often this clears up in childhood. If it recurs later in life, see if there are any childhood issues coming to the fore, or a change in living conditions giving rise to fear or insecurity.

Muscular Pain

Mental attitudes affect the energy flowing through the musculature and can cause pain or limit movement. Muscular pain tends to indicate that psychological pain – anguish, fear, insecurity, guilt, conflict, or even self-punishment – is being expressed through the body.

Pain signifies an aching or longing for something or someone, a deep desire for movement or change, but also an inner resistance to this. Look closely at what is restricting you. What movement do you really want to make? Are there any benefits to your pain, such as extra attention? What is it asking of you? How is it affecting your life? What can you do to ease the tension?

Pain tends to restrict or limit our movement, especially if we are told to stay still. Yet physical movement enables expression of emotion. In not moving, our emotions may also become immobilised and stuck, often the very ones that are trying to find expression through the pain. Exercise, where possible, is essential. Keeping the muscles and joints moving will not only help them to heal but will also help our feelings to keep flowing. Movement also stimulates the release of beta-endorphins, the body's natural painkillers.

Pain can be all-consuming; we lose touch with who we are, apart from the pain. The breath can be used to ease into pain, to soften and release restrictions or resistances. Deep relaxation and meditation increase our awareness and mindfulness, enabling us to see beyond the pain. (See also Chapter 10 for the part affected, Chapter 16 for more on pain, and Chapter 5 for breathing and relaxation techniques.)

Muscle Stiffness

This can be caused after we exercise hard and the following day there is an excess build up of lactic acid in the muscles – the only answer is to exercise some more to get the lactic acid moving! But stiffness can also be due to not having enough exercise, especially in the elderly. Here it indicates stiff and tired thinking patterns, stubborn and resistant attitudes that say there is only one way to do things, with no room for manoeuvre. Stiffness shows a desire for things to stay the same as they are, a holding on to the past. There is an inability to bend or adapt. Not being able to bend means we become rigid and then brittle. Do you need to let go a bit more, to be more spontaneous, playful and loving? What are you feeling so stiff about? What are you holding on to or need to let go of?

Sprains and Strains

Sprains and strains occur when a muscle gets pushed beyond its normal limits and cannot handle the pressure. Are you feeling strained beyond your limit by something or someone? Are you getting pushed or pressured? Is there a mental strain you cannot deal with? Are you trying to do too much to please everyone, and, in the process, ignoring yourself? What needs to be unravelled? A sprain usually occurs when we trip or fall. Do you need to stop and take more time to see where you are going? Are you looking so far ahead that you are missing the present moment? If it is in the ankle, is the ground too weak to support you? Is the direction you are going in creating conflict and confusion? If it is in the wrist, are you doing the right thing, or is your activity creating uncertainty? How can you release the strain in your life? (See also Chapter 10 for the part affected.)

Torn Muscles and Tendons

Similar to sprains and strains, here the stressing of the muscle has gone further, to the point of being torn. This symbolises a mental conflict that is creating a painful wrenching inside, perhaps a conflict of values, or the need to make decisions that are causing a rift. Tendons link the muscles to the bone and symbolise our attitudes and tendencies – when these get torn it indicates that we are being pulled in too many directions at once. Is something tearing you apart? What do you need to do to bring the different parts together?

12

BUDDHA IN THE BELLY
The Digestive System

*W*HEN we are first born our needs are extremely basic – we want food, dry clothes, a warm and safe place to sleep, lots of love, and a few friendly faces to look at. As we grow older these needs do not change much, they just get bigger: we want more food, drawers full of clothes, a whole house with a bed in it, and some loved ones to have fun with. As young babies we do not notice much difference between mother, food and love – usually they come from the same source and do much the same thing, which is to nourish, reassure and love. We are comforted by the smell and touch of a familiar body as much as we are by warm milk. Only as we get older do mother, food and love begin to separate and differentiate. Mother is not always loving, and she does not always give food. Love and food begin to come from different sources and in many forms.

If, as children, we were deprived of food as a means of punishment, we may continue to punish ourselves for what we perceive as wrong behaviour by eating very little for days at a time. If we were made to eat everything on our plate 'because of all those starving children', we may feel tremendous guilt at leaving food and therefore force ourselves to eat *all* the leftovers. If we were fed lots of sweet foods, we may have to realise later that the sweets were actually a replacement for the love we longed for. How often can parents be seen pacifying an upset child with chocolate when the child really wants to be held and soothed? Parents substitute food for love if they were taught to do so, and their children in turn grow up eating instead of loving, each generation continuing the pattern.

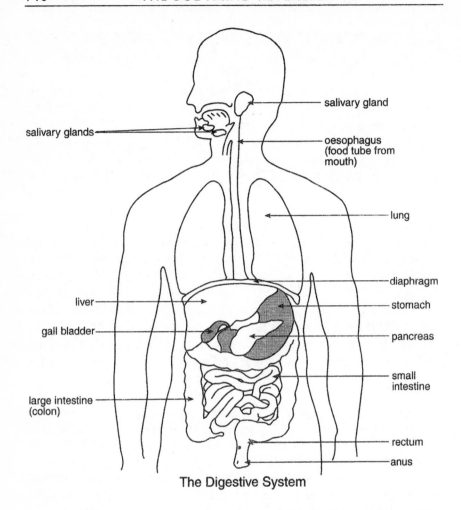

The Digestive System

Love is the most essential and nourishing ingredient in life, so it is understandable that we look for substitutes if that love is either absent or removed. How often do you binge after a broken relationship? Do you take chocolates when you visit your mother to assuage your guilt for not having visited sooner? We use food for emotional support, to satisfy the longing to be comforted or held. Over-eating attempts to fill the emptiness inside. Under-eating attempts to minimise our presence in the world and reduce our demands. In this way, our relationship with food reflects our relationship with ourselves: how far we are able to express our needs, to what extent those needs are met, if we feel worthy of being nourished, or if we feel we should be punished for some indefinable badness.

The love and emotional nourishment we try to find through food is the love every human being deserves to receive. It is, therefore, essential that we learn to give this love to ourselves. Without self-love we will search endlessly for love from somewhere outside, and when we are disappointed or rejected food becomes the obvious substitute. When we have respect and love for ourselves, then we have the Buddha in our belly – we do not need to use food to soothe our inner pain or to gain emotional fulfilment.

Food directly contributes to the formation and maintenance of our entire physical structure and plays a vital role in the healing process – we are what we eat. The type of food we eat represents the level of care and respect we have for ourselves – by applying awareness and discrimination to our consumption we can greatly improve our physical health and energy levels.

As food plays such a vital and important role in our lives it is not surprising that the process of swallowing and digesting means more than just the assimilation of nutrients. It also symbolises the taking in of reality and all the feelings, impressions, experiences and sensations that make up our world. How we feel about that reality affects us physically and, as the digestive system is where the absorption begins, it is here that we invariably find the first signs of discontent or conflict.

♦ THE MOUTH ♦

The entry point for food and liquid, the mouth is the receiver of reality and how that reality tastes – whether it is sweet or sour. The mouth is also the centre of communication, where we express ourselves through sound and speech, or with the lips (through kissing, pouting or snarling). This is the place where the inner and outer worlds meet: a reception area where reality is vetted to see if it may pass through; and a departure lounge for emotions, thoughts, ideas and feelings. Difficulties here may be due to the reality we are taking in or the emotion being expressed.

Chewing begins the digestive process. Through the act of chewing we break down incoming food and information into usable parts. Hence we 'chew things over' when we think about them. How we do this is indicative of our attitude to life: taking small or large bites, chewing quickly or lingering over each mouthful. Do you relish biting into life? Do you sometimes bite off more than you can chew? Or do you prefer to go carefully, taking small bites, but perhaps never accepting a challenge or reaching for new heights?

Do you swallow food without really chewing or breaking it down – do you tend to leap into things without paying attention to the details? Are you trying to swallow your reality without tasting it? Or do you take a long time chewing things over and perhaps get so involved with the details that you lose sight of the overall picture? Is going very slowly a way of maintaining control – perhaps by making others wait for you? In the meantime, do you miss out on experiencing or tasting life?

Mouth Ulcers

The word *ulcer* means 'a corroding or corrupting influence'. Mouth ulcers imply that something is upsetting or corroding, making us feel irritated or attacked. Are you being affected by unexpressed negative or irritated feelings? Are they eating away at you, giving you a 'sore mouth'? What is really making you sore? Who or what is having a corrupting influence? What do you need to do to reduce the acid in your life?

♦ THE TONGUE ♦

Our taste buds recognise only four tastes – salt, sour, sweet and bitter. Yet, from these four, we compile a memory of each taste that stays with us for our lifetime. Flavour is due to air passing from the mouth to the nose – if the nose is blocked for any reason, flavour is usually lost. Does something taste bad? Is it making you recoil? Is it leaving a bitter taste in your mouth? Have you lost your taste for life? The tongue is also used for clear expression and speech. If you bite your tongue, are you holding back from saying something? Are you biting down on your feelings? Have you been saying too much? Have you been too sharp-tongued?

♦ THE GUMS ♦

The gums hold our teeth in place, providing the strength and security from which we can bite on things and chew them over. Do you feel secure in your boundaries and your ability to discriminate between what you want or don't want? **Receding gums** can indicate a lack of strength to get a grip on reality, as if our inner confidence is weakening. If they are swollen or bleeding it implies an emotional conflict or upset. Are you able to stick to your guns – to stay with your beliefs – or do you usually concede to others? The gums are a part of the jaw, and especially the expression of anger or aggression. Are you feeling helpless in the face of adversity? Is the act of defining your boundaries too demanding?

♦ THE TEETH ♦

The teeth develop at the same time as we begin to crawl. Their appearance marks the time when we start being weaned from mother's milk and onto solid food. Difficulties can, therefore, be associated with issues like dependence and asserting independence. The teeth enable us to eat and take in nourishment. **Rotten teeth** in children often reflect the sweet foods they have been given in place of the love they really need. Teeth indicate to what extent the reality we are having to chew and assimilate is either nourishing or damaging. Do you need to discriminate more between what is good for you and what is harmful?

Teeth also clarify communication – we can talk without them but the words will be unclear. Are you being clear in your communication? Are you saying what you really mean? A **tooth absess** indicates that something has *affected* you and is now creating an *infection* – perhaps there is grief or guilt connected to the mother-food-love issue. Are you feeling rejected or undernourished? The abscess is an eruption of negative energy at the very gateway of your being. Both rotten teeth and abscesses may show that unexpressed feelings, such as aggression, frustration or fear, are festering inside.

The teeth form a powerful gate which can shut tight. This is connected to honouring our boundaries, where we discriminate and determine what will be taken in or released. Has something invaded your defences? Are you feeling unable to protect yourself. Through the teeth we bite down and get serious, so problems may also indicate the need to get more involved, or the need to let go and relax.

♦ THE JAW ♦

When we clench the jaw we close off from the outside world; we hold tight so as not to lose our cool. What would happen if you relaxed your jaw? Would there be an outpouring of inappropriate emotions? Or would you be letting something in that you are trying to keep out? **A locked jaw** implies withheld tears, or tears stopped in mid-flow, perhaps through repressed anger. Are you trying to stop something from happening? Do you feel you ought to keep your mouth shut because you always say the wrong thing, or say too much?

Any difficulty with the jaws is usually to do with holding on too tight. We grind our teeth with frustration or anxiety, indicating a build up of emotion or repressed aggression getting locked into the jaw. **Grinding teeth** can be caused by stress and fear – deep relaxation is essential. With children this may indicate repressed feelings against one or both parents, insecurity or fear at home or at school.

♦ THE THROAT ♦

The throat is a two-way bridge, connecting the heart and the head, the mind and the body. It has two major roles: to take in air, food, liquid and reality; and to express outwardly our thoughts and feelings. In this chapter we are primarily concerned with the role of the throat in nourishment. (See Chapter 13 for more on the respiratory and expressive aspects of the throat.)

As part of the digestive system, the throat is vulnerable and tender, yet it sustains our entire life system (it is where we consume the food and liquid that keep us alive). While food is in the mouth it is under our conscious control (we can choose to spit it out if we want) but once we have swallowed, it enters the automatic process of digestion. This is where we surrender control, so here are issues to do with willpower and assertiveness. Gagging on food, or feeling as if we are being force-fed, are both conflicts with personal will.

In exactly the same way as we swallow food, we swallow our reality – thoughts, ideas, feelings, events and experiences. Swallowing is about allowing change to happen. We can resist change by closing the throat or we can trustingly open ourselves to change. To swallow something is to believe it. When we swallow our reality we are accepting it into our being. If that reality is unacceptable we may have to swallow hard, or we will, perhaps, get **a swollen or sore throat**. Are you swallowing your pride? Or swallowing hurt feelings, failure, shame, guilt or disappointment? What are you not wanting to swallow? What is making you so sore? We may not want to swallow our reality, or we may hold back too many of our feelings, particularly if they are unacceptable or inappropriate. Such repression creates great tension and stress and can affect the rest of the digestive system. We need to get in touch with our feelings and give them a voice so they can be heard.

♦ THE STOMACH ♦

Food moves from the mouth through the oesophagus to the stomach to continue the process of digestion. Digestion symbolises the ability to absorb what we need and to let go of what we do not need. Do you know what is good for you? Do you have a tendency to be influenced by things that aren't good for you? Having a healthy digestion means being able to receive from others, and to give to ourselves. Without this there can be a constant craving, a longing to fill hidden needs, or a strong denial and rejection of those needs. The stomach is where we harbour worry – the digestive enzymes churning with anxiety – until we can no longer stomach what is happening. Invariably we use food to pacify that anxiety.

Appetite

Our relationship with food is intimately connected to how emotionally nourished or loved we feel. The act of eating and swallowing is symbolic of taking in and absorbing reality. **An increase in appetite** usually occurs in response to emotional pain, eating in an attempt to fill a bottomless pit inside. A child may eat more in order to get a word of praise from parents because the love that is really needed is not forthcoming. A demanding or devouring appetite indicates a personality who devours information, experiences or relationships, yet may be missing the insights or wisdom they offer by devouring them so quickly.

A lack of appetite can indicate a desire to retreat from the world, not to take in any more. This is often seen in those experiencing a relationship breakdown – they may go for days without food, nurturing the hurt inside – indicating an unexpressed need for love and attention. A low appetite may also occur when energy is being diverted to attend to issues of physical healing – lack of appetite during illness is quite common.

Anorexia Nervosa

This is a condition of near-starvation, where so little food is consumed that the body begins to fade away. It is intimately bound up with the complexities of receiving nourishment and love. In a longing to be nurtured and loved, we reduce our presence so as to reduce our demand for that love. There can be a chronic lack of self-worth, so our own feelings are considered unimportant. This sense of unworthiness is often triggered by guilt or shame. Perhaps love has always been conditional, based on performance and success, or dependent on our giving to others. Yet there is a great longing to be loved unconditionally for who we are. Do you feel you are not good enough, that you do not deserve to be nourished or loved? Do you believe you have to help others and deny yourself? Is it wrong to acknowledge your own needs? There is usually a strong desire to stay small, to be less, not to be noticed, to fade into the background. But less than what? What happens when you are noticed? Are you denying your need for affection?

Anorexia often arises as a result of feeling out of control of what is happening – perhaps due to dominating parents or teachers, or changing life circumstances – and one way to have control is to clamp down on food, which is also a way of clamping down on feelings. Where there is no expression of emotion there is complete control.

This condition is most common in girls, especially as they reach sexual maturity and experience the emotional turmoil that can accompany this period of transition. For many it is overwhelming, especially the physical changes taking place that appear so uncontrollable. Becoming thin takes away any feeling of sexuality, sensuality, desirability or impending womanhood – it keeps the body like a child's: immature and undeveloped. Menstruation can even stop. There is a desire to escape completely from the reality of the body and all the feelings that go with it – especially from becoming a woman. Perhaps growing up is happening too quickly, or social pressures to look and be a certain way are too strong. Loving ourselves, as we are, is essential.

Bulimia Nervosa

This is a combination of eating disorders – secret eating binges, followed by guilt, followed by self-induced vomiting. There is a conflict here between desperately wanting to appear perfect, with the ideal thin body (hence the starvation), combined with a great longing and love for life (hence the desire for food). There is a craving to consume and simultaneously a longing to be free. Caught between the two, we become filled with self-dislike, if not self-loathing, and guilt.

To eat with such desperation (often in the middle of the night when no one can see), or to enjoy a meal only to throw up later, indicates how much emotion is being repressed by the eating. The act of vomiting is a rejection of nourishment, a refusal to allow anything to touch us on the inside. It is a desperate attempt to maintain control over our feelings. As food represents emotion, what feelings are being thrown out (vomited) before they can influence you? What part of yourself are you rejecting so violently? What are you so fearful of?

Obesity

Food and love are intimately bound up, so at times of emotional loss or confusion the stomach appears as a big hole that needs filling.

The food squashes down our real feelings – the more we eat, the less we feel. At the same time we build a wall around ourselves that few can penetrate. Many cases of over-eating develop following deep emotional pain or loss and the excess weight is like a protection against further hurt. It also blocks out our own feelings; we become numb to what is really being felt inside. Grief or shame is often hidden beneath an obsessive appetite. Many women put on excess weight around their hips and thighs following sexual assault – by covering the sexual area the feelings are shut away. Obesity is about a longing for love combined with a fear of loving or being loved, perhaps due to past hurt, loss or pain.

Excess flesh indicates a holding on, an attachment or clinging, particularly to attitudes and thinking patterns that justify our behaviour. It provides a false sense of security – a belief that we are safe from feeling or being hurt. It also implies a loss of control, and an inner hopelessness or lack of self-respect. To shift the weight we need to explore our attitudes – what being heavy means to us, and what feelings the weight is hiding.

Rather than focusing on what is wrong with being heavy, start exploring the benefits. Try writing down all the ways that being heavy is OK for you. What does being heavy enable you to do, or not do? Does it make you feel safe? Look at what issues are being hidden by the excess weight. Can you see what attitudes or feelings you are clinging to? What was happening for you emotionally when you first got heavy? Were you being fed instead of being loved? Did you feel you had no personal power, or had lost control and didn't know how to regain that power? Do you enjoy feeling powerless? Were you in need of love?

Then explore how it would feel to be thin. How would it change you? What would you do that you are not doing now? What parts of your being would be exposed if you lost weight? Would it expose your sexuality? Does this feel scary or unsafe? Would it feel as if you had nowhere to hide? Does being thin imply having to be responsible for yourself? Does it mean emotional involvement?

The bigger we get, the more likely we are to reject ourselves and feel ugly or unlovable. Losing weight occurs through a deep shift in attitude, starting with an acceptance of ourselves just as we are – we need to give ourselves the love we long for. Then we can start working on the layers of fear that lie beneath the excess weight.

Indigestion ✗

This occurs when the reality we are digesting is too bitter or sour, or is proving too much to bear, and we literally cannot stomach it any more. The stomach acid is activated. What reality are you swallowing that is so sour? What is so difficult for you to absorb or is making you feel so acidic? Are you swallowing aggressive feelings – such as anger or irritation? Is your inner aggression towards someone or something rising up? **Heartburn** which can accompany indigestion, suggests we need to find out what the heart is really burning (or getting upset) about.

Nausea

Nausea indicates that something is churning our feelings up in the wrong way. When we vomit, something is making us want to throw up. This is a physical expression of rejection or even repulsion – there is something we don't want to absorb, integrate or deal with. What is making you feel so emotionally repulsed? Is it a part of yourself you are rejecting? What does that part need to do to be accepted?

Stomach Ulcers

These occur when the reality we are dealing with starts to become corrosive, to wear away at our stability or coping mechanism. It may be due to a virus, indicating that something outside is deeply affecting us. We may be taking in too much acidity from others, or our own feelings are eating away at us. Aggravated by the digestive juices, ulcers often arise when we are under too much pressure, worried by financial or work situations, relationships, or our role in the world. Worry is the key word here – it is almost as if the worry itself is eating us. The ulcer creates a feeling of being raw and exposed, as if there is nowhere to hide. There may also be repressed aggression, a desire to get revenge or to lash out at someone. There is a deep need to be soothed and nurtured, to return to the safety of being cared for (as in having to eat baby foods).

♦ INTESTINES ♦

As the food passes from the stomach to the small intestine and then the colon, it goes through a process of breaking down, integration and evacuation. In the same way, the intestines correspond to the absorption and elimination of both our physical and non-physical reality. It is here that we process our 'stuff', where we digest our intake and our responses. The belly is the feeling centre – where we have 'gut feelings', or can get emotionally 'hit in the guts'. Feelings can get locked in here, unable to find expression or release. In the meantime the belly grows big with repressed feelings, or sinks with unexpressed longing.

Most of the digestion and absorption takes place in the small intestine, aided by the liver, the pancreas and the gall bladder. Here incoming information is broken down into small parts and decisions are made about what to do with each piece. This is a process of analysis, detail and discrimination; it is about having the appropriate reactions. Difficulties in this area suggest an overly analytical or obsessive attitude; or being unable to distinguish between what is really needed and what is not.

In the large intestine the matter is finished with, ready to be excreted. This area is about releasing, so difficulties here are connected to clinging to that which has already served its purpose. There may be grief or sadness, a holding on that prolongs the pain; or a fear of letting go, perhaps due to a lack of trust.

Candida

Candida is a yeast infection that can occur in warm damp areas, such as the mouth, intestines, bladder or vagina, sometimes caused by antibiotics and/or a weakened immune system. (For candida in the vagina, see Thrush, Chapter 18.)

Candida in the digestive system suggests fear of being invaded by someone or something, and feeling out of control. It also implies that our normal living environment has become imbalanced or upset, allowing other energies to enter and make themselves at home. Are you feeling particularly insecure? Is something eating away inside you? Are you out of contact with your inner strength and resilience? What is needed to regain your stability?

Colitis

This is an inflammation and irritation of the large intestine – causing bleeding, ulceration and diarrhoea – due to infection, food allergy or stress. Colitis indicates intense irritation and frustration about what is happening and an inability to digest or fully absorb events. In this case, anger may be associated with issues of power and control, or perhaps there is no space in which to express free will. Inflammation is associated with anger – is rage being internalised rather than expressed? If the inflammation is due to infection or allergy, then what is getting inside you and affecting you so deeply? If it is stress, then why are you pushing yourself so hard? What are you trying to prove?

Constipation ⚹

Constipation is caused by a clamping down of the muscles, indicating a mental or psychological clamping down, a way of avoiding our feelings. Fear is the underlying emotion here – a fear of the unknown, of what the future may bring. It is quite common to get bouts of constipation when travelling, moving house or having financial or relationship difficulties – such events create uncertainty about what lies ahead. Constipation is about attachment, and a clinging to the familiar, a holding on to safety and security. It is more common in controlling and fixed personality types, due to a fear of what feelings would emerge without that control. One way of avoiding our feelings is to keep busy which also eliminates the time needed for the body to operate properly: racing out of the house first thing in the morning makes it difficult to have a normal bowel movement.

There are issues to do with authority and power locked into the anal muscles, whether connected to parents and their attitudes to bowel movements when we were young (see also Rectum, below), or towards authority figures such as a boss, religious leader or spouse. Refusing to have normal bowel movements is one of the few ways in which a child can exert his or her will. Having a bowel movement is an act of surrender – constipation is an act of holding on to power.

As bowel movements represent the final letting go, constipation also indicates that there is something not yet finished with; perhaps we have not completed our learning from a situation. The muscle retention is a way of telling us to keep releasing any inner blocks. Learning how to be more playful and spontaneous, can go a long way towards relieving the situation. Most important, though, is learning how to express our feelings and, once expressed, to let them go. The deeper issue is trust – trust that everything will be OK, trust in the people around us, trust that events will flow as they are meant to even without our control, trust in the universe to support us.

Diarrhoea

This can be due to a bacterial or viral infection, or due to stress or fear. In the case of an infection, we can ask what it is that is infecting or affecting us so deeply. Do you feel as if you have been emotionally hit in the guts by something? Are you feeling afraid about something, perhaps your own feelings? If it is due to food poisoning, is something or someone making you feel poisoned?

When we feel we have too much to deal with and our stress levels are rising, we may want everything to be over with as soon as possible. Do you want to run away from someone? Is there something you want to get rid of? Diarrhoea can occur when we feel emotionally disturbed by what we are experiencing but do not know how to assimilate our feelings, such as panic or grief. In this case we are like animals emptying our bowels uncontrollably. Do you appear strong and solid, yet feel helpless inside? Are you actually feeling 'scared shitless'?

Constant diarrhoea means a lack of absorption. Are you rejecting the love and nurturing being offered to you, due to a fear of intimacy? It is important to reconnect with your own inner solidity and strength, to take time to fully experience whatever is happening so you can gain the full benefits.

Irritable Bowel Syndrome

This creates severe abdominal pain, constipation or diarrhoea, and wind. This is not so much a problem with the intestines as with the nerves which cause contraction and spasm in the muscles. It is fairly common, especially as it is often caused by stress. It is connected with maintaining power and boundaries, or with letting go and releasing control. There may be intense fear, a lack of confidence, or the nervousness that arises when confronting unknown situations. Relationships also affect the colon, especially issues to do with intimacy and security. What part of you is getting so twisted? What are you holding on to with such determination that it is distorting? What do you need to do to straighten this part, to unravel the twists? What needs to be released? (See also Chapter 16 for more on the nerves.)

◆ THE RECTUM ◆

Many issues to do with elimination are connected to childhood. A young child has two major ways of controlling his or her parents and that is through refusing or accepting the food they offer, or by refusing or agreeing to defecate. Some children are made to sit on their potties for hours as parents try to impose their power over them. Letting go of the anal muscles is an act of surrendering to the natural rhythms of the body; refusing to relax these muscles indicates a resistance to higher authority and/or a fear of being out of control. Our relationship with defecation is indicative of our relationship with 'our own shit' – our inner pain and darkness – how easily we can accept and let go, or if we cling and hold on.

The anus is the final exit point from the body. It is intimately connected to the mouth as the first entry point, but, whereas the mouth is a conscious area, the anus is more indicative of the unconscious. It is a private, hidden part of our being, tucked away out of sight, so here we often find anger, violation, abuse, perhaps from unwanted penetration. Anger in the mouth is felt in the jaw, while anger in the anus is seen in tight muscles, intense irritation or soreness. Is someone being 'a pain in the arse'?

The area of the rectum is also used to store feelings when we are confronted with a tense or life-threatening situation. This may be as simple as sitting on our feelings during a job interview or first date (we may have a smile on our lips while the buttock and anal muscles are rigid with tension) to a more serious continual tensing of the muscles over many years. What would happen if you let go? Consciously breathe into and release any tension in the rectum and buttocks. How does this feel?

Piles/Haemorrhoids

These occur when we exert a straining pressure during defecation, trying to hurry the process, or because the movement is difficult (see also Constipation, above). Piles can flare up at emotionally tense times, when we are holding on to issues or feelings that should be released, or when we are wanting to get something out of us before we have fully accepted or absorbed it. There is a conflict between pushing out and holding back. This may reflect a conflict between love and loss, surrender and control, or fear and trust.

♦ THE LIVER ♦

As the food passes through the small intestine, digestion is aided by secretions produced by the liver and the pancreas. The liver is one of the most essential organs in the body. It is where poisons get detoxified, fats are converted into energy or prepared for storage, proteins and other nutrients are transformed into usable form, and bile is produced to be stored in the gall bladder ready to break down fat globules. Those suffering from liver problems will suffer from bad digestion, low energy (such as **low appetite** and/or sexual potency), tiredness, perhaps **headaches** or **eye problems**.

If we overdo the level of toxins – such as alcohol or drugs – there comes a point when the liver starts telling us we are taking in more than we can deal with, whether physically or psychologically. Are you going beyond your limits? Have you lost the ability to discriminate between that which is poisonous and that which is helpful? Are you addicted to something or someone that is actually poisoning your system? The nature of addiction is to continue indulging despite our limitations, the toxins we take in covering up deeper toxic states within.

The liver is not just a place where toxins are deposited. In Chinese medicine it is known as a storehouse for anger, particularly repressed anger, which gathers here and may eventually explode outwards. Repressed anger is often the background to addiction (see also Addiction, Chapter 21). Unacknowledged or unexpressed anger leads to depression (anger turned inwards on ourselves) and shame, jealousy or irritability, which further depletes our energy levels and can even damage the immune system. Connected to anger are bitterness and resentment which are seen in the production of bile (see Gall Bladder, below), or guilt, hopelessness, frustration and hatred.

The liver is also connected to deeper issues of meaning and purpose. A sluggish liver leads to depression which makes life appear meaningless. The liver gives life; its health therefore reflects how much we embrace life, or how self-destructive we are – filling ourselves with toxins in order to avoid confronting deeper issues. A healthy liver encourages enthusiasm, creativity, inner strength and resilience.

Hepatitis

This infection of the liver is usually caused by a virus which flourishes in conditions of bad sanitation, especially in poorer areas. It is also transmitted by shared needles amongst drug-users, or through infected blood transfusions. Hepatitis indicates the loss of the ability to distinguish between what is right or wrong, good or bad distinctions become blurred so toxins or poisons are not recognised as harmful. There is a feeling of being overwhelmed, or of having the life drained out of us. Have you lost your self-respect? What is affecting you so deeply that it is influencing your deeper feelings about the meaning of life? If drugs are the cause, what emotions are being repressed or denied and then replaced by the artificial high of the drugs?

♦ THE GALL BLADDER ♦

The bile produced in the liver is stored in the gall bladder. Bile is a bitter green liquid which breaks down fats for easier digestion. A lack of bile means that digestion takes longer and we may feel queasy, indicating an inability to break down or assimilate incoming information, a feeling of being unable to cope. Gall, as a characteristic, means assertiveness, bitterness, spite or malice. Bilious attacks imply an attack of bitterness or anger, rising up from inside. What is making you feel so bitter and bad-tempered? What is so hard to digest or assimilate?

Gall Stones

These form in the gall bladder and if they cannot pass through and out then there is intense pain. The stones are made from congealed liquid, corresponding to congealed or unexpressed emotion. They may have developed through always trying to please or give to others, while feeling bitter that no one is giving to us. The stones take some time to form, so they usually represent resentment that has been building up for a long while. Gall stones indicate the need to soften and ease the bitterness, to realise that it is OK to say no to others and to say yes to our own needs. We do not need to be so resentful to get what we need.

♦ THE PANCREAS ♦

The pancreas produces essential enzymes that break down carbohydrates, fats and proteins. Enzymes enable change to take place. Without the enzymes produced by the pancreas, we are unable to properly digest incoming nutrients and so they pass through in an undigested form, causing **indigestion**, nausea, bloating, even **diarrhoea**. Are you feeling unable to deal with the situation confronting you? Does it appear indigestible or overwhelming? What needs to change for you to be able to digest your feelings? Are you resisting being nourished?

The pancreas also produces insulin and glucogon which maintain the right level of sugar or glucose in the blood. The body needs glucose at all times as a source of energy for the cells. Glucose is obtained from food and is broken down by the digestive system. Whenever glucose enters the bloodstream, the pancreas releases insulin to enable absorption to take place; if there is too little glucose then glucagon is produced to maintain the balance. Blood sugar levels are affected by excess adrenaline, particularly when we are confronted with stressful situations. Pancreatic issues are, therefore, connected with maintaining the right balance in our lives – a balance of giving and receiving, of working and playing, of fear and love.

Diabetes

This occurs when there is not enough insulin to cope with the incoming glucose, or when the pancreas fails to produce any insulin. In either case, sugar accumulates in the blood and is released in the urine, rather than being transformed into energy. Diabetes may have a genetic cause; it may occur as a side effect of drugs; or it can be triggered by emotional stress. It is the sixth most common cause of death and the second leading cause of **blindness** in the United States. Insulin has to be provided either through a change in diet or through insulin injections, depending on the type of diabetes.

Just as diabetics cannot integrate the sugar in food, so it is hard for them to integrate or accept love. Diabetes is particularly related to feeling either a lack of or an over-abundance of sweetness in our lives. This may be through loss or loneliness – children can develop diabetes at a time of parental conflict, such as divorce or death, feeling that they are the cause of the loss, or that the parent no longer loves them; or due to a smothering, excessively loving parent or partner. If diabetes develops later in life it is often associated with obesity, and this shows the link between over-eating to make up for a lack of love or nourishment, and an inability to receive love.

It is hard to be independent if there is a constant dependence on insulin. This creates a dependence on the home – diabetic children may live at home longer than others – and a difficulty in making personal relationships last. There is also resentment at having to take responsibility for ourselves, a desire to be loved but not to have to love, to be cared for without having to give. When the inner sweetness passes straight through and leaves in the urine it causes a sadness or sense of loneliness – diabetics often feel emotionally isolated, unable to give of themselves. Diabetes is also about being able to give love, to both ourselves and others. Healing diabetes is therefore about loving ourselves, and finding balance by developing the ability to both give and receive love.

Hypoglycemia

This can occur when the blood sugar level drops, whether due to excess exercise, a lack of food, or from too much insulin. It may be that we have given out so much to others that there is nothing left for ourselves; we need time to replenish, to come back to our own being, to receive some nourishment. This condition also tends to indicate a desire for affection and a constant need for reassurance that we are loved.

13

THE BREATH OF LIFE
The Respiratory System

TO BREATHE is to be alive – the first breath we take says, 'I am'. The breath is the rhythm of inspiration and expiration that maintains all life, a meeting of two that together create a whole. We breathe the same breath as all forms of life – the same as our loved ones, and our enemies. It is the one place where we all meet equally, where there is no discrimination.

To inspire is to take in breath and give life to form. As we breathe in we are inspired by the outer world and take it inwards; as we breathe out we send our inner world outwards to be shared with others. This is an act of exchange, of give and take. To be inspired is to be uplifted or filled with creativity. Both breath and spirit come from the same Latin root – *spiro*: to inspire is to fill the body with breath and to fill the spirit with divine awareness. Without breath we are merely an inert physical form; without spirit we live a shallow and meaningless existence. To be without breath is to die physically; to be without spirit is to die in our soul.

With the breath there are no edges or limitations; each breath merges into the next. Difficulties with breathing are, therefore, connected to boundaries, to feeling unclear about where we begin or end, and particularly to letting others take over – to breathe for us – by running our lives. Issues of personal control can arise if we feel smothered or unable to breathe for ourselves. With no boundaries we are easily influenced and dominated. The process of giving and taking is out of balance – perhaps we can give but we cannot receive, or we can take but do not know how to give.

If we experience panic or nervousness then the breath becomes shallow and rapid; when we relax we take longer breaths. Short breaths indicate fear or a lack of participation in life. The more

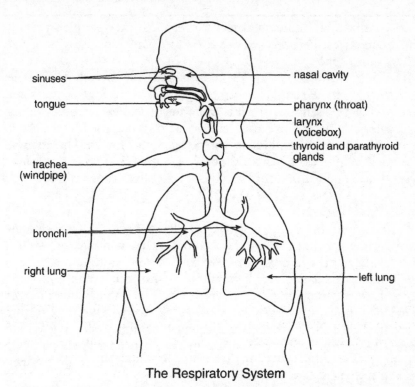

sinuses
tongue
trachea
(windpipe)
bronchi
right lung

nasal cavity
pharynx (throat)
larynx
(voicebox)
thyroid and parathyroid
glands
left lung

The Respiratory System

desire there is to participate, the deeper the breath. When we breathe fully we are owning our own life and personal power. There is an uprightness and openness, a natural dignity. Our boundaries are clear – we know ourselves and our limitations, what we can give and what we need. We breathe freely. (For more on breathing, see Chapter 5.)

The respiratory system centres on the lungs but also includes the nose, throat, larynx, trachea and bronchi. It has an intimate relationship with the blood, as oxygen passes from the lungs into the bloodstream, while carbon dioxide comes from the blood into the lungs for expiration. This relationship will become clearer when we explore the circulatory system in the next chapter.

♦ THE NOSE ♦

Through the nose we breathe in life-sustaining oxygen, so our relationship to life is reflected here: whether we feel at ease with what we are breathing in, or if we want to opt out for a while; whether we feel clear or blocked. The nose also symbolises those times when we push ourselves into areas where we are not welcome

– nose issues may indicate a need to respect other people's privacy and boundaries. Perhaps we need to stop being so nosey and give others more space.

The nose also enables us to take in both the sweetness and the pungency of life. We tend to communicate mostly through the eyes and voice, while our sense of smell is more unconscious. Yet every odour molecule has a unique size and shape, which is recognised by the brain, so we can remember and identify a vast array of smells. There is also the smell of intuition, where the nose is connected to our intuitive perception of something that may not be so obvious or visible.

Blocked Nose

The function of breathing in oxygen is vital yet not always welcome. There are many times when life becomes overwhelming and we just don't want to take in any more. We can't stop breathing but we can put up a resistance so that everything is shut out, as in a blocked nose. Is something getting up your nose? Is there something or someone you want to push away or resist? Are you wanting to pull back from life for a while? Or are you blocking something within yourself – getting stuffy and airless in your attitude? Are you being particularly prejudiced or closed? What do you need to do to open up and breathe freely again?

A blocked nose is also a way of shutting out a smell, closing ourselves off from any memories or feelings attached to that smell. Is there something you don't want to remember? Or is the smell actually an unwelcome insight or intuition about a situation? Are you smelling a rat? Sensing something you would rather not see? Are you blocking off your own intuitive understanding?

Hay Fever

This is an allergic reaction, particularly to pollen. Symptoms are similar to having a bad cold but with very watery eyes and intense itching of the nose and eyes. This is a powerful, emotional response – all the waterworks are on – with strong feelings of wanting to hide or run away. But what are you actually feeling allergic to? What is causing such an emotional outpouring? Is it the sexual potency and fertility represented by pollen? Is it the fear of seasons changing and therefore of time passing beyond your control? Or is there a need for attention, to be special? Allergies indicate an intense emotional reaction to external situations, a reaction of withdrawal, resistance and fear leading to isolation, often induced by stress. If this is the case, what is it you want to run away from? (See also Allergies, Chapter 15.)

Sinusitis

The sinuses are hollow chambers in the head that are a part of the breathing process. To breathe is to inspire, to take in new ideas. As such, sinusitis implies either a pushing away of that which inspires or nourishes us, or an overload of mental work without enough creative energy. Sinusitis means you are feeling irritated or inflamed by something or someone, or even yourself, and this irritation is highlighting a sense of being emotionally or creatively stuck. Are you feeling blocked or limited, unable to break free of old patterns? Are you resisting inspiration or nourishment?

Sinusitis is also connected to repressed grief and unshed tears, especially as there can be intense pain and a high temperature. The pain is expressing the inner anguish, the temperature shows the intensity of feeling – the heat of emotion. What do you need to do to release the blockage, to become unclogged, unstuck? Is there a deep need to be loved? What other senses are being affected?

Sneezing

An irritant can be an irritating person or a frustrating situation as much as it can be a piece of dust. If you sneeze a great deal, is there someone or something that is getting up your nose or irritating you? Or is there something that you need to let go of, to release? Look at the circumstances before you started sneezing – what feelings are you experiencing or holding back? Sneezing is a socially acceptable way of releasing energy and stress. If it becomes a problem, then deep relaxation (see Chapter 5) will help release the stress and calm nervousness.

♦ THE THROAT ♦

As mentioned in Chapter 12, the throat is where we swallow food, water and air – the three ingredients necessary to sustain life. In this chapter we are more concerned with the role of the throat in expression for the throat has a two-way function. Not only do we swallow or take in reality and all the conflicting feelings that go with that, but we also express our feelings in response to that reality.

Sore Throat

The throat is where we swallow the impact of what is happening in our lives, so throat problems can arise when there is a fearful or irritating reaction. It is also where we speak and share our feelings, thoughts and concerns. If there are conflicts with that expression then we may get a sore throat. What are you really sore about? Are you swallowing something that is making you feel sore or inflamed? What is so hard for you to accept? Is something getting stuck in your throat? Is someone choking you, or do you feel choked by your own feelings? Are you holding back feelings such as anger, irritation, frustration or guilt, for fear of expressing them, and in the process causing a build up of energy in the throat? What would you really like to say? And to who? What is needed to soothe and ease your throat?

Coughing

This is a reaction to a stimulus, usually a tickle in the throat or larynx. This tickle can worsen into an inflammation if the irritant continues. Coughing is an attempt to clear the way, to get the irritant out of our system. What is causing you to feel so irritated? Is something making you feel hot or angry? Are you being asked to accept or swallow something you don't want? Is something or someone making you gag?

Coughing may also be due to something we have said or wanted to say, as the cough mechanism is a part of the larynx. Have you said something that was hurtful? Do you now feel guilty or ashamed about it? Or are you longing to express yourself, to let out your feelings? A nervous cough is a way of keeping the lid on inner fears or concerns. The feelings are right there, just behind the cough, but there is too much tension to release them.

(If there is phlegm with the cough, or the chest is also sore, see Bronchitis, below.)

◆ TONSILS AND ADENOIDS ◆

The tonsils and adenoids are a part of the immune system, helping to protect us by filtering out harmful foreign substances. As they are positioned at the point of entry into the body they particularly represent the ability to discriminate between what is helpful and what is harmful.

Tonsillitis occurs when the tonsils are inflamed. This happens when the reality being swallowed contains irritating or upsetting factors; or when we feel unable to protect ourselves and feel vulnerable to whatever is happening. Tonsillitis is most common in children and is associated with difficulty in accepting change, especially as children are usually powerless in choosing what happens. It indicates that the incoming reality is creating anger, fear or an unwillingness to absorb the implications of change. The tonsils swell up so much that it becomes hard to swallow. What is it that you are finding so hard to swallow? Is there something you are resisting? What is inciting such strong feelings?

Swollen adenoids normally occur in young children, blocking the nasal and ear passages. They are also blocking the intake of information, whether through the throat or the ears, so attention needs to be paid to what is happening in the child's life that is so difficult to swallow or to hear.

♦ THE LARYNX ♦

The throat contains the voice box or larynx. The voice is our trademark – no two voices are the same – and the way we use our voice conveys a great deal about our personality – if it is gruff or loud, persuasive or overbearing, timid, soft or caressing. Try speaking into a tape recorder and then listen to your voice. What is the sound saying about you? The voice is our means of expression, of sharing who we are with the world. But expression depends more on tone and intent than the actual words used. Saying 'I love you' with a voice full of venom invalidates the sentiment, in the same way as saying 'I hate you' with a voice full of love.

Difficulties with the larynx are associated with a fear of speaking, or with a repression of feelings. Conflict arises when it is hard to vocalise thoughts or feelings, or if we feel we are always saying the wrong thing. Do you keep putting 'your foot in your mouth'? Through the voice we express our needs and ask for what we want. Does your request get stuck in your throat? Are you speaking for someone else and not finding your own voice? Are you speaking your truth or swallowing it back?

Laryngitis is when the larynx becomes inflamed and we become hoarse or lose our speaking voice completely. It may accompany a bad head cold, be due to excess anger or it can arise when we are feeling particularly nervous about saying something – losing our voice means nothing can be said, so we are emotionally safe. Laryngitis may also be due to feeling that we have nothing worth saying, as when a child is made to believe that whatever he or she says is unacceptable or worthless; or we may lose our voice after witnessing a traumatic scene – there is an overwhelming terror of saying anything.

Finding your voice implies finding courage and independence: you can speak for yourself, stand on your own, you know your own mind; whereas losing your voice implies that you have lost touch with your inner strength, your ability to speak up. What is it you really want to say? What part of you have you lost touch with? What inner voice needs expression?

This is also an area of transformation, where we can accept negativity and transform it through a positive response.

♦ THE THYROID AND ♦ PARATHYROID

The thyroid is in front of the windpipe, while the parathyroid glands lie at the four corners of the thyroid. These glands produce hormones for growth and for cell regeneration and repair; they regulate calcium; they also maintain metabolism and oxygen consumption, playing an important part in the ability to hibernate.

A goitre is where the thyroid gland swells up and can block the windpipe if not treated. Here there may be a feeling of being choked, perhaps by too many responsibilities, or of being overwhelmed by life; there may also be a desire to separate mind and body, so as not to have to deal with deep inner feelings held in the body.

Hyperthyroidism is due to an increase in thyroid activity. There is a speeding up of bodily activities, causing irritability, weight loss, excessive perspiration and weakness. This condition is connected to a fear of responsibility – there may be a desire to stay as a child in that irresponsible, carefree and disconnected state. However it usually indicates a more selfish and self-centred attitude, where we try to avoid dealing with responsibilities by staying very busy.

Hypothyroidism is a slowing down of thyroid activity, leading to depression, tiredness, a decrease in mental and physical activity, slurring speech and low body temperature. The whole system is slowing down, as if the will to live is depressed or we are entering a state of emotional hibernation.

♦ THE LUNGS ♦

When the trachea (the windpipe) enters the lungs it divides into the right and left bronchi which look like an upside-down tree inside each lung. Here oxygen is transferred into the blood supply and exchanged for carbon dioxide. The normal process of breathing –

the inspiration and expiration of air – is carried out automatically by the nervous system, whether we are awake, asleep or even unconscious.

To breathe is to take in and give out – we breathe in, knowing we can breathe out, and in breathing out we know we can take another breath in. However, if there is any fear that blocks this automatic process, any sense that the breath is not a friend but a foe, then breathing difficulties may develop. Children who have been rejected or let down by their parents, especially by their mothers, can lose this trust; as can adults who have experienced abuse, life-threatening situations, or the loss of loved ones.

The lungs are symbolic of independence – the first breath we experience is at birth when we inflate the lungs with air and assert our separation from our mothers. If this is a traumatic experience it can influence the way we meet moments of transition later in life, and the extent to which we are able to breathe deeply and relax into change. This is where we manifest difficulties connected to taking life in or wanting to push it away; or living life for ourselves rather than letting someone else have power over us. The breath responds to our feelings, becoming short and shallow at times of panic, or long and deep when we are relaxed; sadness and grief are experienced in the lungs with great gulping breaths.

Asthma   ⋏

With asthma the difficulty lies in breathing out, a constriction that makes us feel that we are fighting for air. An attack can be provoked by an allergic reaction to an external stimulus such as pollen, to an emotional stimulus, or even to crying or laughing. There has been an alarming increase in asthma over the past few years, especially in children, with a current total of over two million asthmatics in Britain. There is little doubt that much of the physical cause of this increase lies in the corresponding increase in environmental pollution, especially car exhaust fumes. (See Chapter 15 for more on allergies.)

However, pollution does not account for all cases of asthma. As far as the psycho/emotional connection to asthma is concerned, we find two main correspondences. One is our relationship to our mother, as the breath is symbolic of our separation from her. Over the last 15 years, as pollution levels have risen, so also more and more children have been growing up in single parent families – these 'latch-key' children have to become emotionally as well as physically independent at a very early age. Perhaps they are having to breathe for themselves too soon. They may also feel emotionally insecure. Many children and young people feel an increasing fear about the future – about what they are growing up into – as housing and financial problems increase while educational and work opportunities decrease. These social issues deeply affect our feelings about being independent and may therefore affect our breathing.

The emotionally complex mother-child relationship can also include a tendency for the mother to smother or dominate (as if breathing for her child), rather than letting the child discover life for itself. In these cases, the boundaries between mother and child become blurred, leading to a repressed dependence on the mother. Asthma attacks may be triggered by events that highlight the loneliness of breathing independently – that create a separation from mother – such as the birth of a younger sibling, graduation from school, leaving home, or getting married. The asthma attack is like a suppressed cry of longing to return to the womb.

For adults, asthma may develop if we feel smothered by our boss, by too much work, responsibility, or over-demanding relatives, so that we feel unable to breathe for ourselves, unable to express our feeling of suffocation or helplessness. Stress is further increasing asthma, especially amongst white-collar workers and middle management, who are most likely to feel overcome by pressure to succeed, as well as pressure to pay bills and provide for others. There is a feeling of having to do it all alone, a struggling for breath on our own.

This suppressed cry or longing to breathe freely is connected to the second aspect of asthma: the desire to express ourselves but an inability to do so, leading to repressed feelings and even sadness. The out-breath enables us to speak; the inability to breathe out implies that this expression is being held back or impeded. There is a need to get something off our chest, to release all the emotion stored there, but a fear of letting this emotion be expressed – perhaps due to the consequences or a lack of confidence – is holding us back. There is an inner crying, a silent scream of longing. Try holding your breath – breathe in but do not breathe out – and watch the emotions that arise. Usually we feel a great longing to burst, to shout, and it is this repressed longing that can be seen in asthma.

Attacks can be triggered by emotional situations such as anger or heated feelings in a parent or lover, by being misunderstood, or through experiencing grief or loss. When a child is unable to speak for itself, that longing gets held inside, especially if expression is based on confusion or fear of the parents' behaviour. Asthma is an allergy – an over-reaction of the immune system to an antigen. Over-reaction may be the key word here. Is there something or someone who is causing you to over-react? Do you feel your boundaries have been lost? How can you reassert them?

The inability to breathe out indicates a lack of trust that the breath will come back in. Breathing in we are in control, while breathing out demands total surrender. It means that we feel secure the world will support us, and that we will receive the love we need. Asthma is, therefore, about trusting and letting go.

Bronchitis

The bronchi become inflamed due to air pollution such as wood smoke, exhaust fumes, and particularly cigarette smoke. Bronchitis can also be caused by infection from the throat. As the bronchi bring air to the lungs and take used air back out again, they act as mediators or communicators between the inside and outside world. Bronchial problems are, therefore, often connected to being able to share what we are really feeling, and to issues of separation or definition.

Do you need to 'get something off your chest'? Are you coughing and bringing up mucus rather than sharing your feelings? What do you need to release, to let go of? Do you feel smothered by someone? Is there something irritating or painful that you need to externalise? The irritation may be to do with yourself, perhaps a feeling that you have done or said something regrettable. Or are you feeling overwhelmed by your circumstances? Are you finding it difficult to maintain your sense of individuality?

This area is also connected to our taking in of separate and independent life, through the breath. Any doubts, uncertainties or insecurities we may feel about being separate or alone can manifest here. Below the irritation you may find deeper feelings, perhaps of sadness, guilt or shame. Are you experiencing conflict about asserting your independence or boundaries? Have you recently ended an emotionally dependent relationship? Are you feeling overwhelmed by what you are taking in?

Hyperventilation

This is particularly associated with stress. It is estimated that one in ten people suffer from hyperventilation, where the breathing becomes so shallow and rapid that there is an excessive loss of carbon dioxide. The imbalance between oxygen and carbon dioxide upsets the acid/alkaline balance, creating faintness, dizziness, confusion and feelings of unreality, panic attacks, headaches, tingling or numbness. This is usually due to unconscious fear or anxiety. Where is the imbalance in your life? Are you giving out too much and need to give to yourself more? Are you fearful of breathing deeply, of taking life in? Learning how to breathe more fully, and especially how to do abdominal breathing, is essential, as is deep relaxation. (See Chapter 5 for more on relaxation and deep breathing.)

Pneumonia

This is an inflammation of the lungs, so here we need to look at what might be so deeply inflaming our feelings about breathing – the taking in of life – whether it be something we are taking in from outside, or something within that we are unable to express. There are hot emotions here, as well as pain and exhaustion, depleting our energy. The act of breathing is the act of living. Are you feeling exhausted or overwhelmed by the burden of having to cope and keep going? Is there a longing to stop and take some time out? Do you need help but feel unable to ask for it? Do you feel knocked about, as if someone has knocked the wind out of you?

The relationship of breath to spirit is often seen in this illness, as mystical or spiritual experiences are not uncommon in those suffering from pneumonia. It can distort our relationship to the physical world, which is normally maintained by the rhythm of the breath, and this distortion can act like a window through to another level of reality.

14

THE RHYTHM OF LOVE
The Heart, Blood and Circulation

THE HEART is the centre of the cardiovascular system, with a network of vessels taking blood all around the body. Oxygen and other essential nutrients are taken to every cell via the arteries, while de-oxygenated blood is carried back in the veins. The pumping of the heart provides the power that propels the blood.

The heart and blood correspond to our relationship to love. As blood gives life, so love gives life meaning and direction. With love and life come their opposites: fear and death. Love is expansive and all-embracing, reaching out to other beings; while fear is contractive and exclusive, pulling back from participation. Love embraces fear, but without love fear becomes hate. The more we open our hearts, accepting ourselves and all beings, the more love grows and fear diminishes. Without love, life loses all meaning; when the heart stops, life goes.

The heart symbolises all aspects of love, from the romantic to the divine. We call people cold-hearted or heartless when they appear to lack love or warmth; warm-hearted or big-hearted when they are loving and kind. We leave our hearts in different places, have our hearts broken, feel them flutter with joy or beat loudly with passion.

The heart contains only pure, abiding and constant love, like the unconditional love a young child feels for all beings. However, years of conflicting or hurtful experiences lead us to repress or deny our love, creating a heart that is locked away, unreachable. Added to this, our society views expressing love as sentimental so we hide our feelings behind embarrassment or fear of rejection. Disconnected from the power of love, life becomes superficial, uncaring and lonely. Without a strong connection to the love within us, we are cut off from our source, alienated within ourselves; a closed heart sees a world full of imperfection, mistrust and abuse.

♦ THE HEART ♦

The type of cynical, self-centred attitude, leading to frequent anger and aggressive behaviour as described above, is now being identified as a high risk factor for cardiovascular disease. Lifestyle is also an important predictor. Overwork, excess pressure and stress lead to a weakening of the entire system, but most importantly they limit the amount of time available for exercise, relaxation, play or loving relationships. Too much alcohol debilitates the liver and immune system; while smoking causes an 84 per cent increase in adrenaline which puts extreme stress on the heart. A diet rich in fat, particularly red meat and dairy foods, can increase the number of **heart attacks** and cause a hardening of the arteries, or **cancer**.

Together these risk factors point to a lifestyle lacking in self-care, self-respect and inner nurturing. This is usually due to the pursuit of material gain at the expense of emotional balance; to a need to be in control, especially over our own feelings, perhaps because of painful memories, past hurt or trauma; or because of grief, depression and 'broken-heartedness' due to the loss of a loved one. A closed heart can mean that we are deaf to our own need for love.

Healing the heart therefore involves healing the inner wounds, fears and hurts, releasing the barriers and letting go of the resistance. It is about accepting and coming to love ourselves. If we deny our own needs, then our love for others will be limited and conditional. When we accept our own imperfections, then we can accept all beings as they are and love unconditionally, recognising the humanity we all share.

Learning to open the heart, to listen to, respect and trust what we feel in the heart, is one of life's most powerful teachings. Even though the heart may appear illogical or irrational, intuitively we know that it is more real and meaningful than all the arguments the head may use to counter it. An open heart sees the inherent beauty within each being. There is no room here for self-centredness. Instead there is a greater awareness of the whole of which we are each a part. The open heart experiences a depth of love that is not dependent on anyone or anything else. It is simply there, just as the sun is there, shining equally on all.

TRY IT YOURSELF

Breathing Into Your Heart

Take a moment to stop reading and to breathe into your heart.

- Sit comfortably, close your eyes and breathe naturally, but breathe into the area of your heart – the heart space in the centre of your chest. Feel it opening with each in-breath, releasing any tension with each out-breath.

- Continue for a few minutes, letting yourself relax into this. Do you feel this space? Are you experiencing the depth and magnitude of feeling contained there? Just breathe naturally, without effort, and let yourself sink into the heart.

- When you feel ready, gently open your eyes.

As described in Chapter 10, the heart is where we point when we say 'I' – we know it to be our true self. From the heart, all our passion, adoration, devotion, fear, anger, hurt, desire, yearning, gratitude and joy are expressed: through the mouth with words and intonation and kissing; through the shoulders, arms and hands, when we express our feelings in hugging, holding, caressing, pushing away or rejecting; and through our sexuality, by caring and sharing. The upper back reflects the back of the heart – the denied and repressed feelings that we push away, the anger, resentment or bitterness. The chest reflects the heart we show the world. Is it pushed out, creating a false image of a strong heart? Or does it sink inwards, as if the heart has been beaten down so much it has finally collapsed?

The heart is a powerful organ which does not give way easily – without our even needing to be aware of it, it pumps continually throughout our entire life. A heart disease means a lack of ease has entered into this great system, a deep discontent or unhappiness.

Angina

Angina means tightness and refers to the tightness of the chest experienced when a narrowing of the arteries prevents blood and oxygen from reaching the heart. It is usually triggered during exercise, or by excessive mental or emotional stress, times when the demand for oxygen is increased so much that it outstrips the body's ability to respond and there is a breakdown in the balance of supply and demand. Less exertive activities, such as smoking or over-eating, can precipitate angina, as can worry or over-concern for others.

As angina is a result of restricted blood vessels, so it indicates a constriction in our ability to receive. This applies particularly to receiving love and nurturing, or being able to ask for help or advice – there is a strong desire to stay in control, to do it all ourselves. This reduces our inner resources, so when the demand grows the supply is not there: we have nothing to give. The tightness of the chest implies the conflict between the need to replenish and the inability to receive. It can also indicate where we are giving too much to others and not to ourselves.

Angina is reversible and often causes no lasting damage. But it is a strong warning from the body – a flashing red light – that we are overdoing it, and in the process ignoring vital needs. Do you need to be in charge and find it hard to ask for help? Have you become hostile or aggressive, uncaring about others if they stand in your way? Has making money or being successful become more important than walking in the country or playing with your children? Is too much being demanded of you and do you feel unable to meet that demand? Or are you too involved in other people's problems? Angina is saying that the balance in our lives has gone, the pendulum is swinging too far in one direction. Most importantly, it is asking us to pay more attention to the feelings in our hearts.

Heart Attack

This is the number one killer in the Western world, the incidence of which has doubled every 20 years since 1900. A heart attack is caused by a blockage of a coronary vessel supplying blood to the heart, a thrombosis, or a sudden spasm when the heart muscle is starved of blood. It may be triggered by excessive exercise, stress or emotional trauma, or from a long build-up of deposits until the arteries can no longer function properly. Or perhaps by a combi-nation of causes, such as a heavy smoker who drinks 3–4 cups of coffee per day and eats a high fat diet but gets little exercise, and is then emotionally traumatised by the death of his or her partner.

The mind plays an important role here, especially if we are normally more involved with mental activity than with heart activity. The head and the heart need to be balanced so we do not become locked into the intellectual, rational and mental part of our being while losing touch with our deeper feelings. If there is too much cerebral activity and a simultaneous increase in stress or pressure, then the heart becomes energetically cut off. Do you have an awareness of your heart as a vital centre of life within you, or is it simply a pulsating mechanism? Do you tend to deny the importance of your feelings?

Love is the natural expression of the heart, yet we spend most of our lives denying its true expression. A heart attack implies that the heart is being attacked by a build up of unexpressed hurt, loss, grief, or resistance to love. The heart is desperately trying to get our attention, to break down the limitations. Are you putting your heart in a cage so you cannot feel anything? Are you holding on to pain or hurt from the past, refusing to forgive? Without deep, heartfelt involvement, life can appear meaningless. This leads to depression and sadness, a sense of not belonging. Do you need to put more heart into your life? Have you lost heart or just want to give up?

Normally the blood flows continually; it has its own rhythm. Are you in touch with the natural rhythm of life that moves within you? Or do you regiment your life and fill every space with scheduled activity? When blood vessels contract and go into spasm, the constricted circulation of the blood affects the heart. Are you focused so completely on work that the emotional side of your life is constricted? Are you suppressing your emotions so they take up less space in your life?

For many people a heart attack is a turning point that changes their attitude and at the same time saves their lives. It is an urgent request for us to review our lifestyle, behaviour, relationships and, more importantly, our priorities. This is a golden opportunity to explore all the aspects of our being that have been locked away for so long, to rediscover the beauty and love that is our birthright.

Heart Rhythm

As the heart is the centre of our deepest feelings, so its rhythm responds to those feelings, increasing at times of stress, shock, fear, terror, passion, elation or joy. It normally returns to its natural rhythm as we relax. An increased heartbeat that does not easily return to normal indicates the need for greater emotional balance and inner relaxation. Do you feel out of rhythm with your life? Are you easily upset or do you feel emotionally insecure? How can you find greater balance and a calmer rhythm in your life? Be aware of your breathing – deep breathing (see Chapter 5) will help to ease the tension. In deeply relaxed states it is normal for the heart rhythm to slow down.

♦ THE BLOOD ♦

Through an intricate maze of arteries, veins and capillaries, the blood reaches every cell in our bodies. The blood consists of plasma, red and white cells and platelets, and it has a complete impression of our physical individuality contained in the DNA – the genetic code. In the womb we are connected to our mother through the blood system and, from that shared blood and genetic inheritance, to our entire history. Difficulties to do with the blood are, therefore, often connected with family conflicts.

Just as the blood contains an imprint of our physical individuality, so it also contains the deep feelings that form our emotional identity, and it is responsible for distributing those feelings throughout our being. There is normally an equal flow of give and take as the arteries carry blood from the heart outwards (sharing the feelings in our heart with the rest of our world) and the veins bring the blood back to the heart (bringing the feelings we receive from others). Any imbalance indicates a conflict concerned with being able to give or receive, or issues to do with emotional involvement and the expression of love.

Anaemia

This is due to a lack of haemoglobin in the blood. **Iron deficient anaemia** may be due to poor diet, blood loss as in menstruation, or supply not meeting the body's demand for iron during pregnancy. **Pernicious anaemia** is due to a lack of vitamin B_{12} (folic acid) caused by dietary deficiency, or by a lack of the substance needed in the stomach to absorb B_{12}. In both instances it is important to look at lifestyle and attitude. Lifestyle habits may include an insufficient diet, where we are not recognising our real needs. Have you been working too hard and not caring for yourself? Do you think your diet is unimportant?

As the blood corresponds to the sharing of our love with the world and the receiving of love into ourselves, anaemia indicates a weakening of the force that enables us to respond energetically to life. Have you lost the desire to be involved? Do you feel you are not worthy of being loved? Is there a fear of opening yourself to the power of love? Do you feel overwhelmed or exhausted by emotional demands? A lack of iron suggests a lack of strength and resilience. Have you lost your motivation and sense of purpose? What is needed to rebuild your strength?

Blood Pressure

Our blood corresponds to the life energy within us, the movement of love and vitality throughout our being. Blood pressure can be raised by exertion, shock, conflict or passion. **High blood pressure** is usually due to increased pressure and stress, or anger and similar hot emotions. If it does not normalise easily then it is known as **hypertension**. This is a leading cause of heart attacks and strokes, affecting up to 25 per cent of the population worldwide.

Those who have high blood pressure are often over-active, as if doing everything possible to avoid themselves. Activity is a way of averting aggressive or emotional impulses – high blood pressure is symbolic of feelings not being expressed or even acknowledged, creating a build up of inner pressure. As the emotions begin to spill over, physical difficulties can develop. It is essential that we learn how to read the signs before damage is done, and to connect more deeply with what is seething just below the surface. These are hot emotions which, if ignored for too long, may cause a great deal of damage. What is getting you so heated? Are you applying the pressure yourself or is it coming from outside you? Are you trying to avoid something that is making you angry or upset? If high blood pressure is due to panic or fear, we need to recognise the insubstantiality of external events and to reconnect with our inner balance. Breath awareness and inner conscious relaxation are essential (see Chapter 5).

Low blood pressure implies a resistance to entering into life fully and fearlessly. There is an inner weakness and a desire to pull back; we are unable to stand up without feeling dizzy or overwhelmed. This indicates a powerless or hopeless response to pressure, an inability to meet life face to face, a giving up attitude. Do you feel unable to cope with the demands on you? Do you feel overwhelmed? What do you need to do to connect with greater reserves of inner strength?

Low blood pressure also occurs in those who meditate a great deal, but here it is due to a deep level of serenity and calm, where all the inner tension is released. Rather than being overwhelmed by life, there is a total lack of resistance, a merging of oneself with all life.

Circulation

Poor circulation, which in its worst form is known as **Raynaud's Disease**, usually affects the extremities – feet, hands, ears and nose. The parts affected become pallid and/or purple and invariably numb and cold. It also causes **chilblains**, which are swollen, red, itchy and hot areas on the toes, fingers and nose.

A lack of circulation indicates that the blood is not going far enough to reach the extremities, as if there is not enough blood to satisfy demand, or it is withdrawing into itself. As the blood represents the circulation of feeling, of love and life, poor circulation implies a weakening of that force. It is associated with being unable or unwilling to reach out to touch or be intimate, a fear of contact or of being grasped by someone or something. It can show a depletion of inner reserves, or a desire to pull away and redirect our emotional involvement. There is a fear of being vulnerable or exposed, and so we act like snails, pulling our outer extremities inwards.

Do you feel you have nothing to give, no love to share? Do the parts of you that meet the world feel threatened, shy, ugly or unlovable? Are you wanting to withdraw from a relationship or situation where you no longer feel emotionally involved? Do you feel cold or numb to a relationship? What do you need to do to feel warm or emotionally expansive? What needs to change for you to be able to reach out with love?   ⋇

Coronary Artery Disease

Arteriosclerosis is a hardening and narrowing of the arteries, more common as we grow older. **Atherosclerosis** is an accumulation of plaque or fatty deposits in the arteries, leading to a constriction. A thickening of the walls means that less blood can pass through, which can lead to a restriction in the blood supply to the heart or even a **heart attack**.

The arteries and veins transmit life-sustaining oxygen and essential nutrients, as well as communicating feelings and emotions. The blood contains our unique individuality, while the vascular system provides the walls within which we are contained. But these walls can also be the limitations or restrictions we impose on our communication. Are you holding yourself back from sharing or receiving? Are you limiting your emotional involvement or interaction? Narrow or blocked blood vessels imply a breakdown in the balance of giving and taking. Have you become narrow in your outlook? Unable to accept others' views? Is this because you are trying to do too much and not recognising your own needs, not seeing where you need to give to yourself? Do you deny yourself love? Do you pretend you can manage on your own and that you do not need any help?

A lack of love in our lives, perhaps from childhood, means we grow up with a hardened attitude, especially towards emotion. Are you overly critical? Are you very rigid or fixed in your attitudes, inflexible with your feelings? What happens if you soften your attitude, become more willing to love and to receive? Fatty deposits in the vascular system imply that negative emotion, such as guilt or shame is slowly building up and clogging the system. Do you let your feelings build up inside before they finally burst out? Do you feel clogged or stuck? What would happen if you shared your feelings? What can you do to increase the flow of energy in your life? How can you release the restrictions?

Haemorrhage

This is an acute loss of blood, whether external or internal. It is like an outpouring of emotion, a release of deeply held feelings that we may not have been conscious of, or have been unable to express. But they are so powerful they have to find an outlet. The bleeding is like a pressure valve blowing. It is a blasting out of life-giving energy. Have you been keeping your feelings locked inside? Do you feel attacked on a deep level with no way to express yourself? What do you need to heal this emotional outpouring?

Thrombosis

This is a blood clot which blocks a vein and may move to the lungs or heart. The fluidity and vitality of the blood has become congealed and stuck, causing a lack of movement and the potential for disaster. Movement means change, whereas being solidified implies a resistance to change, an inability to flow or concede. As the blood carries life and love giving energy, a thrombosis implies a blocking of that energy. Where have your feelings become congealed, stuck, solidified or unresponsive? What change are you resisting? Are you clinging to a situation for fear of what will happen if you let go? Are you blocking off something within yourself?

A thrombosis is much more common in the veins than in the arteries, indicating that it is in receiving, rather than in giving, that we are most stuck. Are you able to give *and* take? Are you willing to receive nourishment and care from others? Or do you push help away and try to do it all by yourself? It is also most common in the legs, implying that there may be a fear of the direction or movement that lies ahead. Are you fearful of an impending emotional change? Do you feel stuck to the ground you are standing on, as if embedded in concrete? What do you need to do to release the blockage, to begin moving again?

Varicose Veins

Varicosity occurs when the valves in the veins fail to do their job, which is to let the blood flow upwards but not come back down again. The blood therefore collects in the vein and causes swelling. This is found in the legs, where the muscles usually help to keep the blood flowing upwards. It often happens when someone is standing for long periods or during pregnancy, both activities putting extra pressure on the valves.

The veins carry the blood back to the heart, representing our ability to receive love and be nourished by that love. The failure of the valves indicates difficulty with being able to receive love leading to an inner longing to collapse. When due to standing for long periods, it is connected to feeling unsupported – hence the need for *support* stockings. Do you feel you are standing alone, with no nourishment or love sustaining you? Or are you resisting the nourishment being offered? Do you long to give up completely? What part of you is collapsing inside?

If due to pregnancy, it may be connected to inner fears about having to be responsible for another person. So often all the attention is on the child-to-be, while the mother may be feeling confused and insecure. Are you able to express your fears or do you feel ashamed of them? Are you receiving the help and support you need? Do you fear you will not love the child, or will lose the love of your partner? What do you need in order to feel more supported?

15

PROTECTOR OF THE CASTLE
The Immune System

THE MAIN FUNCTION of the immune system is to recognise foreign substances and prevent them from doing us any harm. This represents the ability to protect ourselves against invasion; it also implies an awareness of the relationship between inside and outside, to what extent we are influenced by that relationship, and the ability to discriminate between what is us or is not us – between the self and the non-self. If the immune system is over-active towards *external* antigens, such as bacteria or pollen, then an allergy can develop; if it is under-active then an infection develops; if it is over-active against an *internal* antigen then it can start destroying itself, as in **auto-immune diseases**; if it is under-active then abnormal body cells will develop, as in **cancer**.

The immune system works in two main ways. Firstly, when the system encounters a foreign substance (such as bacteria) an antibody is formed by B-cells in the blood. As each substance is dealt with, an immunity develops against future invasion by the same antigen. Vaccination was developed on this basis. This is also how infectious diseases help build resistance and strength, and why childhood diseases like measles or mumps occur only once.

The second aspect is cell-mediated immunity, which occurs through specialised cells in the blood. T-cells destroy the invading substance (helper T-cells sound the alarm, killer T-cells do the destroying, and suppressor T-cells sound the retreat when the job is finished), and macrophages engulf the foreign cells and clean up the debris. T-cells originate in the bone marrow and are then sent to the thymus gland for maturation, before entering the bloodstream. As their main job is to identify and destroy abnormal cells they have to recognise what is harmful and what is harmless.

The word 'tolerance' is used to describe this discrimination between self and non-self, so we attack only non-self substances. 'Intolerance' is the inability to distinguish between what is harmful and what is not, where the non-self actually appears as self. Such a process of discrimination is a vital component of our sense of identity – the ability to define our own thoughts and feelings, rather than being easily influenced by others.

The thymus gland is of the utmost importance in maintaining the strength of the immune system – in China it is known as a source of *chi* or healing energy. It derives its name from the Greek work *thymos*, meaning 'soul or personality', indicative of its relationship to our sense of identity. The thymus is also known as the seat of fire because of its close connection to the heart. For instance, when we are in love, feel confident, or have an open, positive frame of mind, it is usually quite hard to get sick; conversely, when we feel depressed, lonely or sad we can catch cold or get ill quite easily. It appears that the emotional state of the heart can energise or deplete the thymus gland, which in turn influences the health of the immune system.

A solid emotional support system gives us greater resilience and strength to resist influence or external invasion: the more love we experience, the better we feel about ourselves and the less likely we are to be depressed. If that support system is weakened – whether through loneliness or loss – the ability to resist attack is also weakened. The immune system becomes exhausted, just as our tolerance of stress or grief becomes exhausted.

This is not to deny the impact of chemical toxins in our air, food and water, which is enormous. The immune system tries to maintain harmony by tolerating and balancing internal states with external ones. If the external substances become overwhelming, or have abnormal patterns, then the immune system can get pushed beyond its tolerance level. In the same way, if the level of emotional toxins rises, this also undermines its strength.

The lymph glands are another important part of the immune system. The fluids in the body are transported to these glands and collect in the lymph nodes so any foreign substances can be attacked by antibodies or T-cells. Swollen lymph glands, such as in the armpit or groin, indicate that the immune system is working to fight an infection. Included in this system is the spleen which filters the blood to remove waste, old blood cells and foreign substances, and infuses the blood with new immune cells.

The word 'spleen' means moroseness and irritability, so difficulties here indicate that, rather than filtering out the waste, there is a harbouring of old or stagnant thoughts and feelings. This creates disruption or indigestion, and an increase in irritability. A strong spleen encourages clarity, compassion and sympathy, as the blood is freed of negative influences.

Auto-immune Disorders ✳

Normally the immune system is able to identify which substances are foreign or potentially harmful and which are harmless. When it starts attacking itself in the same way that it attacks foreign substances, then auto-immune diseases develop, such as **rheumatoid arthritis** (see Chapter 11), **lupus** and **AIDS**. In these cases, the ability to differentiate becomes so confused that the self appears as the non-self.

The questions we need to ask, therefore, are about our feelings for ourselves. These questions are not easy to answer, as they demand great honesty. Do you feel as if your life doesn't really matter, or is not really valid? Are you carrying guilt, shame or blame from the past that is wearing away your self-esteem or self-respect? Do you have an underlying dislike or hatred of yourself? Do you spend your time helping others but refusing help yourself? What needs to change for you to be able to embrace yourself, to bring this part of your being into a loving and loved place?

As this condition is one of attacking ourselves, we need to see where we are negating our own inner beauty or undermining our love of life. Are you overly critical of yourself? Constantly putting yourself down? Disappointed in yourself? Or is someone else wearing away at you, corroding your sense of worth?

AIDS

When an invading substance enters the body, the immune system normally sounds the alarm and goes to work. However, when the HIV virus enters the body, it not only invades the T-cells but it also shuts off the alarm. This leaves the body open to attack not just from HIV (which appears to be the precursor of AIDS) but also from invading substances such as bacteria, fungi and other viruses. With AIDS the body becomes vulnerable, no longer protected from infection. The immune system loses its boundaries, becoming unable to distinguish between self and non-self.

From recent research it would appear that two of the main psycho/emotional characteristics that AIDS carriers share are a sense of victimisation or a tendency to suppress emotions. The populations where AIDS has predominantly manifested are those least respected by society at large: the poor in Africa, drug users, prostitutes and gays. There is a very natural tendency for these groups to feel victimised or to deny the truth of their feelings. For instance, even those homosexuals who are open and honest about their sexuality know that society has yet to be so accepting, and the majority will spend many years feeling ashamed or guilty. For some, telling their parents of their sexual preference is the hardest thing they have to do, others never feel able to do it, knowing the pain and guilt it will generate. Prostitutes and drug users live in fear of being caught, while the poor are victims of numerous political battles and social prejudice. Even haemophiliacs are a vulnerable social group, having to spend their entire lives being protected from injury.

The fact that the HIV virus is transmitted through blood and semen can give us valuable insights into the disease. Blood represents the circulation of love from the heart through all parts of our being, containing within it life-sustaining oxygen; while semen represents the expression of love from one to another, containing within it the potential for further life. Yet it is through these two essential life-giving fluids that a latent cause of death is transmitted.

Love and life are indivisible. Without love, life has no meaning; without life, love has no expression. Without love – or a love of life – there is depression, hopelessness, an endless search for fulfilment. There may be self-hatred, self-abuse, anger or fear that shuts us off from the feelings in our hearts. Does the transmission of the virus imply that love is lacking? Does an inner defencelessness attract the virus, or does the virus create a defenceless state?

And to what extent is the transmission dependent on being received? It would appear that to receive the virus there has to be a shared or similar emotional environment; if there is no receiving pattern, no receptive place, then the virus is not transmitted. This is seen in the many cases where one partner is HIV positive but the other, despite unprotected sex, remains negative. Does the strength of the love between the two partners provide protection?

With AIDS has come the growing awareness of how love heals, as if the virus itself awakens us to see where the heart is closed. It is extraordinary how many AIDS patients, particularly in their last months or weeks, connect with unconditional love. Families are healed, parents accept children who were previously rejected, friends and lovers openly care for each other, inner conflicts are resolved. I have seen few illnesses that focus so deeply on love and the opening of the heart.

Paul Krueger, a dear friend who died of AIDS as this book was being written, wrote a song called 'Finally Free':

One day when I woke up in despair
A rising sun broke the darkness there
And on the horizon what did I see?
A hundred of God's angels flying so high
My heart took wing, my eyes could see
The voice of my soul cried 'I'm finally free!'
And then to my surprise
Everybody flew to meet the angel band
The people of hate and the people of peace
All the opposites of the human race
The Mother and the Father too
The devils in me and the angels in you
And when the holy hour had come
In freedom we flew into the sun
We took no hate, we took no guns
The game was over, the battle done
Finally free, I'm finally free, I can fly like an angel.

There are also those people who have received AIDS accidentally –
as through a blood transfusion – and who do not fall into any of the
above categories. It is at this point that our understanding of the
implications of AIDS needs to expand. We need to recognise it as an
illness of our times, a reflection of the harm we are inflicting on
every form of life, not just ourselves. As we cut down the rain
forests, pollute the oceans and deplete natural resources, cases of
AIDS, child abuse, cancer and heart disease are rising. Perhaps
nature is trying to tell us, in the only way she can, that the time has
come to find a deeper level of tolerance and harmony, to realise that
the way we are behaving, as a race, is intolerable.

The energy of love is all-powerful – it should be the determining
force of our lives. But, with our massive over-population and abuse
of planetary resources, we have become hostile and resistant to one
another, more inclined to inflict harm than to share love. The
ignorance of our essential connectedness is all too destructive. AIDS
is a wake-up call to us all – not just those who are individually
affected – to connect ever more deeply with our love. (See also Sex,
Chapter 18.)

Allergies
Allergies are when the immune system over-reacts too strongly to an
external stimulus – causing sneezing, watery eyes, **hay fever** and/or
breathing difficulties. (See also Asthma and Hay Fever, Chapter 13.)
This implies that our tolerance or balance is upset and we are over-

reacting to a normally harmless substance.

It is as if the external world has become an enemy, something to be feared and resisted. Fear leads to withdrawal but, in refusing to allow anything in, we are also unable to let anything out – to express our feelings. We are being irritated by an irritant – and it is making us irritable! The reaction is an emotional one, as there is crying and a runny nose, as well as difficulties with breathing, or receiving and taking in. Are you over-reacting to an emotional situation? Is there a desire to be rid of something or someone that is causing a strongly irritated reaction? What or who are you actually feeling allergic towards?

Seeing the world as hostile or potentially aggressive can be due to repressing our own hostility or aggression. It is more socially acceptable to have an allergy than it is to scream or hit out. It signifies an unwillingness to communicate, a withdrawal from connecting or sharing with our world. Before the allergy symptoms developed, were you feeling hostile or resistant to communicating with someone? Were you wanting to scream or shout? Did you feel yourself withdrawing inside, pushing those feelings down?

Often the feelings being repressed are directly linked to the cause of the allergy. If we look closely at what the allergy symbolises, then we can get closer to the part of ourselves that we may be rejecting. For instance, pollen is symbolic of sex and fertility and the wildness of nature. Are you resisting the release of passionate or wild feelings within yourself? Is there a fear of fertility or reproduction? This also applies to **perennial rhinitis**, the allergic reaction to house dust, pet fur, mites, feathers, even face powder. What is it in your life that these substances represent? What is making you pull away from them so dramatically? Animal fur relates to the instinctive, animal-istic aspect of our nature, while a dust allergy may indicate a fear of dirt or contamination. But life is not clean, well-ordered or under our control. It is full of dirt, passion, play and disorder. Is a fear of your own deeper, more uncontrollable aspects making you keep a tight hold on yourself to resist freedom?

Food allergies have increased in recent years. To a large extent this is attributable to an increase in the use of chemicals in farming and food processing. There is also no doubt that certain foods, such as coffee, peanuts, shellfish or wheat, can cause extreme physical reactions, and many adults are allergic to dairy products.

However there may also be psycho/emotional reasons. If the list of food allergies is a long one then you may want to look more closely at issues of control or power. Does it make you feel special because you cannot eat in certain places or eat the same food as others? Is it actually hiding a need for attention and love? Is it a reason not to participate? In rejecting certain foods, are you actually rejecting certain aspects of yourself? Is it easier to blame the food than to look at your own behaviour? A food allergy indicates a pulling back or resistance to fully enter into life.

Cancer

After heart disease, cancer is the most common cause of death. There is no doubt that we are facing an enormous increase in carcinogens (cancer-producing agents) in our environment – the rise in the use of chemicals and the adulteration of food are producing substances totally foreign to our bodies, so that the ability to combat abnormal cells is seriously undermined. However, although we are all exposed to these carcinogens, not all of us develop cancer. It would appear that it is a combination of environmental and psycho/emotional factors that most affects the immune system.

Abnormal cells grow in the body all the time but the immune system usually deals with them effectively and there is no residue. With cancer the abnormal cells are not stopped by the immune system; instead they are able to grow and spread. A cell that is *abnormal* has become wayward, even rebellious, behaving differently to other cells; rather than fulfilling its role in support of the whole it goes off on its own. In this sense, cancer can be seen as reflecting the human condition. Rather than being concerned with the welfare of all, the emphasis is on the self, but such behaviour undermines the survival of the whole. And, just as the cancer cell becomes isolated, so we can become isolated from ourselves, cut off from our real feelings.

An accumulation of problems or stress can create this state of inner alienation. Stress includes emotional shock or trauma, such as the death of a loved one, divorce, sudden loss of one's job or financial security. Such trauma can seriously undermine our sense of purpose or identity. In turn, this suppresses the body's natural defence system. The two years preceding the onset of symptoms is the most critical time, particularly if strong feelings are not fully acknowledged or released but are buried inside, pushed away or ignored. Those feelings have energy that does not just dissolve.

There are certain characteristics and personality traits that seem to be more prominent in those prone to cancer. Their common theme is a lack of personal respect or care, to the point of isolation from our own feelings. These characteristics include helping others to the detriment of ourselves – denying our own needs due to believing that others must come first; the inability to express negative feelings, especially those of anger, shame or fear; long-held resentment or guilt, often from childhood, that may never have been expressed; a sense of powerlessness, as when another person is emotionally stronger or more dominating; feeling worthless, unimportant, or not good enough; and an inner hopelessness leading to what has been termed 'acceptable suicide'.

Obviously not all cancer patients have these characteristics, for cancer is nothing if not multi-faceted and indiscriminate. There is undoubtedly a mystery factor involved here. But cancer has lessons for us all – about our attitudes towards ourselves and each other, about accepting and loving unconditionally, and especially about loving ourselves. Many cancer survivors have spoken about it being connected with a lack of self-care, saying that their healing came as they began to honour themselves more deeply. Most especially cancers give us the chance to re-evaluate, to take stock and be more honest about our feelings, and to clarify our priorities.

It is important to remember that cancer is not contagious, is not something alien that enters the body and takes over. The abnormal cells grow within us – they are as much a part of our being as any of our other cells. If cancer represents an alienated part of ourselves, then rejecting or isolating it further does not encourage healing. Opening ourselves to love means loving the cancer, bringing it into the heart, accepting it as an expression of ourselves.

There are many ways we can work with cancer – through creative visualisation, deep relaxation and meditation, with diet or the many complementary therapies available. Being able to share our feelings – whether through counselling, group therapy or talking to a friend – is a vital aid to recovery. When we acknowledge the alienation, the disconnection from our feelings, we can bring those isolated parts of ourselves back into the whole – understanding the function and part of the body that is affected helps indicate which part of ourselves is being ignored or pushed away.

It is essential to strengthen the functioning of the immune system – which means strengthening the desire to live. Those who develop a fighting spirit, mental resilience and vigour, who do not reject themselves, appear to have a greater survival rate. This is about developing an 'I want to live' attitude. It means finding what is meaningful, looking deeper to discover the real purpose of life.

Common Cold and Influenza

There are many different versions of the **common cold** although the symptoms usually include a runny nose, watery eyes, stuffy or painful sinuses, a sore throat and sometimes a cough. It may start in the chest and move up, or start in the nose and move down. In all cases, it occurs most often in those whose immune systems are already in a weakened state, perhaps due to overwork, stress or emotional issues. A strong and healthy immune system will not easily succumb to a cold, even when surrounded by those who have.

When we cry, our nose runs. When we have a cold, our eyes water. Colds, runny noses and crying are all related. We often feel the same helplessness and despair, the same need for comfort. Tears and mucus are both ways of releasing emotions that have been pent up inside. So, if you have a bad cold, you may want to see if there is some crying or grieving you are repressing, some deep feeling that has been pushed aside. Unshed tears will find their way into the nose, whether due to sadness, frustration or guilt. A cold often follows the death of a loved one or some form of emotional shock, particularly if grief is not acknowledged; it may imply that we have gone emotionally cold or are being cold to our feelings. Colds are common, just as it is common not to show how we really feel.

Are you frustrated at work and unable to express this? Or are you feeling mentally and emotionally overloaded – to the point where the pressure is overwhelming? A cold not only releases the feeling but gives us a few days off – the time we need to find our balance. It also makes everyone else keep their distance. Are you actually wanting to push someone away? Feeling fearful of intimacy? Are you in need of some time out to be with yourself? A cold can be a cry for love and attention, a need to be cared for, to be mothered. Are you longing for comfort but unsure of how to ask for it? Or a cold may indicate a time of change and transition, when there is too much happening at once and we need to shut off for a while, slowing down our intake to allow for assimilation.

Influenza – which includes a high temperature and aching muscles – sends a clear message that some time out is needed. The word *influenza* means to 'come under the influence of', implying that someone or something is having a strong influence on us, perhaps making us doubt what we think or feel for ourselves. This can undermine our sense of identity or purpose and we need time to reconnect with our own feelings. Influenza is also nature's way of getting us to take a break, to help build our inner strength. It often occurs at times of seasonal change – perhaps it is the body's way of clearing out toxins and debris, of having a 'spring-clean'.

Herpes Simplex
The herpes simplex virus affects the genitals and mouth, with fever blisters or **cold sores** that burst and leave a crust. A particular

characteristic of herpes is that it stays with us for life and outbreaks are unpredictable. However, it appears that the most usual time for an outbreak is following emotional stress or conflict, particularly around the theme of relationships, as herpes invariably brings any form of intimacy to a halt. There may be hurt, sore or sad feelings that need to be released. Is there someone you feel sore about? Is the relationship a meaningless one, only based on sex? Does intimacy make you feel fearful? Are you being asked to be intimate too quickly? Are you finding it hard to communicate?

Guilt can also be connected to herpes – perhaps guilt from past sexual activity, or the belief that we are somehow bad or dirty. Is someone or something reminding you of previous guilty or shameful behaviour? An infection in the genitals or the mouth implies that we are really wanting to stop what we are doing, to pull back into ourselves. Herpes means no one can get too close, so it allows us time to be with ourselves. This can also apply to work or financial difficulties (especially for men), with the pressure to succeed making us want to withdraw.

Infection

Infections are encouraged by our lifestyle and environmental issues, such as hygiene, sanitation and personal habits – smoking increases the risk of infection by lowering immune response, as does a poor diet.

However, even if we live in the most sterile and germ-free environment, infection is still possible as it is more than the presence of germs or bacteria that causes an infection. There also has to be a weakness in the immune system. For instance, one person in an office catches a cold, two others then get it, but two others do not. The contaminant is equally contagious to all five, so there must be another factor that creates the difference. 'Chemical stress weakens the immune system, inactivity weakens the immune system and, finally, our negative emotions weaken the immune system,' says Dr Norman Shealy in *The Creation of Health*. 'The new field of psychoneuroimmunology now suggests that emotions may be the final straw that causes the immune system to decompensate.'

Being *infected* indicates that something or someone is *affecting* us to the point of weakening the ability to protect or defend ourselves. Is someone undermining your sense of self? Do you feel invaded or contaminated? Is someone or something making you feel intolerant, insecure or fearful? Have you been overworking – getting out of balance? Have you been feeling depressed, sad or out of touch with your deeper feelings? All these can deplete our inner resources. Exploring *where* the site of the infection is will deepen understanding of its significance. (See Chapter 10 for the part affected.)

Inflammation

To be inflamed conjures up strong images of hot, fiery passion, redness and anger. Are you feeling angry and fired up about something? An inflammation is swollen and sore – can you find what is making you feel this way inside? There is a war going on between an invading substance and your inner being; your immune system is fighting against the non-self in order to maintain balance. Perhaps you are failing to acknowledge this war within yourself. Is there a battle going on between what is acceptable and what is not? Between right and wrong? Between your own beliefs or feelings and those of someone else? What has penetrated your defences? (See also Chapter 10 for the part affected.)

ME (Myalgic Encephalomyelitis)/Chronic Fatigue Syndrome

This illness includes severe muscle pain, muscle weakness, debilitating exhaustion, with headaches, allergies and sometimes fever. It can last for years and can affect anyone at any age. It tends to develop following an infection, such as **glandular fever**, when the immune system remains in a weakened state indicating it is of viral origin or due to an immune malfunction.

ME seems to be symptomatic of the present age, an illness that has developed in response to increasing pressure to succeed, often at the expense of our own dreams or aspirations. Some ME characteristics include thinking that we are not good enough and need to keep pushing to be better or achieve more; or a giving up and inner lassitude that denies any sense of purpose; a tendency to be image-conscious and uneasy with ourselves; a strong desire to be in control so that it is very difficult to ask for help – despite finding it hard to cope alone; and a resistance to taking care of ourselves – such as having to watch our diet – because it all seems so unfair and such an effort. So, on the one hand, there is a fear of failure and on the other hand there is a lack of effort or self-love.

It is very interesting that this illness is called ME (although in the US it is known as CFIDS – Chronic Fatigue Immune Deficiency Syndrome). More than any other illness, ME seems to generate self-obsession. We become immersed in our own problems and issues and talking about ourselves – the 'poor me' syndrome. This shows how ME is connected to the ego. The need to focus on ourselves is perhaps due to a fear of being lost in the crowd, not being noticed or recognised, or because we want to be seen as special or different. Perhaps we are not honouring ourselves on an inner level. Are you doing what someone else wants you to do rather than heeding your own desires? Are you trying to live up to others' expectations, and making these more important than your own feelings? Or are you feeling trapped, caught in a state of emptiness? In either case there is a growing alienation from ourselves, a disconnection from who we are inside, and particularly a loss of spirit. It is as if the disconnection from our inner spirit or true self leads us to over-compensate by becoming excessively connected to the ego or superficial self.

As there is no motivation or clear direction, all movement forward comes to a halt – muscles ache or collapse, exhaustion takes over. There is a longing to give up, to be free of all the effort it takes to be human. ME provides a hidden place where we cannot be reached, a shelter from the storm. There is always an excuse not to participate, not to get a job, to socialise or to be intimate. This may be due to having been overloaded with responsibility, leading to an inner exhaustion; but it can also be due to others having previously filled that role in our lives and a fear of facing that responsibility ourselves, or a fear of failure. This is a very loud cry for attention.

The weakness of the immune system indicates a loss of inner aliveness, resulting in an inability to protect ourselves. There is no strong 'I want to live' message. It takes a deep commitment to be able to go beyond the ego – the self-absorption and obsession – to reconnect with our inner spirit, with our true purpose.

Shingles

Shingles is the **herpes zoster** and **chicken pox** virus, usually affecting adults and the elderly at times of immune weakness, as when we are stressed or emotionally traumatised. It affects one or more nerves, most often in the chest, occasionally in the face, causing redness and intense pain along the nerve pathway where blisters can form and burst. It implies a deep anxiety, an inner pain that has been building up over a period of time. As the nerves are our means of communication, shingles is like a cry of pain demanding attention and tenderness, a rawness where we feel vulnerable and weak. Our body is telling us to stop helping others and to start helping ourselves, to ease the stress and tension communicate our feelings, and to take time to nourish and love ourselves.

16

CENTRAL CONTROL
The Nervous System

THE NERVOUS SYSTEM controls and coordinates the body's movements. Receiving information and impressions from the senses, it relays that information to the brain – the centre of the nervous system – which is responsible for our thoughts, personality, movement and behaviour. From the brain, information is relayed through the *central nervous system* by way of the spinal cord, with peripheral nerves taking messages to and from the spinal cord out to all other parts of the body. The *automatic nervous system* is a separate relay of nerves which maintains the automatic responses within the body, such as breathing, heartbeat and digestion.

The brain forms the largest part of the nervous system, each section dealing with a different part of our being, whether it be hearing, seeing, thinking, emotions, speech, breathing or walking. The left cerebral hemisphere controls the right side of the body and vice versa, each side having quite distinct areas of functioning. (See Left and Right Sides, Chapter 10.) At the base of the brain is the hypothalamus which is a major nerve centre. Through the pituitary gland, the hypothalamus controls appetite and thirst, sleep patterns, sexual urges and temperature. The pituitary gland regulates physical growth, puberty and pregnancy, and releases powerful endorphins that not only act as painkillers but also as anti-depressants. It is in charge of the entire endocrine (hormone) system with many of its orders coming from the hypothalamus.

Also a part of the endocrine system is the pineal gland, which is connected to mental aptitude and sexual rhythms. This small gland, called the 'seat of the soul' by Descartes, can be seen as a two-way link between spirit and matter, between the abstract and the relative.

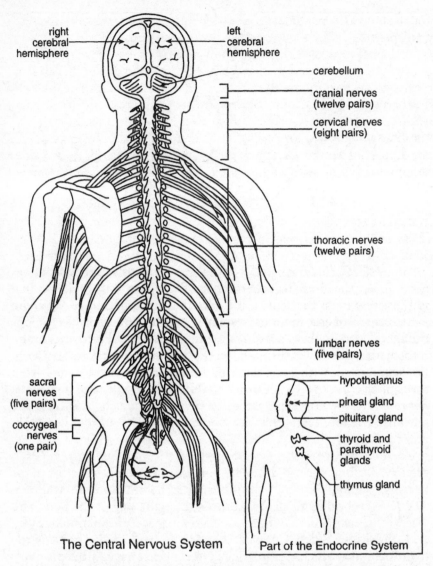

right cerebral hemisphere

left cerebral hemisphere

cerebellum

cranial nerves
(twelve pairs)

cervical nerves
(eight pairs)

thoracic nerves
(twelve pairs)

lumbar nerves
(five pairs)

sacral nerves
(five pairs)

coccygeal nerves
(one pair)

hypothalamus

pineal gland

pituitary gland

thyroid and parathyroid glands

thymus gland

The Central Nervous System   Part of the Endocrine System

This indicates the intimate relationship between the mind, the endocrine system and the nervous system – between how we feel and how we behave, our emotions and our physical state.

Neuropeptides, known as messenger molecules, are found in the areas of the brain governing our emotions, in the immune system, and throughout the nervous system. They are chemicals that transmit information, whether it is a thought, a feeling or an experience. In this way the mind and body are inextricably linked. 'Neuropeptides are the bodymind's *lingua franca*, a web humming with information and intelligence,' writes Barasch in *The Healing Path*. 'Our thoughts and feelings are mediated by neuropeptides; some diseases secrete neuropeptides; they are key to the healing response.'

As the nervous system is the communication network that links all the various parts of our being together, so any damage to this system means a collapse in communication between the brain and part of the body (as in a **stroke**). It can mean an increase in sensitivity leading to hypersensitivity and extreme nervousness; or to **numbness, neuralgia**, or **paralysis**. As in a telephone exchange, there are numerous communications going on at the same time, crossing and interchanging with each other. A fault in any one area can affect may other areas, creating a blockage or system failure.

Headaches

There are numerous reasons for headaches. Some may be indications of other issues taking place in the body, of hormonal imbalance (such as during menstruation), of allergies, fatigue, or of more serious head or brain disorders. Headaches in general are the body's way of saying we are going too fast, doing too much, overloading the circuit, and are out of touch with our inner needs. The blood vessels are getting constricted, limiting the oxygen supply to the head. This implies an inner tension that is resisting going with the flow and is constricting or holding on inside.

Headaches can be caused by:

- unexpressed feelings – such as anger, resentment, frustration, even rage – that build up and create inner pressure
- worry, self-doubt or fear of failure, creating self-dislike and disconnectedness
- pride or arrogance, stubbornness and rigid thinking patterns, where we hold on tight to what we think is right, thus narrowing our views and restricting our sensitivity
- a resistance to events or circumstances, making us want to opt out of participation
- taking on more than can realistically be coped with, leading to overwork, stress, and tension between the head and the body (between thought and action)
- a desire to control, especially combined with a strong will or perfectionism, or equally a feeling of being out of control
- excess mental absorption or self-centredness leading to a lack of physical grounding and a lack of contact with the heart and inner feelings
- tension and stiffness in the neck and shoulders resulting from poor posture, creating a split between body and mind

If you experience headaches frequently try keeping a diary, noting the times and the surrounding circumstances. Include the food eaten within the previous few hours, and the psycho/emotional environment. Describe the headache, its location, duration and severity. Describe your feelings prior to the headache. In this way, you can build a picture of what is happening, especially if there is any repetitive behaviour or attitudes. Are you resisting someone or something? Putting too much energy into your head while forgetting your heart? Trying too hard to be perfect? Or trying to do everything without asking for help?

Migraines

Due to a restriction in the supply of oxygen to the brain, migraine headaches can last for many hours and include nausea, vomiting and the need for complete rest in a dark room. Physical causes include allergies to foodstuffs, particularly chocolate, coffee, cheese, red wine or wheat. A restriction in oxygen implies a restriction in the life-force, a holding back from full participation, a desire to push away what is happening and completely retreat into ourselves. Migraines are often connected to psycho/emotional expectations not being met, or a fear of failure.

Bodymind causes include:

- attempting to completely repress our feelings, particularly anger and rage, so that they create a build up of nervous tension and extreme frustration
- a tendency to be a perfectionist or to control, putting undue stress on behaviour, with a fear of spontaneity or emotional expression
- strongly repressed sexual feelings, often because of their seemingly uncontrollable nature
- great expectations and anticipation, creating inner stress
- unfulfilled plans and deep disappointment, a feeling of being let down
- fear of being unable to do everything that is asked of us, or extreme introversion which resists involvement, or a terror of being asked to be involved
- needing to be loved and cared for – a silent cry for attention

As with headaches in general, it is important to keep a diary of the times and duration of migraine headaches, alongside what foods are being eaten and the psycho/emotional atmosphere. Make a note of all your feelings prior to the migraine, and see if you can pinpoint the cause – whether it be a food allergy, medication, stress or an emotional reaction.

It is important to catch a migraine before it is full blown, and, if possible, to normalise the blood vessels. A good way to do this is to take a few minutes, sitting or lying quietly, and visualise your hands becoming warmer and warmer (see p. 54). Inner conscious relaxation and breath awareness meditation (as described in Chapter 5) will also help.

Nerve Pain

We do not like pain and usually do anything possible to get rid of it. Yet pain is the body's way of getting our attention. It is most especially a way of telling us that something is wrong, that we need to stop and look at what we are doing, to find what change is needed. If we simply numb the pain, then those messages go unheard and further difficulties may arise. Pain is normally triggered by an accident, injury or strain, but invariably there is an underlying weakness in the area affected by the injury. For instance, although you may strain your back by bending over while gardening, you will probably find that the painful area is also connected to a psycho/emotional issue that needs your attention. It is easy to blame the accident for the pain, for facing inner pain is more demanding. However, the two are inextricably linked. Physical pain is like a signpost, showing us where we need to connect with psycho/emotional pain.

Pain makes us realise just how impermanent we are, how fragile the body really is. Confronting our own vulnerability often reveals a need for love and attention, a nurturing that we may have been longing for without realising it. Are you being nourished? Are you able to ask for help? Pain indicates that we are holding on tight, so we need to work at letting go. It creates a prison. Are you feeling trapped by negative feelings, such as revenge, guilt or shame? Is there someone or something you are holding on to? Is an inner pain demanding attention? What part of your being is hurting so badly? What needs to happen for the pain to ease or be released?

When we experience pain we usually take painkillers, get drunk, or try to distract the mind. All this helps, but only temporarily – the pain is still there when the diversion has passed. A different way of dealing with pain is to enter into it unreservedly, completely, opening ourselves to receiving whatever the pain is saying. To sink into it as rain sinks into soft earth. 'Several laboratory experiments with acute pain have shown that *tuning in* to sensations is a more effective way of reducing the level of pain,' writes Jon Kabat-Zinn in *Full Catastrophe Living*. 'You are trying to find out about your pain, to learn from it, to know it better, not to stop it or get rid of it or escape from it.'

This is vital, as fear only makes the pain worse through added tension – fear of being ill, fear of not being able to work, fear of being an invalid. By entering into the pain we confront the fear. Ask the pain to tell you what you need to know, to show you where you are holding on tight and why. Open yourself to letting go. Breathing into the pain is one way to do this. Pain usually makes us hold our breath in an attempt to counteract the tension. Breathing into the pain, especially deep breathing, enables the muscles to relax and the tension to release. This will help the pain recede. Direct your breathing into the area that is hurting, let your breath fill the cells with oxygen, and visualise the pain softening and receding. (See also Chapter 10 for the part affected, and Chapter 5 for breathing techniques.)

Pinched Nerves
Here there is the feeling of being squeezed, compressed or gripped tight, as if someone or something is constricting our normal flow of energy. This may be due to excess stress putting pressure on the surrounding muscles or bones. Find the place in your psycho/emotional being that is being held so tightly or that feels so squeezed. Do you feel trapped by someone or something? (See also Chapter 10 for the part affected.)

Sciatica
Pressure on the sciatic nerve, due to a **prolapsed disc** or **pinched nerve**, causes a shooting pain in the back, buttock and down the leg, whether standing or lying down. Prolapsed discs are connected with pressure and stress, or a burden that is weighing too heavily upon us (see Chapter 11). Nerves are to do with communication and sensitivity. A pinched nerve implies that we are being squeezed or gripped hard by something or someone.

As the sciatic nerve affects the hips and legs, it is associated with the ground we are standing on or the movement we are making. There may be unexpressed anger or frustration about a situation we cannot stand any more, or a feeling that we can no longer stand on our own and need more support. Can you find the inner need and express it? What pain are you sitting on or holding back? Is someone or something restricting your freedom to move? It may be indicating a doubt or fear about where you are going and your ability to cope with what lies ahead. Are you feeling trepidation about the future? What is needed to release the pain?

As sciatica often occurs during pregnancy, it is important to check your feelings about having a baby. Are you feeling fearful of the impending responsibility? Do you feel alone, unsupported? Pregnancy is not always joyous; it can also be confusing, fearful and uncontrollable. What do you need to feel more at ease? Are you getting enough support?

Numbness

Numbness is a lack of sensation in the nerves. It implies a withdrawal of feeling, perhaps because there is too much pain for us to absorb in that place. Numbness is a way of denying the pain, of pushing it away, of forgetting that part of ourselves. It indicates an inner deadness, a detachment from feeling, even a giving up or hopelessness. It may be caused by stress or pressure, making us want to stop, withdraw, pull back, and especially, not feel. Is there someone or something you don't want to feel? What part of you are you pushing away? Are there feelings you have withdrawn from? Long-lost hopes or dreams? What needs to happen for you to be able to accept that part? To bring it back to life? (See also Chapter 10 for the part and side affected.)

Paralysis

Although there are various reasons for paralysis – injury, virus, **stroke** – the message the body is giving is much the same. Paralysis implies an inability to continue the way we are. Something has to change, concede, surrender. This is often associated with issues of power and control, the need to dominate or rule, in contrast to a world that is essentially fluid and uncontrollable; the result is a system that gets jammed or overloaded with stress. Or there may be an intense fear of what is happening, of what lies ahead – perhaps due to shock or trauma – and therefore a pulling back and resistance to any forward movement. Paralysis means no movement and, therefore, no expression of feelings.

Paralysis also means being dependent on others, having to be cared for and looked after, which is the exact opposite of being the one in charge. It can be very hard to accept such a situation, giving rise to tremendous bitterness and anger, which only adds more tension to the body. (See also Chapter 10 for the part affected.)

Multiple Sclerosis

This is a degenerative disease of the sheath surrounding the nerve fibres which can occur in any part of the brain or spinal cord, leading to sclerosis of the nerves. MS may remain dormant, occurring only occasionally with symptoms that pass, or it can move through progressive cycles of recovery and relapse in a process of slow degeneration, in which the body becomes ever more limited in movement, particularly the legs.

To move is to emote, to bring to life our emotions and feelings. MS restricts and limits movement, implying that our expression of feeling is becoming more and more withdrawn or held back. Are you moving in a direction you do not want to go in, perhaps following someone else's directive rather than your own volition? Do you feel unable to stand up for yourself? Have you shut down your feelings in order to keep everything immovable, so you do not have to deal with change?

There may be deep resentment about having to cope as an adult, a reluctance to take responsibility, or a feeling of lost opportunity. Often there is a great deal of suppressed anger or rage, with little or no forgiveness towards others (a bitterness, as if the world is responsible for all our problems), but this anger is hidden behind a polite exterior. In repressing these emotions, all our feelings get held back – a state of emotional denial – so there may be little expression of joy or love.

MS invariably means that we become dependent on others as the body degenerates, as if we are literally *de-generating*: regressing back through the generations to become like a child again. Does this indicate a fear of being a responsible adult? Is there a fear of failing as an adult and desire to return to the safety of being dependent? How can you begin to regain your personal power? To find your sense of self and purpose, your own direction? What feelings are you resisting? What is needed for them to be released?

Stroke

This is due to interference with the blood supply to the brain, which stops that part of the brain from functioning. A stroke on the right side of the brain will affect the left side of the body and vice versa. **High blood pressure** can be a contributing cause. A stroke usually results in partial **paralysis** and speech difficulties.

In this situation the blood vessels – the means we have of expressing love and transmitting life-sustaining qualities throughout our being – become constricted and are involved in shutting off a part of the brain, the centre of the nervous system. This leads to a restriction in our movement, which is also a restriction in the expression of our feelings. A stroke is a way of stopping life from proceeding, an emotional resistance or holding back against further change or movement, often due to a fear of what lies ahead.

Most strokes occur later in life, when they are connected to our fear of aging, facing sickness, loneliness and death. This fear may be combined with a strongly controlling personality finding it increasingly difficult to accept getting older and a loss of power, while also unable to express feelings of need, helplessness or love. It implies a deep fear of financial insecurity or anxiety about lack of family support. There is a high incidence of strokes when the elderly are moved into retirement or nursing homes, showing the insecurity and fear, triggered by the loss of familiar surroundings. However, the incidence of strokes in younger people is on the increase, implying that excess stress can cause considerable overloading of the nervous system. It is a serious warning that time is needed to relax and bring more balance to our lives.

Epilepsy

This is where the brain has a seizure, linked to an electrical or nerve disorder. It may be *grand mal* – a complete loss of consciousness with shaking and convulsions and a falling to the ground, with possible frothing at the mouth and biting of the tongue – or *petit mal* which is far less severe, being a break in consciousness for only a few seconds or longer. Seizures are seemingly unpredictable, but there are links to previous head injuries or birth traumas. Alcoholics and drug addicts have a higher incidence of epilepsy. Causes may also include metabolic imbalances.

By its nature, an epileptic fit represents an internal breakdown, an explosion, triggered by unexpressed pressure that overloads the circuit. It is as if we are being 'seized' by emotion. It implies a great struggle taking place between our inner world and the world around us.

Through not being able to express our inner fears, insecurities or concerns – whether real or imagined – the pressure builds up inside until there is an overload. Such a break in consciousness implies a separation between relative reality and our inner perception. The separation may also be between ourselves and the divine, for epileptic fits are known to occur during mystical states of emotional frenzy or devotion, as if the level of ecstasy being experienced is too much for the human brain and a circuit break occurs.

17

KEEPER OF THE BALANCE
The Urinary System

THE FLUIDS in the body correspond to the emotional aspects of our being, which give our lives direction, purpose and meaning. Just as the blood corresponds to love, so the urine corresponds to emotions that are finished with, and no longer needed. If they were not released we would soon drown in our own negativity! This system of waste removal maintains an essential balance; it is a purifying process that keeps our bodies in harmony. Kidney and bladder problems, therefore, tend to arise when we have difficulty letting go of emotions – particularly negative ones – and the feelings become blocked inside.

♦ THE KIDNEYS ♦

The main function of the kidneys is to extract unwanted substances from the blood. To do this the kidneys have to discriminate between what is harmful and what is beneficial. Are you able to see what is good for you and what may be potentially damaging? Can you recognise what needs to be released?

The kidneys work hard at maintaining an acid-alkaline balance in the blood. This is an essential balancing of opposites – hot and cold, right and wrong, masculine and feminine – symbolised by the two kidneys in relation to each other. Issues here are especially connected with relationship, whether imbalances in our relationships with others – particularly with our primary partner – or imbalances of the masculine and feminine energies within ourselves. The kidneys are

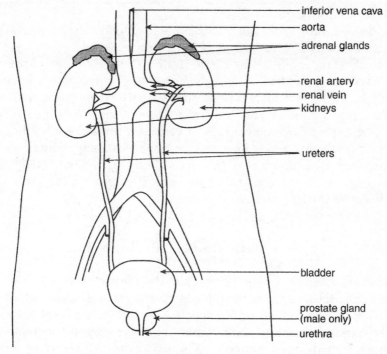

inferior vena cava
aorta
adrenal glands

renal artery
renal vein
kidneys

ureters

bladder

prostate gland
(male only)
urethra

The Urinary System

also involved in the production of red blood cells, indicating their relationship to generating love throughout our being. Are you experiencing difficulty in your relationships? Are you holding on to emotional issues that are creating an imbalance? Repressing anger or fear? Are you able to let go of past difficulties? Where do you need more balance in your life?

Situated on top of the kidneys are the adrenal glands (see below). These produce adrenaline which is released in response to fear. In Chinese medicine the kidneys are seen as the 'seat of fear'. Kidney problems are particularly concerned with fear connected to relationships, such as unexpressed grief or emotional insecurity.

Fear motivates us into action or immobilises us into inaction. This indicates the important connection between the kidneys and the joints – between the ability to express ourselves and move on. Uric acid is normally excreted by the kidneys, but if it is not released it can build up in the joints, as is the case with **gout** causing painful swelling and immobility. Gout particularly affects the toes, implying specific deeper fears about what lies ahead. (See also Gout, Chapter 11.)

Kidney Stones

Condensed substances such as uric acid and minerals, which are normally passed in the urine, begin to separate and slowly gather more substance, like a snow ball, until a stone is formed. This can be extremely painful. Condensed matter represents condensed thought patterns and emotions, particularly to do with fear and grief. They are like unshed tears that have become solidified. There may be an outward appearance of ease, but inwardly a holding on to sadness or insecurity. This may be due to past experiences – such as unresolved grievances – that have built up, unexpressed, until they begin to take form and cause pain. Recognising the inner fear or negative thought pattern is essential.

♦ THE ADRENALS ♦

The main function of the adrenals is the release of adrenaline, the hormone associated with the flight-or-fight response which is activated by fear, stress or danger. This would be fine if the adrenals only responded to *real* danger, but they also respond to *potential* danger, which may simply be stress from a screaming baby combined with the telephone ringing, one too many roadworks causing long delays, or an alarm call during the night. Stress tells our body to get ready to fight the situation or to run from it, when in fact neither response is appropriate. This means that the adrenals are continually activated, causing extra wear and tear on related organs, with a corresponding increase in exhaustion, muscle ache and digestive problems. With nowhere for the adrenaline to find an outlet, stress accumulates in the body.

The fact that we have two adrenal glands, one on each kidney, implies a need for balance, especially in our relationship with the world. Without this balance we can build up excess fear or irrational anxiety, we can push too much and suffer related disorders. In order to avoid damaging the adrenals it is essential to spend time relaxing and creating more equilibrium in your life. (See Chapter 5 for deep breathing and relaxation techniques.)

♦ THE BLADDER ♦

The bladder is a grapefruit-sized bag, a holding area for waste liquid before it is released. One of its greatest attributes is its ability to expand and then shrink, according to the quantity of urine passing through. The release of specific muscles enables the urine to pass, usually as the pressure is building. The relief at releasing the pressure is obvious.

This symbolises the releasing of emotion and the resulting relief when the emotion is out, rather than in. For instance, it is quite usual to want to urinate after a particularly emotional confrontation or experience, as if all the fear of the experience is released in the urine. This happens at moments of extreme fear when we find that we have wet ourselves, as seen in animals who urinate when confronted with a fearful opponent – the release of the urine clears the system of upset feelings and leaves us ready for action.

Bladder problems are about the need to let go of our emotions – to release and move on rather than hold tight; or about the ability to adapt – to accommodate different circumstances and different feelings – versus the desire to cling to the past.

Cystitis and Urinary Infection

This is an irritation of the urinary system, indicating that we have become inflamed by our inner emotions, making us hot and irritated – we feel pissed off! It is painful and difficult to pass urine, just as it is to let go of negative feelings. Many cases of cystitis are linked to times of relationship conflict or breakdown, whether between partners, or parents and children. At such times there can be an abundance of negative emotion, much of which is not released, and so the confusion, grief, anger, fear and hurt all build up inside. It is not easy to express the hurt when a partner leaves, or the feelings of abandonment, loss and loneliness. More often we cling to a relationship even when the time has come to let go. A relationship breakdown involves change. It usually means moving from being co-dependent to being independent, and this transition can be fraught with conflict.

Cystitis often occurs on a honeymoon, as such an intimate situation can release deeper feelings – love brings up everything that isn't love – and we blame or get irritated with our partner, when really it is our inner changes that need to be dealt with. Is there some deep grief arising? What inflamed feelings are you holding on to? Is there a fear of intimacy? What is needed to help you release these feelings?

One way to help heal cystitis is to drink lots of pure water – to flush ourselves through with pure emotion – or to do some good emotional releasing, like pillow bashing! For children experiencing difficulty in relation to their parents, it is very important to help the child to talk through his or her feelings, perhaps with a child counsellor.

Frequent Urination

The bladder can expand its capacity, but if we are not able to expand into a situation emotionally or psychologically then we may find we are having problems, such as frequent urination, as the pressure builds in the bladder.

This may be due to feeling an urgency or hurry to do things, or feeling squeezed by circumstances. It may be due to an excess of emotions – an emotional overflowing. It is also indicative of not wanting to deal with deeper feelings or their consequences – they are being released quickly so that they do not have to be fully acknowledged. Are you taking on more than you can cope with? Trying to do things so quickly that nothing gets done properly? Or wanting to get something out of your system without really acknowledging it? Frequent urination implies an inability to adapt to different circumstances or to expand into new experiences. It may also be a way of avoiding interaction, always having an excuse not to participate. In men, this condition is often caused by an **enlarged prostate** putting pressure on the bladder. (See also Prostate Problems, Chapter 18.)

Incontinence

As incontinence is the result of a muscular action that has collapsed or weakened, it implies a tendency towards mental feebleness or inability to focus energy, an attitude of hopelessness or inner collapse. No longer able to adapt to different circumstances, to expand or contract as necessary, there is instead a giving in, especially to grief, loss or fear. Incontinence indicates the inability to control our feelings, so there is a continual, unstoppable outpouring. Or there may be a feeling of being powerless, as if we are helpless victims and can do nothing for ourselves. This can occur when we feel abandoned, isolated and without personal power, as when the elderly are moved into nursing homes.

Bedwetting

Bedwetting indicates a tremendous need to express confused or upset feelings but with no means of doing so. As it occurs most often in children, it is usually due to emotional pressure from family, friends or school. Perhaps there has been a divorce, physical or psycho/emotional abuse, constant teasing, academic failure or some other trauma. There is an inability to express these feelings so they build up inside. Bedwetting is a cry for help. It is a response similar to crying – a releasing of inner emotions – but far more uncontrollable and unconscious. And, as it happens at night, it is like a hidden secret, a dark pain. There may be a deep grief, guilt or shame; or a need to cry that is felt to be unacceptable, perhaps due to fear of a reaction from the parents – often the father – or teacher. It is essential that such a situation is treated with love and tenderness, providing a chance for the inner fears to be expressed.

HIS AND HERS
The Reproductive System

THE REPRODUCTIVE ORGANS and the hormones they release – oestrogen and progesterone in females and testosterone in males – affect sexual maturity from childhood through puberty. In the ovaries are formed the eggs and in the testes the sperm, both needed for life to continue. These organs also contain all our ancestral knowledge; only through the meeting of opposites can this continuity be achieved. We cannot have male without female, just as we cannot have light without darkness, or giving without receiving.

As we mature into adulthood we get to know our sexuality, the shape or size of our bodies, the nature of intimacy and sharing; rarely are two people alike in their feelings or needs. Problems in the reproductive system are often connected to problems with relationships and sexuality: issues of acceptance or rejection, communication or the lack of it, experiences of trauma or distrust, self-dislike or confidence. Sexual repression, hurt or abuse can lead to low self-esteem, and from there to an increase in aggression, a desire to dominate or manipulate, loneliness, marital breakdown or depression. Our innermost feelings about our bodies are of prime importance, influencing all other aspects of our lives. However, much of our sexual behaviour develops as a result of social pressure to conform.

Each culture throughout the world has its own stereotype of what a man is meant to think or feel versus what is expected of a woman. In the West, this stereotyping determines that men aren't meant to cry or show emotional weakness, women aren't meant to be aggressive or strong, men don't clean houses, women don't fix cars, and so on. This creates images of men being macho and brave and women being soft and weepy, which influences our sexual behaviour – men are dominant; women are to be dominated.

As no one is purely masculine or feminine (we all possess aspects of both), such stereotyping has alienated men from their ability to be caring and sensitive, and women from their assertiveness and power. The feminist movement began to dig into this entrenched way of thinking, giving women permission to explore their masculine qualities. But men have yet to emerge in the same way. In the Tibetan tradition, wisdom is seen as being a feminine character-istic and compassion as masculine, yet women are only just beginning to claim the depths of their insights and few men have the courage to be gentle and merciful. Instead, men are thought of as having the brains and women as the care-givers. Until we re-establish a true balance within ourselves, we will have to deal with the effects of such stereotyping and its influence on our health.

♦ HIS ♦

It is traditional to think of the male as dominant, not just in sexual relationships but also in worldly and political matters. Religion is extremely patriarchal, as shown by the widespread outrage when the Church began to ordain women priests; while the number of female politicians is still extremely low. Women are just beginning to enter the upper echelons of the business world, but the boardroom remains a largely male stronghold. Enormous pressure is placed upon men to live up to these images of domination or leadership. They are meant to be intelligent and capable, brave in the face of adversity, never wimpish, helpless or demonstrative.

In the light of this, it is not surprising to find men having difficulty sharing inner conflicts about their masculinity – how can doubts or fears be aired in an atmosphere where you are meant to be all powerful? When you are taught that brave boys don't cry, then personal conflicts have no means of expression, no way of being acknowledged.

Yet many men feel unable to live up to the typical male image. Considering themselves to be failures in the eyes of society leads to feelings of inadequacy, helplessness and stress, which can translate into difficulties in sexual organs or sexual functioning. There are feelings of confusion about sexuality and performance, and how to cope with social responsibilities. Unable to accept their own feminine nature, any such qualities in other men are condemned and thought of as weak. Rather than dealing with these feelings in a constructive way, they get buried by excess alcohol, sporting activity, television or work, deepening the confusion, the lack of communication, the separation of feelings from reality.

Throughout history, however, there has been the image of the warrior – the fearless yet tender-hearted male who is in balance with both his masculine and feminine energies – with both strength and tenderness, wisdom and compassion. Here the qualities of masculinity are not dependent on competition, aggression or exerting power, but on the protection of all beings, equally. The warrior is fearless, not by pretending he feels no fear, but by accepting his fear; through acknowledging his weaknesses he gains strength. The warrior is one who knows the depths of his own heart and feels the pain of all beings – none are rejected, denied or abused.

This image encourages us to explore what it means to be male. Just as the feminist movement created an opportunity for women to question what it means to be a woman, so men need to do the same. For times have changed, roles are no longer so clearly defined. In most families the man is no longer the sole breadwinner, yet in sharing the money-earning is he also sharing the child-rearing, the laundry, the cleaning? Who cooks dinner? Who stays at home if a child is sick? A recent documentary celebrating 75 years of the feminist movement highlighted a woman who worked in a post office alongside her husband. 'We do the same job at work, but I also get to cook and clean and deal with the children. So where's the equality?' she asked.

The social pressure to deny or hide our feelings, combined with the male ego that finds it difficult to surrender, causes tremendous resistance. If a man does share his pain he may be called an 'old woman', yet the warrior teaches us that when a man acknowledges his feelings he is made stronger, not weaker – that the more he loves, the more fearless he is. Women's exploration of their assertive and intellectual qualities should provide an impetus for men to acknowledge their insecurities and fears, to discover their tenderness and love. For modern man, then, the challenge is to open the heart, to make friends with his feelings, to be fearless in his compassion. The actor, Richard Gere, recently featured in a woman's magazine, said how making movies is easy but opening your heart is the real challenge.

Impotence

The size and strength of an erect penis is invariably compared to a man's capability and power in the world: a strong and assertive male is presumed to have a large and healthy erection. The inability to get or maintain an erection can, therefore, be devastating to a man's confidence, undermining his sense of purpose, acceptance or desirability.

In most cases impotence is due to psycho/emotional issues. The communication between a man and his partner is of prime importance, especially if the partner is demanding too much emotionally, or subtly undermining his masculinity; or if there are concerns about conception taking place. There may be a fear of his partner, perhaps due to emotional threats; a fear of entering in and being consumed by her, or lost within her power. He may be playing the submissive role, losing touch with his innate masculine qualities, or have conflicting feelings about his sexual preferences. Impotence is also linked to child abuse. Memory is stored in the soft tissue, so memory of past abuses can be found in the penis; impotence can occur when there is a build up of guilt or shame, or something that has not been shared.

It may be caused by stress at work, focusing too much energy in mental activity, away from physical expression; or if he is being asked to perform beyond his normal capacities at work and is unable to maintain his energy at home; or perhaps he is being emasculated at work by a critical or aggressive boss. It may also be due to a lack of work, as happens after retirement, causing a feeling of no longer being of any use.

Beneath all these possible causes lies fear – fear of losing control or being powerless, fear of sharing real feelings and intimacy, fear of having to stand up for ourselves, to achieve or perform. These fears lead us to repress our feelings, become a perfectionist, deny spontaneity, and keep a tight hold on sexual expression.

Potency is an expression of masculinity, power and superiority – to lose this is to lose one's own manhood. It can lead to marital breakdown, deep depression, even suicide. Finding the inner cause is essential in order to restore self-esteem and self-acceptance. Inner conscious relaxation (see Chapter 5) is important. It is also vital to recognise that true masculinity is not dependent on sexual performance, but on a deeper, more meaningful relationship with ourselves.

Prostate Problems

Situated close to the bladder, the prostate produces some of the fluid necessary for the sperm's passage and therefore for the continuation of life. Problems here occur more as we get older. As the prostate is connected to reproductive ability and performance, it often reflects the conflicts and concerns experienced in aging. Retirement can make a man feel that he has lost his purpose as the breadwinner; he may see himself as useless and worthless, his power draining away. Problems with the prostate can also be associated with financial loss or difficulty, and fear of having material security reduced or removed.

Many men feel emotionally undernourished or out of touch with love, but do not know how to reach out to find that love. Some may have used sex to find love, but with prostate problems they may find this difficult and so they become even more emotionally isolated. An enlarged prostate also puts extra pressure on the bladder, causing an increased desire to urinate, even if there is nothing to pass. This indicates difficulty with expressing these inner feelings of confusion and longing.

The Testicles
The sperm is the source of life and needs to be treated with respect. The testicles are the containers for that life, so they also contain all the inner fears and confusions connected with sexual desire and hidden yearnings. **Cancer of the testes** is the commonest form of cancer in men aged 20 to 35, perhaps indicating the enormous amount of conflict and confusion many men have about their sexuality and potency.

♦ HERS ♦

The role of women has changed enormously in the past century, going from not having the vote to becoming heads of state; from being housewives to having both careers and families. With the advent of birth control, women can choose to have sex whenever they want without fear of pregnancy, to have a child or not, and to have control over their future. All these factors have radically changed their relationship with men.

Although many women prefer to be independent and enjoy working, these changes have created a tremendous shift in how we view femininity – what it means to be a woman, what it *feels* like to be a woman. How is a woman to be assertive at work during the day, a caring mother in the evening and a seductive lover at night? How does she cope with having a heavy period at the same time as conducting a vital business meeting? Or dealing with menopause while trying to teach a class? Or having a sick child at home and sick patients to be seen at work?

Learning how to balance these opposing forces means facing the challenge of balancing the masculine and the feminine: being assertive without being aggressive, feeling equal to men without losing the ability to nurture and care, being worldly as well as intuitive. Gone are the days of all women being submissive, emotional and helpless. Increasingly women are reclaiming their voices and their wisdom is being heard.

But, at the same time as women gain greater freedom, we are also seeing an increase in female reproductive difficulties such as **breast cancer** and **premenstrual tension**. There are growing conflicts to do with having children, being able to mother adequately, perhaps not wanting children but feeling guilty, or not being able to conceive and feeling a failure; and sexual problems to do with wanting to dominate or be more assertive, feeling put down by men or treated as inferior, or feeling guilty and shamed by past abuse.

The image of the warrior is equally relevant for women as it is for men. This image reminds us that fulfilling our womanhood is not dependent on having an ideal body, bearing children, being a perfect mother, being a passionate sex partner or even a successful career person. The feminine nature is one of insight and intuition, the 'wise woman', combined with the depth of love and compassion of the open heart. The ability to conceive and create a child is symbolic of a woman's tremendous creativity and ability to change within herself – to give birth to new aspects of her inner being. These new aspects develop more easily the more she is able to truly accept and love herself for who she is. The feminine nature is also about surrender – not on the level of surrendering to a man but surrendering the ego to the higher dimensions of spiritual understanding.

The Breasts

The breasts are the most prominent symbol of femininity, the most stared at, commented on, agonised over, and exposed part of the female body. Women rarely like their breasts, believing they are either too small or too large, too high or too droopy. Social conditioning requires them to be a certain size and shape in order to be attractive, yet few women fit this requirement. Hence the enormous number of breast enlargements and reductions that have taken place over the past 20 years, often to the detriment of the woman's health. Breasts create embarrassment, insecurity, shyness and shame, as well as pride and confidence. They influence a woman's sense of identity, how she feels about herself and her attractiveness. Some women are never able to touch their own breasts, feeling fearful or repulsed, completely unable to accept this part of their being.

The breasts are also a source of nourishment, nurturing and

caring, an expression of the heart, a sacred and tender place. They offer nourishment to a new being, not only providing life-sustaining food but also comfort and security. How often do we see a child snuggle up to the breast, despite being long past suckling? This same comforting quality can be present in a sexual relationship, offering a partner a place to feel safe and nurtured. Through the breasts, a woman shares her love, giving a part of herself for the benefit of another. But this can involve an inner conflict. Being unable to have children, being embarrassed by milk leaking out, or having difficulties with feeding, can all give rise to guilt, shame or self-dislike.

There may also be a tendency to over-nurture, treating a grown person as a child, keeping them 'close to one's breast'. Or, equally, there may be a tendency not to nurture oneself, to always put others first, denying any personal need for care and love. A woman may also feel under-nurtured in her relationships, not honoured or nourished by her partner or children, leading her to feel rejected, no longer valued as a woman. In an attempt to gain that love, she undervalues herself. All these issues can give rise to breast problems.

Breast cancer is undoubtedly connected to the increase in environmental carcinogens, but there are also psychological and emotional issues involved. Cases have grown in number at the same time as more women are leaving their traditional homemaking role and entering the work force. Sometimes called 'the feminine wound', breast cancer tends to indicate a conflict between being both an object of desire and a nurturing mother, or between being both assertive and receptive. Do feelings associated with being female cause you confusion? Do you enjoy your breasts or are you repulsed by them? Has your femininity been abused or rejected? Do you feel you have failed as a woman or mother? Are you being nourished and cared for? (See also Chapter 15, Cancer, and Chapter 10, Left and Right Sides.)

The Vagina

This hidden entrance to a woman's being is where she can easily feel exploited or violated. The ability to open and surrender is an expression of the feminine nature but it is a tender and sensitive activity, easily damaged by force or brutality. This is where our conflicts with sexuality manifest – issues of past sexual abuse, sexual rejection, a fear of being out of control, guilt or shame over past acts, or a fear of intimacy.

A vaginal or uterine prolapse indicates a collapse or loss, a sense of having no control over what is happening, a feeling of hopelessness and helplessness. As a prolapse tends to occur more often either after childbirth or after the menopause, it can indicate feelings to do with losing control, as if our body is no longer ours, and in the process we fear we have lost our femininity. This is often combined with feeling either sexually unattractive or rejected, or no longer desiring any sexual involvement.

The Womb   ✗

The womb is the centre of creative life, the darkness from which light emerges, the female heart. Issues that can arise here are, therefore, deeply connected to our inner world, our darkest and most primordial feelings. These are particularly to do with being a woman and/or a mother. Feelings of doubt, guilt, failure, shame, fear, resentment, hurt, loneliness, being unnourished, being unable to nourish – all these and more are connected with the womb. A hysterectomy can seem like the ultimate rejection of womanhood, generating feelings of hopelessness, that we are of no more use, that we have lost our creativity, or that we are no longer desirable. It is vital to reconnect with the essence of womanhood that is not dependent on whatever organs we may have, but is the light of wisdom shining deep within.

The Ovaries

The ovaries represent the source of life or creativity within a woman. This does not just apply to creating new humans but also to creating new life within ourselves. Conflict in this area is connected to what extent a woman feels alienated from her creativity (from being alive within herself) or has lost respect for life. **Ovarian cysts** can create menstrual problems or hinder pregnancy. This is indicative of deep conflicts connected to being a woman or becoming a mother. There may also be a hidden hurt – perhaps from past sexual abuse.

Cervical Cancer

The incidence of cervical cancer is second to breast cancer. It can indicate conflicting feelings about sexuality, particularly resentment, hurt, rejection or fear. It is linked to sexual activity where participation does not always equal enjoyment. There may be a feeling of being disgusted by sex, alongside a belief that we have to 'do our duty' by complying and putting our partner's needs first. It may be due to having been a victim of sexual abuse, leaving us feeling dirty or violated. Or there may be a deep longing and desire, a yearning for sexual activity that is socially unacceptable, creating shame. All the issues to do with the vagina (above) are relevant here, especially ones concerning past abuse, or a rejection of our femininity. (See also Chapter 15 for more on cancer.)

Fibroids

Fibroids in the uterus and cervix tend to show that mental patterns accumulated over a long time are beginning to solidify. These often concern issues of shame or guilt, conflict or hurt, connected with childbirth, mothering or our own childhood. As this is the area where we nurture new life, there may be conflicts about nurturing – perhaps giving to others while feeling unnourished ourselves. Are you being nurtured? Do you need caring for? The womb is symbolic of where new aspects of our being can be developed and new ideas created, so difficulties here may imply a fear of change and newness, or a desire to keep everything the same by blocking our creative forces.

Frigidity

The sexual act is very different for men and women. Whereas for a man there may be a fear of entering into and being consumed, for a woman there may be a deep fear of being penetrated or invaded by another being. During sex a woman opens and surrenders herself, an act that can leave her feeling powerless, without protection – before penetration there is still a measure of safety, but after penetration any defences are destroyed. In surrendering there may also be a sense of losing something that, once lost, is irrecoverable. The inability of a woman to share sexually often reflects deeply held inhibition or a fear of intimacy, perhaps from childhood, or due to past abuse or sexual trauma.

This particularly applies to orgasm. Inherent in orgasm is a quality of uncontrollability, of spontaneous free-falling. For some women this is terrifying, especially to those who cling to order, perfection or control as a means of security. Any form of emotional expression may be difficult, the feelings locked inside while a smooth veneer is offered to the world.

Frigidity implies a tremendous holding on to control by clamping the muscles tight. This may be due to conflicting sexual preferences, or it can arise when a woman is shamed by her erotic desires and so blocks all feelings in her body. She may feel ugly and unattractive, wanting to hide her body from others. It may be that refusing sexual admittance is the only power a woman has in her life, or she may believe that sex is dirty, that it makes a woman into a whore – such feelings often develop in childhood due to her parents' attitudes to their own sexuality. Sex should be sensual and pleasurable, but will be unbearable if pleasure is seen as an immoral indulgence. Was your mother fearful of sex? Was she abused by your father? Were you abused? What were your childhood messages about sex? Were you told it was wrong? Deep relaxation (see Chapter 5) and connecting with the fear of feeling will help (see also Sex, below).

Thrush

Candida is a yeast-like organism which infects warm damp areas, such as the mouth or intestines. In the vagina it is known as thrush. It is normally kept in check by the acid/alkaline balance in the vagina, but if this balance is upset – whether through psycho/emotional causes or because of antibiotics killing the natural flora – then the yeast flourishes, causing a heavy, white, foul-smelling discharge with irritated membranes.

The discharge is indicative of discharging feelings, particularly ones that are not considered acceptable. An infection implies that something is affecting us in an irritating or angry way, and is proliferating inside. Is intimacy giving rise to conflict? Are you being intimate with the right person? Do you feel sexually abused or exploited? What has happened to upset the balance within you? Are there hidden feelings of guilt or shame, or repressed sexual longing? Is something affecting you so deeply that it is breaking through all your defences?

If thrush recurs then we need to see what issues are not being dealt with, but simply repressed each time they arise. It can help to keep a diary of psycho/emotional events, noting diet as well, and correlating these with any outbreaks. Using live, natural yoghurt in the vagina is an excellent remedy.

Menstruation and Premenstrual Syndrome

The monthly period is the woman's reminder of her essential femininity. It means surrendering to the body's natural rhythms, to the flow of life that goes on within us, beyond our conscious control. There are many variations on the 28-day cycle, most of which are perfectly normal. However, stress, trauma, a lack of nourishment, weight loss or illness can all cause menstruation to stop for a while.

As periods are a reminder of fertility, **period problems** may be connected to a desire to get pregnant, or to a fear of parenthood. Problems also indicate an inability to surrender – if we resist the flow we create a dam, behind which our feelings gather. The issues are usually connected with feelings about our womanhood, which may include confusion about our role and what being a woman actually means, or resentment towards men. The hormones involved in maintaining this monthly rhythm have a powerful influence on our psychological and emotional state. The body is asserting itself and asking us to take this time to be more reflective, meditative or creative. It is not always easy to do this in the midst of a busy schedule.

Premenstrual Syndrome (PMS) can be very debilitating and affects about half of all women. Caused by the changing hormones, the effects vary but may include: moodiness, depression, weepiness, irritability, sudden outbursts; headaches, sometimes migraine; food cravings; a need to be alone; fluid retention, causing bloatedness in the lower abdomen, puffy hands and feet, and weight gain; swollen and/or painful breasts; constipation and/or intestinal swelling; a tendency to be clumsy and accident-prone, or vague and forgetful. Some women feel unable to cope for anywhere from a day to a week.

It is important to recognise that PMS is on the increase at the same time as the role of women is changing. The more women go out to work, the harder it is to surrender to the rhythms of nature. It is not easy to cope with a period if we are also having to do a demanding job that requires clear thinking, or wanting to look our best while feeling bloated and swollen. Women get caught between the pressure of work and the longing to be quiet or restful at this time. Add a large measure of guilt, a lack of self-love, even some shame, and certainly some stress, and is it any wonder that women dislike having periods and that so many are experiencing menstrual problems?

Do you resent having a period? Or are you resenting having to work? Do you feel you are struggling to prove yourself as a woman? Would you rather be a man? Do you prefer to dominate rather than surrender? Does this monthly reminder of your femininity fill you with disgust? Do you find it hard to flow with nature, preferring to be in control?

Pregnancy and Childbirth

Most women find pregnancy a joyful time. However, society places some very high expectations on a pregnant woman – she is meant to be happy, to be looking forward to having a child, to be radiant with good health – despite the reality that pregnancy can involve a mass of doubts, fears, resentments and insecurities. Not only are there tremendous and uncontrollable physical and hormonal changes taking place, but the idea of actually having a child to care for can be terrifying. For some women it marks a farewell to youth and freedom, a sudden thrust into adulthood.

It is totally natural for any woman to feel anxious and fearful. What she most needs is strong and unconditional support so that she does not feel so alone. Some of the difficulties experienced in pregnancy are indicative of these inner feelings. Exercise (see Chapters 8 and 9) and deep relaxation (see Chapter 5) are essential to release inner tension and fear.

Most births are completely normal, with few complications and a quick recovery. Childbirth is, after all, a natural process and not an illness. It is certainly one of the most powerful moments in a woman's life. However, complications in childbirth do occur, no matter how prepared the mother is. There are two beings at work here and each has their own agenda. Unconscious fears can unexpectedly arise as a woman suddenly confronts the reality that she has to get the child out – even though it seems impossible – and in so doing there will be a separate person demanding attention. In theory this sounds fine; in practice it can be daunting. How will she know what to do? Will she be able to cope as a mother? With every birth there is a death – the death of one and the birth of two.

Being able to relax, let go and breathe into the fears will help release the tension, as will being able to express whatever feelings are arising. Most important is accepting whatever happens and not feeling guilty or ashamed if the birth does not go as planned. The essential thing is to bond with the child and recognise the blessing of the new life. A gentle, loving, supportive and caring environment will do much to ensure strong bonding, as well as a more peaceful and trauma-free child.

Post-natal depression is connected to all the issues mentioned above – in particular to the tremendous shift that is needed in order to care for this new person. The responsibility can be overwhelming, frightening and exhausting, leading to anxiety, guilt and shame. There may be issues with her partner not fully understanding. The act of childbirth may also trigger past memories within the mother of her own birth or childhood, and if these memories are uncomfortable then depression and grief may replace the joy of becoming a mother.

Breast-feeding problems can develop due to inner conflicts about making the change from lover to mother, or a fear of being intimate in this way. There may be feelings of resentment, compounded by guilt, inadequacy and helplessness; the new responsibility of caring for another life can be daunting; or there may be a tendency to over-mother. A new mother can also feel very unnurtured or unappreciated as the baby gets all the attention.

Menopause

The menopause is a time to give 'men a pause'. In other words it is a time for a woman to tune into and find herself. This 'change of life' occurs when her relationship to herself and to being a woman moves into a different phase. No longer involved with fertility or having monthly periods, the time has come to discover who she really is as a person. Having played the roles of wife and mother, she is free to find her true identity.

However, this situation can also be very threatening. The main fear is that she will no longer appear sexually desirable to her partner, that her body will become overweight and lose its attractiveness, or that she will lose her sex drive. For many women, being a mother is the central reason for existence. Without that role, what can a woman do? What is her purpose? Who is she? There may be a great fear of aging, of uncontrollable change taking place. Few women enter this time without trepidation and concern. Some may become depressed. Others may reject themselves as no longer being worthy. As the menopause is a stopping of the blood flow, it indicates that we may stop loving ourselves, as if our feelings are drying up inside.

The symptoms of menopause are related to these issues. **Hot flushes** indicate the fire of anger or fear, the heat of resentment or insecurity; the body is burning the past, releasing all the old ways of being. **Sweating** is the release of emotional energy, an outpouring of emotion washing away who we have been and preparing for the new. **Vaginal dryness** is linked to the fear of becoming sexually unattractive or incapable, making our sexual feelings contract.

It is essential to put extra energy into loving and caring for ourselves. This is an important time to make friends with who we are, to create anew, to discover a new direction. Rather than being the end of something, let this be a beginning, an opening into our fullness. There is tremendous freedom after the menopause, a time for the true woman to emerge – the wild woman, the wise woman, the free woman!

♦ TOGETHER ♦

Infertility

Being able to have a child is normally taken for granted – as we grow into adulthood it is usually a question of *when* we will have a child rather than *if* we will have one. To discover that this is not going to happen can be devastating. In particular there are feelings of being out of control, powerless, a victim, that life has no meaning, leading to depression or deep despair. And infertility is increasing – in the United States one out of every six couples of childbearing age experience problems with conception. In some cases this is clearly related to the effects of environmental pollution, or it is due to genetic causes. However, there are also many psycho/emotional issues involved.

High stress levels can affect sperm production and ovulation, as well as hormone production. Even the stress generated by trying to get pregnant can hinder conception, as seen in couples who adopt – thereby removing the pressure to become pregnant – only to find themselves conceiving soon afterwards. Infertility is also connected to childhood abuse that has not been acknowledged or resolved, creating an unconscious fear of having a child, perhaps even the fear that at a later date we will abuse our own child in the way we were abused. There may be fears of passing on violent traits or mental disabilities. Or there can be very powerful fears of responsibility, feelings of inadequacy or not being able to cope, especially financially.

Childlessness can make the future appear very empty, but it also provides an opportunity to look closely at how we feel about ourselves. Many people have children in order to give their lives meaning, rather than finding the source of joy within themselves. Are you dependent on having someone to love and care for? Do you feel life has no meaning or purpose without a child? Do you feel you have nothing of any value to offer the world yourself?

There are many people who chose not to have children, and others who cannot but who do not let it hinder them. In these cases we invariably find they have a strong relationship with themselves, have made friends with their circumstances, and discovered a purpose to life that is deeply enriching and fulfilling. Very often they are in the creative or caring professions, using their nurturing energy to the benefit of many. If it is physically not possible to have a child, for whatever reason, then let it be a time to reconsider, rediscover and enrich ourselves. There are many ways we can share our love with other beings, and many beings in need of the love we have.

Sex

Despite the media telling us that sex is something that everyone loves and usually participates in at least four times a week, each individual's sexuality is different. There is no norm, no right or wrong. Desire can come and go, and be stronger or weaker depending on numerous other factors in our lives. The gonads – the endocrine glands associated with the reproductive organs – have an energetic relationship with the pineal gland in the mid-brain which is associated with spiritual awareness. The balance of sexuality and spirituality can, therefore, influence our desire level – we often have less sexual desire when we spend time in meditation or prayer, but more if we are involved in physical activity such as sport or dancing.

Sexual energy is a force so powerful that it forms the basis of certain esoteric spiritual practices, can stimulate higher states of consciousness, unite two people in a bond that is stronger than blood, and dissolve inhibitions that free the spirit. Sex completes the human equation, where two become one. Through our sexuality we share our love and caring for another being, and discover a freedom and beauty within ourselves.

Orgasm releases all control, boundaries and limitations. As a result there can be a tremendous outpouring following orgasm, a release of long-held emotions, a letting go of fear. But such ecstasy does not always come without difficulties! To release control – to allow the body to express itself – takes courage. Being intimate with another human being is fraught with inhibitions, coloured by past experiences of abuse, hurt and fear. The closer we come to each other, the more these issues arise. If they become overwhelming we pull back into our separate selves, unable to reach out into the shared space.

To be intimate is to allow another being into our inner world, either by sharing our love and friendship, or by sharing our passion and sexuality. Intimacy is seeing another as they are – 'intimacy': *into me you see*. In the moment of shared ecstasy there is total intimacy as the individual self no longer remains, the 'I' dissolves. One way of maintaining a degree of safety from such closeness is to have a deep friendship – a heart connection – with one person, while having a physical relationship with someone else. In this way, one part of us is always held back, private and protected. It is far more challenging to have the two together. When that happens there is nowhere left to hide – the intimacy of both heart and sexuality with the same person demands a profound level of surrender and trust.

When we are able to open the heart and completely give of ourselves, the transformational power of sexual energy can awaken. This energy is misused if sex is used for domination or power, for perversion, abuse, or when there is no reciprocal emotional connection. Misusing sexual energy can result in sexual confusion, psychological trauma, emotional breakdown, depression, and/or disease. Sex should not be taken lightly – heedless sexual activity can cause pain.

Sexually Transmitted Diseases

A sexually transmitted disease is a transmitted *unease*, an inner longing or unhappiness trying to find release through physical pleasure. It tends to occur when sexual energy is misused or abused. Are you being physically intimate with the wrong person, with someone you do not have real feelings for? Or are you being sexually active in a way that, deep inside, you are not actually enjoying? Such unease may imply guilt or self-dislike, feeling that we are somehow dirty, or perhaps that we are knowingly abusing someone. The feeling of self-dislike can be so great that we continue to abuse, or allow ourselves to be abused, as a form of punishment.

Sexually transmitted diseases have become progressively harder to cure. From **syphilis** to **gonorrhea** to **AIDS**, they are a warning that we need to pay attention to how we are using our sexual energy, that we need to bring more respect, both to ourselves and others. The disease creates a space in which we cannot be intimate or have sex, so we have an opportunity to be with ourselves and look at our behaviour. Such diseases are a loud cry that all is not well with our sexual energy and our feelings about what we are doing; that deeper issues of resentment, abuse, fear and self-rejection are being ignored. We are out of flow with the natural energy of our whole being. (See Chapter 15 for more on AIDS.)

19

DEFINING BOUNDARIES
The Skin

THE SKIN, which includes the hair and nails, is one of the largest and most remarkable organs of the body. It is waterproof, washable, elastic, self-mending and tactile. It protects us against water loss and water intake, while allowing us to perspire; it defends us against infection and exposure to foreign substances, and it regulates our temperature.

Through the skin we face the world, and are known by it. The skin flushes with anger or shame, blushes with love or embarrassment, goes white with shock, breaks out in goosebumps in cold or anticipation, or sweats with exertion or fear. Every emotion creates a response in the skin that can be electrically noted. It reflects what food we eat, how much sleep we have, and our alcohol consumption.

The skin is the outermost expression of our innermost being: through it we relate and communicate with others. It represents our outer limitations, within it we are contained and held. It forms a boundary between ourselves and the world, a meeting place of inner and outer. Difficulties with the skin are, therefore, often connected to difficulties with communication, especially if that communication is threatening our boundaries in any way.

Touching passes through those limitations, crossing our boundaries by reaching into our feelings. Touching is the most basic form of communication, transmitting love, tenderness, healing, security, confidence, safety and passion. A baby can die if it is not touched enough, while adults can develop serious mental illness and trauma without human contact, as if they are shrivelling up inside a shell.

Touching is a natural part of intimacy, but physical contact is not always pleasant; it can also trigger a fear of being hurt, or of feeling exposed and vulnerable. A fear of touching shows a deeper fear of sharing ourselves, perhaps due to previous touching that was abusive. There may be feelings of being unclean or ugly, a sense of shame or guilt.

The face is the part of us that meets the world first and on which we are most often judged. We spend an enormous amount of time and money attempting to improve our faces to make them socially acceptable, providing a smooth veneer to hide our feelings behind. Faces can be open or closed, relaxed or tense, trusting or suspicious, happy or sad – the face shows everything that is going on beneath the surface. The more we frown, the more the muscles will take on that furrowed look; the more we smile, the more the face will appear at ease.

Conflicting emotions, self-confidence, self-dislike, inappropriate passions, withheld feelings or anguish – all these are expressed on the face in the form of **blemishes, rashes** or other **skin irritations**. **Very dry skin** implies a withdrawal of emotion, keeping ourselves back so as not to have to deal with communication or feeling. **Oily skin** implies an excess of emotions – often passionate or angry ones – that are not finding release. Each facial blemish is like an inner pain finding form.

Acne

Usually occurring in our adolescence and early twenties, acne represents an eruption of all the conflicting and tormented feelings locked inside. At this time of life it is very hard to feel good about ourselves. Everything we do seems to be either stupid or wrong; there is little self-esteem and much self-dislike. Life appears unfair, as if we are being picked on personally, when in fact it is our own inner torment that is causing us pain.

The confusion involved in moving from childhood to adulthood is enormous. It is a time when we are tentatively discovering who we are as individuals, while powerfully strong sexual urges that have no means of expression are awakening. Fantasies abound, any touch from another person can cause the hormones to leap with desire. Acne reflects the depth of emotion surging through the body – the longing for release finds expression in the eruptions. This is a cry from within to stop attacking ourselves, a plea for us to accept ourselves and find our inner beauty.

Acne Rosacea

Occurring most often in middle-aged women, this condition leads to a reddening of the cheeks and nose due to dilated blood vessels, followed by pimples. Usually associated with poor diet or smoking, alcohol and **cirrhosis of the liver**, it also indicates suppressed anger or resentment – issues connected to the liver energy. As acne rosacea affects the face, it is to do with feeling unnoticed and unacknowledged by others, giving rise to bitterness and frustration.

Athlete's Foot

This itching, cracking and soreness between the toes is caused by a common fungal infection which is easily spread in places such as locker rooms or swimming pools. The toes represent our concern with detail, and in particular with the direction we are going in and what lies ahead. Do you need to deal with some details that are becoming irritating? Is something affecting you, making you sore, or getting under your skin? What is making you crack at the edges? Are you walking in the direction you want to go in?

Boils

Boils are caused by an infection of a hair follicle when resistance is low and bacteria multiply. They indicate an eruption of angry and inflamed emotions, or of incensed thoughts, focused on a partner or parent, or even on ourselves. These feelings may have been fermenting or gathering energy for some time before the boil appears. The emotions are literally boiling over, coming to a head, wanting to burst. Boils on the face tend to indicate that we are feeling angry about something we do not want to face up to or deal with; if they are on the back it is more likely to be an issue that we are trying to hide from. Who is making you boil over? What is making you want to burst out? (See also Chapter 10 for the part affected.)

Bruises

When we hit something and get bruised it implies that we are going in the wrong direction or doing the wrong thing. We are, symbolically, hitting a brick wall. Are you trying to do too much and in the process not looking at what is coming towards you? Are you looking too far ahead, rather than paying attention to the details? Do you keep bumping into the same issues inside yourself? A bruise is sore and tender, it needs comforting. Is this how you feel? Sometimes it gets livid. Are you expressing your anger or keeping it locked inside? Is someone emotionally hitting you? Constant bruising can indicate that we are feeling beaten up by life; it reflects a victim attitude that says we just have to suffer whatever comes. Do you need to take more responsibility for your situation and not allow things to keep punching you down?

Burns

The issues involved here concern our relationship with the world. It implies that we are playing with fire and need to be more attentive, especially to areas of emotional danger as a burn means a loss of our protective cover. Are you feeling particularly vulnerable or defenceless? Are you getting burnt by someone? Small burns are reminders to watch the details, be aware of limitations, be careful not to reach out too quickly without first checking what is there. Larger burns indicate that some very hot emotions – anger, frustration or pain – are burning up inside. Do you feel burnt by your experiences? Burns create tremendous tenderness and often mean there can be no physical contact with anyone else. Do you need time to yourself, time to be alone? Time to heal not just the outer wound but also the inner wounds? (See Chapter 10 for the part affected.)

Callouses and Hard Skin

Areas of hardened and thickened skin indicate that thought patterns – such as fear or prejudice – have become hardened, unmoving or stuck. To be callous is to be hard and unfeeling. A build up of skin deadens our ability to feel and receive input. It is like a protective wall, preventing any trusting or open communication with others. Have you become hardened or insensitive? Closed off from others or from your own tenderness? If the callous is on the feet it indicates that the ground we are standing on has become solid and fixed; there is no allowance for change or movement, or going with the flow. Rather, there is a resistance, an inner stuckness.

Cuts

A cut is like a mental wound, a psychological hurt due to something outside us (as a cut is caused by an external object and not by an internal eruption), or due to our extending and reaching out too far. Are you giving too much? Or reaching beyond your limitations? Cuts affect our powers of protection and weaken our boundaries. Has something or someone broken through your defences? Small cuts may simply be reminders to be aware, to pay attention to detail, to watch how we are being affected psychologically or emotionally by our environment. Are you missing details that are important? Large cuts indicate that we may be feeling cut up about something, cut to pieces or cut off by someone, and this is leaving us feeling unprotected and raw. There is nowhere to hide; our boundaries are exposed. (See also Chapter 10 for the part affected.)

Dermatitis

Dermatitis is a term that covers a wide range of skin irritations caused by stress, **infections** or **allergies**. An irritation implies that something is bothering us, causing the edges of our being to react. Skin problems are a way of keeping the world at a distance. Is someone or something affecting you or getting under your skin? Or are you feeling over-exposed, vulnerable and sensitive?

Eczema indicates an extreme sensitivity to the circumstances and emotions around us. It limits physical contact as if creating a bubble in which we can't be touched. Are there areas of contact and communication that are causing irritation? A fear of intimacy? Are you locking yourself inside for fear of coming out? Are you isolating yourself when really you want to be in contact? Are you being overly sensitive to someone or something?

Flaking or peeling skin implies that our boundaries are thin and insubstantial, easily giving way, indicating that we are easily influenced by others and have little sense of our own identity. It can also mean we are like a snake shedding its skin, getting rid of old ways of being so that the new can emerge, but we are unable to let go, are fearful of release. We need to peel away the old layers of thinking.

A rash implies that we are acting too hastily or that something is really bothering us. Are you taking more risks than you should? Are you jumping to conclusions before you hear the whole story? Is someone making you feel hot or very irritated? Have you done something you are ashamed of and now feel guilty? Or are you feeling particularly allergic to someone or something?

Itching is a scratching on our surface – either something inside is trying to get our attention because it wants to get out, or something on the outside is beginning to irritate us and get under our skin. Itching makes us mad with frustration. What is trying to get out? Does something need to be voiced? Or is someone really bugging you? The act of scratching is an attempt to scratch out the offending cause. Is there something or someone you are trying to get rid of? Scratching may also indicate repressed aggression. Do you really want to hit someone? (See also Chapter 10 for the part affected.)

Melanoma

Skin cancer is on the increase, as the ozone layer develops holes and we are over-exposed to the harmful qualities in the sun's rays. This disease is directly related to the environment, especially in countries like Australia. However, melanoma also occurs in people not exposed to harmful sun rays, where there is a stronger psycho/emotional component.

Melanoma implies that our boundaries are being penetrated. Have you been particularly affected by stress, emotional tension or inner conflict, leaving you feeling unprotected and exposed? There may be issues of self-dislike or a lack of self-care; complying with other people's wishes and not heeding our own needs; or deep-rooted conflict over physical contact and touching. (See also Chapter 15 for more on cancer and Chapter 10 for the part affected.)

Sweating

The sweat glands are part of the body's temperature control system, so when the heat gets turned up we cool the body down with water. **Excessive sweating** usually occurs when our emotions are getting too hot and we need a release – we are steaming up inside with embarrassment, shame, anger or passion. **Cold sweats** are associated with fear, particularly a deep fear of communication or confrontation and with feeling insecure and unprotected. Sweating is also due to exceptional nervousness or shyness, indicating a need to become more relaxed and at ease with ourselves.

Verrucas and Warts

Both caused by a virus, verrucas appear on the feet while warts can appear anywhere. There are two main bodymind connections. One is the feeling of being invaded and having a strong reaction to such an invasion. When a virus takes hold it is like something penetrating our outer layer of protection and this generates feelings of repulsion or disgust – we feel exposed and powerless, as if we are a victim of this other energy. Is something eating away at you? Has something got past your boundaries and is now making itself at home in you? Verrucas dig into the feet and can be quite painful. They can stop us from putting our feet down fully. Is there some situation which is bugging you but you are not doing anything about? Do you need to be firmer or clearer about asserting your needs?

The other aspect is self-dislike or rejection of certain parts – we can feel so negative about a part of ourselves that it becomes a separate, ugly thing. Warts may be due to a belief that we are unlovable or unattractive. Very often the part of the body affected represents strong feelings of shame or guilt that we wish we could hide or cover up. It is necessary to bring love to these areas – to recognise each one as an essential part of our whole being. (See also Chapter 10 for the part affected.)

◆ HAIR ◆

Hair is produced by hair follicles within the skin. A hair actually consists of cells which are pushed up the follicle and harden as they die. The shape of the follicle determines whether our hair is curly or straight. Each hair follicle contains a small muscle which stands the hair upright at times of fright. **Hair growth** can be affected by excess stress and tension which restricts blood flow to the muscles, as well as by lack of exercise which slows the circulation.

Dandruff

Flaking dead skin on the head symbolises an accumulation of old ideas and thought patterns, ways of being that are no longer needed – a layer of dead tissue that we need to let go of. We may think we are not clever enough, or think of ourselves as being 'flaky'; or perhaps we are stuck in behaviour patterns that are limiting our expression and there is a desire to break free. It can also be that too much energy is in the head and we need to come into the body through more exercise, which also increases the circulation and improves skin condition.

◆ NAILS ◆

Nails grow from a layer of cells which, like hair, harden as they die. Our nails reach out into the world so they represent our attention to details – they are often affected when we are going through a time of change and get caught up in major events but miss the smaller issues. They also play a protective role, as they are a version of claws, normally used for grasping or fighting. Very long nails are saying keep clear, keep your distance, although the aggressive potential of long nails is also an invitation to sexuality and passion.

Nail-biting is strongest at times of nervousness, tension or insecurity. It indicates a deep self-dislike as we are biting at ourselves, gnawing away at our own being, as if we are trying to eliminate something. It is often connected with a fear of expressing sexuality or assertiveness; it is a way of limiting any aggressive or sexually dominating tendencies. There may be a deep fear of what would happen if that energy was released. In a child, nail-biting may indicate that family dynamics are limiting the child's full expression of assertiveness, passion or creative communication.

20

GETTING FOCUSED AND TUNING IN
The Eyes and the Ears

THE EYES AND EARS enable us to perceive our world through sight and sound. These sensory impressions can be so affected by trauma that our capacity to see or hear clearly becomes distorted. This is especially so with children. Events such as murder, war or severe accidents, hearing our parents fighting, or being verbally rejected or abused – all these can make us want to stop seeing or hearing, to withdraw our senses, and instead to create a fantasy world inside ourselves. Difficulties to do with sight and sound are, therefore, often linked to repressed emotion, fear, or a rejection of the outside world in preference for our own inner world.

♦ THE EYES ♦

Through the eyes we see or sense others, and we are also seen and known – the eyes are the windows of the soul. They may be empty and lifeless – as if no one is home – or bright, sparkling and lively; they may be half-closed, the inner person hidden from sight, or wide open with nothing to hide; they may be filled with anger or fear; they may appear hard and calculating, or they may be soft and filled with tenderness.

Images created from the nerve impulses are sent to the brain by the retina, so clear sight does not depend on the eyes as much as on having a functioning nervous system. If we do not feel comfortable with what we are seeing our vision may become distorted to make it more acceptable; we may deny or close off from the vision, seeing only what is right in front of us and not what lies ahead, or we may only see what lies further ahead while being blind to the immediate details.

However, we do not just see physically, we also see psychologically and emotionally as demonstrated through the use of such phrases as 'I saw the depth of his feelings', or 'I see your point of view'. To see is to perceive, to sense, feel, comprehend and know. Our perception is invariably coloured by our own feelings; we see the world according to our upbringing, education or religious beliefs. It is rare for two people to perceive a situation in the same way. Sight problems can sometimes be due more to our *perception* of events than to what actually happened.

We have the ability to close our eyes and thus to discriminate between what we see and what we don't see. We can cut out the immediate horrors but eventually we have to open our eyes again. Difficulties with the eyes or with eyesight may revolve around issues of accepting or rejecting what we see, and the emotional effect of what is being perceived.

The most common solution to eyesight problems is to wear glasses. This is sometimes unavoidable, although many children are prescribed glasses without first being taught eye exercises that could greatly improve their sight, while psycho/emotional reasons for poor sight are rarely investigated. Soon we are dependent on the glasses to be able to see clearly.

Glasses provide a place behind which to hide. They not only enable us to hide our own feelings but they also act as a filter to block out the intensity of life. Making the shift to contact lenses can be an enormous emotional challenge, as there is no longer a safety barrier between ourselves and others. Do you use your glasses as a shield? How do you feel when you take them off – defenceless, exposed?

Blindness

Although the loss of sight often has genetic, environmental or disease-related causes – as in **diabetes** – it may also be connected on a psycho/emotional level to the desire to cut off from what we are seeing, when simply closing our eyes is not enough. This may be due to shock or trauma, or prolonged abuse, when we can no longer reconcile ourselves with the world around us. If we cannot see it then we can pretend it is not there. Blindness allows us to avoid what is happening as well as avoiding our own feelings of fear, horror, anger or sadness. Blind people often develop a bright and colourful inner world – much as those who are deaf may do – a fantasy world untouched by external reality.

If your sight is getting dimmer, are there issues you are avoiding looking at? Are you projecting your own images onto people, making them appear different to how they really are? What needs to be brought out into the light of day rather than shut away in the dark – past memories, accumulated shame, a deep fear? Is there something in yourself you do not want to see? Are you creating a fantasy world in preference to the real world around you?

Cataracts

Cataracts cause the lens to become progressively more cloudy and opaque, making the vision blurred. As this is most common in the elderly, it indicates a fear of seeing what lies ahead – the dread of impending helplessness, sickness and loneliness. It may occur when we create a mental image of what will happen in the future and then live in fear of this occurring. Withdrawing behind the cloudiness creates the illusion that nothing is really changing. Cataracts also occur through malnutrition, even in younger people, as we contemplate a future without enough food or shelter, a future devoid of nourishment and nurturing. Cataracts represent the lack of light in our lives.

Conjunctivitis

This is an infection causing weeping and swelling, redness and soreness, indicating an inflamed response to what we are seeing. There is anger, sadness, a build up of conflicting emotions – something we are seeing is giving rise to this outpouring of feelings in our eyes, creating intense irritation and annoyance. This is relieved only by bathing the eye and cleansing the sight, or by closing the eye and closing off from what is being seen. As there is so much liquid around, is there some crying or grieving you need to do? What is making you feel so sore?

Glaucoma

With glaucoma there is a build up of pressure of fluid in the eye due to a blockage of the drainage canals indicating an accumulation of unexpressed emotion. This indicates a resistance or fear of seeing what lies ahead, causing a slow loss of sight until it is reduced to tunnel vision. It is as if the world is narrowing down to only what is right in front of us, while the rest is blurred. This condition is often due to sadness, a build up of unshed tears, or a sense of loss and inability to adapt to change. It is more common in the elderly as they witness changes within themselves or changes beyond their control, and feel sadness at something going that is familiar or comforting. Do you really need to cry? Is there a fear of what lies ahead? A longing for things to be different to how they really are? A desire only to see what is right in front of you and no further?

Hypermetropia or Far-sightedness
Here we are able to see into the distance but what is close up is blurred. This can indicate that the reality around us is not so easy to deal with or accept. It is easier to focus on distant, faraway images, ones that involve imagination and creativity rather than on the details or facts that make up our immediate world. Far-sighted people tend to be more extrovert and active, keeping busy and involved in projects or other people's lives, but they are less likely to take time to look within, to meditate or be reflective. There may be a fear of the present, perhaps due to past abuse or conflict, so the emphasis is on the future. There may also be difficulty in forming close intimate relationships. It is important to look at any resistance we may have to accepting our immediate and intimate reality.

Myopia or Near-sightedness
Myopia is usually due to contracted eye muscles. This contraction may have been caused by witnessing a trauma as a child, followed by a tensing of the eyes in an attempt to block out the vision. With this condition the world immediately in front of us is clear, but the far distance is blurred and hazy. It is as if the sight has been pulled in or retracted, perhaps due to a feeling that the future is insecure or fearful, that it is easier to avoid it by focusing on the present. There may be a tendency to become quite introspective, solitary or shy, or perhaps obsessed with detail. Myopia implies a need to hide within ourselves, often due to fear, or a lack of clear self-image.

Tearfulness
Tears keep our eyes moist and help to protect them from infection or irritation. They are normally triggered by our emotions, so if we do not release those emotions but keep them bottled up inside we are more prone to being infected – or affected – in the eyes. The release of tears helps cleanse and protect the eyes, thus ensuring that our vision does not become blurred; in the same way, releasing our emotions ensures that we stay clear within ourselves. Tears come spontaneously and they make it impossible to hide what we are feeling, whether it be sadness or joy.

Crying is not easy for everyone. If children are told not to cry they learn to suppress their feelings. Boys, in particular, are often told that crying is a sign of weakness, so they grow up being unable to express their real feelings for fear of appearing a sissy. Instead of crying, many will have a **runny nose, hay fever** or **sinusitis** – all ways of releasing the fluids of emotion.

Crying can also be used as an emotional bribe. Children cry unnecessarily if they know it gets them attention, adults cry if it makes others feel sorry for them. It is important to be able to discriminate between genuine tears and superficial ones, or where tears are being used to express a deeper need for affection.

✦ THE EARS ✦

Able to detect minute vibrations in the air, the ear translates those vibrations into electrical impulses that are sent to the brain. We hear words, music, sounds of pleasure, sounds of pain, sounds that give us joy, sounds that make us cry out. Difficulties in the ears are directly connected to our ability to cope with what we are hearing. We cannot close our ears to unpleasant sounds as we can our eyes to unpleasant sights; our only recourse is to become hard of hearing or deaf. The ears also maintain our sense of balance – through them we are able to remain focused and in a state of equilibrium.

Hearing has many aspects. On the one hand it is just a matter of receiving sound and transmitting vibrations to the brain. From another point of view hearing is actually about listening. Being able to listen is quite difficult – our own pain or discomfort may get in the way and stop us from being able to really hear what someone else is saying; or our thoughts may distract our attention from simply being present with another person. We may hear the words but real listening is different – it means hearing the intent, the story behind the words. To listen is to hear with awareness and presence; to receive someone else without judgement means putting our own issues on hold and being fully open and receptive.

It may be that we have never been really heard or listened to. How often were your parents too distracted or busy to listen to your stories, your conflicts? Does 'never mind dear' or 'not now, I'm busy' sound familiar? There is a natural longing to be heard, acknowledged and recognised. The lack of such recognition can lead us to feel locked inside, unable to share, alienated from communication. When someone else really hears us and receives what we are saying there is a tremendous sense of relief, an offloading – we are known. Hence the proliferation of psychotherapists!

Hearing is also about listening to our own inner voice – our own needs and feelings – and responding to these. Sometimes it is easier to talk to a friend or to keep a journal so we can hear our words. Listening inside is as vital as listening outside.

Deafness

There are both genetic and environmental causes for deafness, but a lessening of the ability to hear (from being **hard of hearing** through to **complete deafness**) also implies a withdrawal from communicating or participating in what is being heard. This can occur in response to hearing too much pain and anguish, when what we are hearing becomes overwhelming, or we have heard enough. Or we may be so shut off from ourselves that we cannot open to hearing others – our own issues stand in the way. It may occur when a partner or parent is very dominating or loud; if we witness parents shouting or abusing each other; when we are being made to feel insecure, unsafe or fearful; or if we are constantly told we are worthless, ugly, or a hopeless case.

Difficulties with hearing are a way of cutting ourselves off, not just from other people but also from our own voice. If we cannot hear we do not have to deal with our response to what we have heard – we do not have to experience our own feelings of anger, hurt, rejection, fear of insecurity. We can live in a fantasy world where everything is fine and everyone is happy. Deafness may indicate such anger at what has been heard that it makes us pull back inside ourselves, creating a separation from the outside world.

Normally we cannot separate nice sounds from bad sounds – if we cut out only bad sounds we cut out the good ones too. But psychologically we *can* do this. For instance the elderly often have very selective hearing – they are only able to hear nice things but nothing unpleasant! As we get older we want to stop hearing any demands that are being made on us, or even stop hearing life going on around us, especially if a loved one has died and we can no longer hear that familiar, loving voice. Deafness creates a barrier behind which we can hide without being bothered. We can be left in peace, alone with ourselves.

Fluid in the ear, which blocks sound, indicates an accumulation of feelings. In children a loss of hearing is often associated with emotional and psychological factors so it is important to make sure that the child has a means to express any hidden feelings and fears, perhaps to someone not involved with the immediate family. The child may develop a fantasy world, a secret and private place where the characters are completely different to the ones in normal life.

Earaches and Ear Infections

An ache in the ear is like an ache in the mind or heart – something we are hearing is causing inner anguish or confusion. Children are particularly prone to earache because they do not know how to express their feelings, especially anger or fear. The feelings get bottled up inside, making them want to close their ears, to stop the sound coming in. Earache can also develop if we have been listening to others but feel that no one has been listening in return. Our ears are aching with the woes we have heard, but we are also full of our own issues and need an ear to talk to. Or it may be that we have refused to listen to someone and now feel guilty about closing ourselves to them.

An infection in the ear indicates that what is being heard is affecting us to the point of causing an inflamed or hot reaction. What are you hearing that is making you so angry or enraged? Or is it that no one is listening to you?

Tinnitus

This ringing in the ear is the ears' way of getting our attention, especially if it drowns out all other sounds. It is a reminder to really listen to what is being said, rather than being distracted or unaware. Tinnitus often increases with stress – at times when we are likely to be paying less attention, whether to others or to ourselves and in particular to our own needs. All our energy is focused outwards. The ringing makes us focus inwards, forces us to listen to our own voice, to pay attention to feelings, to what is going on at home.

Loss of Balance

Within the ear is an area called the labyrinth which consists of three semi-circular canals, each at an acute angle to each other. Fluid moving between these three canals indicates to the brain the position of the head and the body, and the angle between the two, in this way maintaining a sense of balance. This keeps us upright, centred and clear in our direction. It is the balance between heaven and earth, between self and other, between inner and outer.

Losing our physical balance is synonymous with losing our sense of dignity and inner security. If this happens we need to look at how balanced our lives are, if there are areas where we are getting unbalanced or unhinged. A stressful situation or emotional trauma may create a loss of balance and an inner dizziness – we don't know in which direction to turn. Losing the ability to discern makes us feel as if the world has been turned upside down. Do you feel unbalanced? Out of order? As if everything is in the wrong place?

21

ALL IN THE MIND
Mental Disorders

THE MEDICAL approach to mental disorder is fraught with confusion over what is a real illness and what is 'only in the mind'. Doctors tend to view illness as real when there are physical characteristics that can be monitored, labelled, or changed with drugs. Illnesses that do not have obvious physical symptoms are not so easy to diagnose, or even to accept as valid. Someone suffering from depression is quite likely to hear a doctor say that there is nothing the matter that a good holiday won't cure. Few doctors are taught how to deal with mental or emotional issues; most tend to believe that such problems are a sign of weakness and we should just pull ourselves together and get on with life.

From a bodymind perspective, *every* illness has a psycho/emotional connection; some are simply more obvious than others. There is no clear separation between what is happening in the mind and what is happening in the body. Both the physical problems that arise and the mental battles that rage within us can be due to a lack of self-acceptance, or a separation from our true nature. Finding a way through these issues means making friends with ourselves and seeing beyond our apparent limitations.

Mental and emotional disorders are real and they are not necessarily cured by medical intervention. Anti-depressants tend to numb *all* our feelings, not just the depressed ones, leaving us feeling half-dead or zombie-like. This is not a cure. Most of the therapies available aim to make us normal according to society's idea of what normal is, although more holistic and sympathetic systems are now emerging that treat the whole person, recognising that each of us is a unique individual with specific needs.

For most mental problems, it is extremely helpful, if not essential, to practise inner conscious relaxation, belly breathing, or breath awareness meditation (see Chapter 5). These techniques not only relax and release inner stress and tension, but they also enable us to see ourselves more objectively and clearly.

Addiction

Addiction covers issues as diverse as alcohol, drugs, smoking, food, sex, sugar, coffee or gambling. In general, addiction tends to arise from a longing for something more, a need to satisfy an inner yearning or pain. Causes may include external pressures such as financial difficulties, emotional traumas, or growing up in a stressful environment with emotional and/or physical abuse. There can be a deep need to hide or obliterate our problems, but this is not necessarily a conscious process. Alcohol makes us feel that everything is fine. Cigarettes enable us to swallow back our feelings. Drugs take us into a different world where we don't have to deal with the realities of this one, as well as giving us a false sense of grandeur. Food replaces the love we crave and smooths over the cracks in our lives. All these numb the pain inside, alter consciousness, or fill an inner emptiness. The substance provides a sense of security and enjoyment that is far easier to deal with than the pain. By not feeling anything we can maintain an illusion of happiness.

But addiction is not necessarily a numb and happy state. Deeper inside is the knowledge that we are destroying ourselves. The craving continues, no matter how much we consume. This gives rise to guilt and shame, leads to depression, or is projected outwards as anger. There is a deep, rarely acknowledged fear of where we are going to end up; a self-dislike, even hate, that eats away at our ability to recover. How can we even begin to love ourselves when we see such desperation acting itself out each day?

If we can recognise the craving, and its underlying causes, then we have a chance to let go of the addiction. But in so doing we inevitably have to confront the problems that the addiction was hiding – to deal with the past abuse or fear of failure – and to begin to heal these issues. Healing addiction is about our ability to accept and make friends with who we are. It is about facing the reality of our feelings rather than running away from them, and bringing that reality into a place of love.

Alzheimer's Disease and Senile Dementia

This is a degeneration of the brain leading to senility, confusion, incoherence and sometimes abusive or violent behaviour, as well as severe memory loss and delusive imaginings. As this mainly tends to develop in the elderly, we need to look at what is happening to that part of our society. For a loss of memory is indicative of losing our history, our roots or past. In the West we treat our old people as a nuisance. Aging is not honoured; retirement is not seen as a time to share one's wisdom with younger generations. Those who loved and cared for us as we grew up are more often than not discarded as having long since served their purpose.

Whether living at home or in a retirement centre, elderly people have invariably gone from a position of power, whether as the main breadwinner or as the matriarchal head of a family, to a position of helplessness or powerlessness and often extreme loneliness. There can be deep fear about financial survival or how to deal with worldly matters. Unable to look after themselves and not knowing how to cope, a once strong and useful person can become weakened and feel worthless or fearful of what lies ahead. Is it surprising that they begin to lose their minds – to become irrational or forgetful?

Senility includes childishness and the need to be looked after like a child. This can indicate a fear of being alone and growing old, a longing to turn back the clock and be irresponsible and cared for again, rather than having to deal with life in its present form. It is a desire to go back to the past, to how things used to be. Alzheimer's disease can include violent behaviour and total lack of cognizance. This implies an altered state of consciousness, a different perception of reality, due to fear of what lies ahead, or in preparation of the transition.

Depression

In most cases of depression there is a range of physical symptoms such as exhaustion, **insomnia, headaches, reduced or excessive appetite** or **constipation**. Depression affects both the body and the mind, creating a tired, lethargic, heavy feeling, a loss of vitality and energy, or **muscular pain**; a hopelessness or sense of not being worthy or good enough; guilt, shame, worry and helplessness. There are undoubtedly hormonal and even environmental causes of depression, as well as psycho/emotional ones.

The inner cause is invariably found in stress from deeply held, unresolved feelings or traumas that get depressed or pushed down, in an attempt to push them away. The word depression comes from the Latin *deprimo*, meaning 'to press down' or 'to press under'. Causes may include pressure from overbearing parents to achieve success, shame arising from sexual abuse, a longing to express violent or aggressive tendencies that turns to guilt, or feelings of worthlessness leading to an inability to cope. It may be due to the loss of a loved one, or a traumatic experience such as war – events that create hopelessness, despair, and loss of purpose in life. Many elderly people are depressed by the thought of what lies ahead – the loneliness of old age and death. Without meaning there is no reason for being. Depression is a way of giving up without actually dying, a desperate and silent cry for help.

Healing is about making friends with ourselves so we can reconnect with spirit, with real purpose, and discover a deeper joy that is not dependent on external circumstances, but arises from within ourselves. Physical movement – such as dance, yoga or exercise – is particularly good for healing depression. As the body moves, so it begins to release the mind. (See Chapter 9 for more on movement.)

Insomnia

Sleep provides us with the means to regenerate and recuperate, but it is also a time when we surrender the ego and have no control. For many this can be terrifying – there is a fear of what will happen without our awareness. For some, insomnia is the accumulation of stress and worry, the mind filled with doubts or fears; for others it is due to a lack of exercise, or too much television, alcohol or caffeine. Sleep is similar to death, so insomnia may be connected to the fear of dying. Surrendering is the opposite of what we have to do during the day when we are faced with competitive work situations, screaming children, or endless traffic. Being able to come back into a sense of ourselves in a relaxed and quiet space can be very difficult.

We cannot control sleep, nor can we make it happen; it has a rhythm of its own that is activated by our letting go. There are important issues of trust here: we need to trust what will happen during the night, that the world will be OK without us, that if we let go nothing will fall apart; trust ourselves and trust others. Deep relaxation (see Chapter 5) is essential, especially before going to bed.

Nervous Breakdown

This is a conflict in ourselves with our darker aspects – the ones we usually repress. If we are unable to deal with our inner fears, guilt, shame, or feelings of victimisation, these aspects can take over our rational, ordinary mind. Due to overwork, stress, or emotional trauma, a nervous breakdown implies a breakdown in communication within ourselves. The pressure or demands of life have pushed us to a place where we snap. There is a psycho/emotional breaking apart, leading to irrational behaviour or deep **depression,** sadness and fragility; we may become irresponsible, withdrawn or hyperactive. Everyday events become impossible to deal with and our normal perception begins to crumble, we can no longer make sense of our world. There seems to be nothing to hold onto, nothing solid we can relate to. The usual means of communication becomes confused.

A nervous breakdown is a loud cry for help. It can also be a prelude to spiritual transformation, a breaking down prior to a breaking through. A nervous breakdown destroys all our normal ways of seeing things or even thinking about things – all the old patterns are gone. In their place, as healing occurs, can come a deeper awareness, more meaningful priorities, and a stronger connection to spirit. During this time it is important to stay grounded. Dance, exercise, or physical activity is vital.

Nervousness and Anxiety

Being nervous to an extreme level indicates a lack of contact with the inner self. Lacking self-esteem, self-respect or even self-awareness, we are not grounded in our own being. This creates a nervous fear of attack from others, a wariness that the world is not a safe place to be, an apprehension that may have no real cause. We are more likely to suffer from **muscle tension, stiffness, eating disorders, heart palpitation, excessive sweating** and **headaches**. Extreme nervousness is often connected to severe stress and anxiety about failure or loss. Spending time getting to know ourselves, especially developing our confidence and self-respect, and learning how to relax (see Chapter 5), are essential.

Panic Attacks

Panic attacks occur when our strength or ability to cope becomes undermined. Fear overrides all sense of balance or reason and we can no longer see that the fear is irrational; it simply dominates our entire psyche. Some sufferers cannot even leave their homes for fear. This is due to feelings of worthlessness, helplessness and vulnerability; or to an increase in external demands and pressures, stimulating fear and powerlessness. We slowly lose touch with our own understanding and become more dependent on what society projects as real. All perspective is lost, creating fertile ground for fear to develop. Panic attacks occur when fear takes over. Deep breathing and relaxation (see Chapter 5) are essential, as is being grounded in our bodies through movement or exercise.

22

ENERGY CENTRES
The Chakra System

THERE ARE seven major energy centres in the body, located at specific areas in the spinal column. These are known as chakras. They are levels of consciousness that influence our perception of reality; they also connect the physical with the metaphysical, each chakra influencing the health of the organs and limbs within its area. Chakras are like energy gateways within our being, through which we can gain access to ever greater states of consciousness. Although each chakra is described separately, they work together vibrationally, the energy flowing freely between each one. It is our greed, fear and lack of self-love that will block or limit the flow of this energy.

The chakras may be represented as a wheel or mandala, by a specific colour or sound, or as a lotus flower. The lotus arises from the mud, through the water, to emerge in the light; as such it symbolises our own growth from the realms of darkness and ignorance to the awakened state of enlightenment. Beginning below the base of the spine and moving upwards to the top of the head, the chakras reflect this movement from the more instinctive, self-centred behaviour, through the exertion of the ego, to ever higher states of compassion and wisdom.

There is an enormous wealth of understanding about this great Indian tantric system. Here we are primarily concerned with the bodymind connection of each chakra.

♦ MOOLADHARA – ROOT CHAKRA ♦

The first chakra is located at the perineum, halfway between the anus and the genitals. Here we find our most basic and instinctive

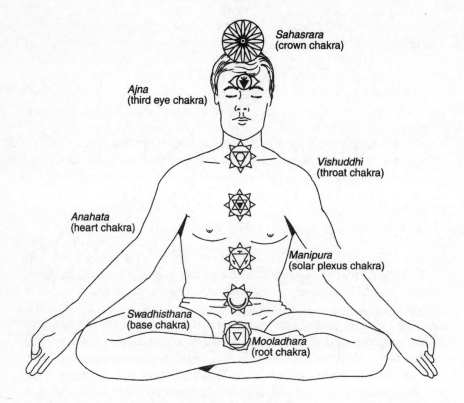

Sahasrara
(crown chakra)

Ajna
(third eye chakra)

Vishuddhi
(throat chakra)

Anahata
(heart chakra)

Manipura
(solar plexus chakra)

Swadhisthana
(base chakra)

Mooladhara
(root chakra)

The Chakra System

qualities of survival and self-protection. This chakra is connected to our history and ancestral energy – the sense of belonging to a particular family and having a valid place in the world. When this chakra is stimulated and awakened we meet survival challenges with optimism and creativity. Our attitude will be one of trust in the world and acceptance of others. We will feel grounded or 'rooted', with a strong desire for life. If the energy is inactive then we will cower in the face of difficulties and rely on others to solve our problems; we will fear being able to provide, whether financially or emotionally. There will be suspicion, paranoia and personal greed – the 'I come first' attitude. There may also be a fear of not belonging, of having no safety or support, even of being suicidal.

The attitudes we hold towards ourselves, our families, and our ability to survive are all shown in the way we walk, the posture of the spine, the way we hold our head, areas where we are tight or stiff. The physical connections to this chakra are found in the skeletal and muscular systems, particularly in the back, pelvis and legs, as seen in **back pain** or **sciatica**. These areas are all related to our ability to stand our ground, to feel safe and rooted in the world.

This chakra is also related to issues of stress and fear that are found in the kidneys and adrenal glands. This can cause **digestive** or **bowel problems** such as **irritable bowel syndrome** or **constipation**. These issues are to do with trust, particularly in trusting that the world is not a threatening place and that it will support us. This chakra is related to all forms of creativity and manifestation – where there is no ground or the soil is weak, then creation cannot flourish. When we are well rooted and established within ourselves, then the flower within is free to blossom.

The practice of yoga is particularly important for opening this chakra as it enables a release of any tension in the spine.

✦ SWADHISTHANA – BASE CHAKRA ✦

The second chakra is located at the base of the spine. It is connected to issues of desire, sexuality and reproduction, as well as financial issues. Having secured our ground, we now need to deal with the details of living. This covers a vast area; it determines how we feel about intimacy, communication, sharing, relating, birthing and parenting, money and the world of exchange, trade or business.

As we emerge out of the realm of survival in the first chakra, the energy is that of continuation of the species and of exploring pleasure, especially sexual desire. However, desire can lead to greed and the longing for more, in the belief that more will bring greater pleasure. We forget how intricately pleasure is linked to pain. Sexual energy is often mishandled or abused, leading to guilt, shame, confusion, deceit and relationship breakdown; conflict over sexual issues can give rise to problems in the genital organs and related areas.

Issues in this chakra also revolve around feeling inadequate financially, ie poverty consciousness, or being unable to cope with the business world. There may be feelings of being impoverished compared to others, of devaluing ourselves and losing self-esteem.

This chakra can influence all or part of the reproductive organs, including menstrual issues, menopause, the lower back, the bladder and elimination. It also relates to the lower belly, the core of our inner strength and emotional groundedness. If the potential of the second chakra is undeveloped it will give rise to excess **exhaustion, low appetite, low sexual desire**, feelings of helplessness, or an inability to cope. When it is fully developed it will give rise to us feeling balanced and at ease with our sexuality, in touch with our intuition and gut feelings, and able to function responsibly in the material world.

Dancing – especially free dance – is very good for stimulating the second chakra.

♦ MANIPURA – SOLAR PLEXUS ♦ CHAKRA

The third chakra is located in the spine, behind the navel. Emerging out of survival and procreation, this is where the individuation process starts – the development of the ego, self-consciousness and power. This is where we assimilate information and digest our world, where we manifest basic fears and desires, such as rage or the need for control. The energetic connection is to the digestive system, which includes **stomach problems** and **eating disorders** such as **anorexia** or **obesity, liver problems**, or **addictions** – issues of fear and control.

As this chakra is associated to power, it relates directly to our feelings about ourselves, in particular feelings of being worthy, valuable, likeable and confident. When the third chakra is unawakened it gives rise to a false sense of power, with delusions of grandeur that cloud our perception. It includes a fear of power or authority, of being intimidated, fear of trusting others or even ourselves, or a fear of responsibility. There is a weak sense of ourselves; we need to be told what to do and need authority in order to act, rather than being able to take the initiative for ourselves. This weak self-image can also manifest in a need to dominate others.

This area has tremendous energy which, used positively, gives a purpose and direction to life. It is the energy of politicians and teachers, of entertainers and athletes, of people who want to get ahead – sometimes at any cost. It is also the seat of intuition, where we 'feel something in our guts'. Taken further, this is the area of psychic awareness. However, this energy can be misused to exploit and manipulate others, as seen in dictators or those who lust for power, such as Hitler or Stalin.

The process of becoming an individual is one of finding our own power. This is not a power over others but is our inner authority and emotional strength. An awakened third chakra is where we have a healthy, positive and confident sense of ourselves.

Breathing and concentration techniques are important for this chakra, as they release tension in the solar plexus.

♦ ANAHATA – HEART CHAKRA♦

The fourth chakra is located in the spine, directly behind the centre of the chest. Moving from the development of the individual at the third chakra, this is where we evolve into a truly loving person by opening our hearts. Is is where the deeper qualities of service and compassion develop.

An unawakened heart chakra is seen in a closed or cold heart, unable to warm to others or even to truly care about ourselves. Everything is either sensual and sexual, or rational, logical and intellectual, but the inner feeling is missing, there is a lack of depth and warmth. There may be feelings of being unlovable, a fear of loving, or a holding on to past pain – a lack of forgiveness creating untold misery; there may be bitterness, jealousy or deep sorrow. Instead of love we find aggression and guilt, hard-heartedness, prejudice or bitterness.

The heart chakra is associated with the thymus gland, heart and lungs. Conflicts manifest in **breathing difficulties, asthma, bronchitis** or **pneumonia**, or in **heart conditions** such as **angina,** or **circulatory problems**. These are issues to do with embracing life for ourselves, rather than being dependent on others, and unconditionally loving both ourselves and others.

An open heart chakra is an infinite source of love and compassion – the more the heart opens, the more love fills our being. This is about awakening to a real love for ourselves, to seeing the true beauty that lies within, and to developing profound loving kindness for all beings.

Meditations that focus on the development of loving kindness and forgiveness stimulate an opening of this chakra.

♦ VISHUDDHI – THROAT CHAKRA ♦

The fifth chakra is located in the neck, directly behind the throat. From an awareness of others and the development of loving kindness, we move into expressing that love – this is the awakening of the throat centre so that our true voice may be heard.

The fifth chakra is energetically associated to the throat and mouth, and with expression and assimilation. The throat is both the entrance to our whole being, through which we take in nourishment, as well as the exit point for our feelings. A throat chakra that is not activated will restrict that flow of energy, hindering our ability to receive love or express ourselves. We will lie, cheat, or insult. It may feel as if we have no voice, that we are not being heard, or perhaps we are fearful of speaking up for ourselves. This is seen in all **throat, mouth and teeth problems**, also **neck and jaw trouble**, and in **addictive behaviour** such as **over-eating**.

The throat chakra forms a bridge between the head and the body, the mind and the heart. When it is activated it energetically opens our whole being, enabling clear communication, a flowing of energy between the mind and the heart. Then there is a balance of wisdom and compassion, of thought and feeling, of giving and receiving. When this chakra is open we can transform negative to positive, poison to nectar, and we can speak our truth. Chanting and singing will enable the true voice within to be freed.

◆ AJNA – THIRD EYE CHAKRA ◆

The sixth chakra is located behind the centre of the eyebrows. Symbolised as a third eye, this chakra is the eye of wisdom that looks from within and sees the truth. It is associated with the mind and the development of higher consciousness, and in particular with the development of perception and intuition. Where the ego was so predominant in the solar plexus, here the ego is dissolving as consciousness expands beyond the individual self. This is the eye that sees through the limitations of human existence to the transcendent wisdom of the enlightened mind. Insight is the key here – insight into the nature of all things.

An awakened third eye chakra is seen in a lack of self-awareness or any sense of higher consciousness. There will be a fear of the inner self or anything introspective or spiritual, leading to **nervous behaviour, paranoia** or distorted images of reality. This results in rigid, fixed or closed thinking patterns and attitudes, and a resistance to new or different ideas, especially spiritual ones. If our attitudes are negative, critical or prejudiced, then they are reflected in every part of the body. This chakra affects the nerves, the senses and the immune system. **Brain disorders, headaches** and **senility** can all result.

The balance of head and heart is essential for complete awakening. The wisdom of the mind gives direction to the compassion of the heart, just as compasion gives warmth and love to the clarity of insight. One without the other is incomplete – insight without feeling, or mercy without discrimination.

It is also necessary to distinguish between the mental energy that can lock us into the intellectual levels, and truly spiritual energy that opens us to the brilliance within. Through the third eye chakra we have the ability to penetrate into the nature of reality and to discover the truth within ourselves. This is not an intellectual pursuit.

Both creative visualisation and meditation encourage the third eye to open.

◆ SAHASRARA – CROWN CHAKRA◆

The seventh chakra is located at the top of the head and is seen as the penultimate human experience, where the 'I' dissolves into cosmic consciousness. Personal desires are purified and all activity becomes selfless. This is not so much the end of the journey as the beginning of the real journey – the emergence of the true human. Rarely is anyone evolved to this level as it means the complete dissolution of the ego and a rebirth into our Higher Self.

When this chakra is not awakened then it is reflected in a strong ego and a resistance to spiritual growth. Because this is the final awakening, the resistance is greater. This can lead to **depression** and sadness, for life seems to have no meaning. It takes tremendous commitment and trust to maintain the journey. Most important is the development of faith, whether in an external God, guru, or the divinity within ourselves. Without faith there is an emptiness, a vacuum or spiritual void. The energy associated with this chakra is that of surrender – the full surrendering of the ego – the individual self – to the divine self that is limitless and all embracing. It is associated to the whole physical body as this chakra affects every aspect of our being: physical concerns are whole body ones connected to issues of losing purpose and direction.

Silent meditation is the key to *Sahasrara* (enlightenment). As we enter into the spaciousness between thoughts we activate the potential for complete awakening.

RESOURCES

Bibliography

Achterberg, Dossey & Kolkmeier, *Rituals of Healing*, Bantam, 1994

Akong Rinpoche, Dharma-Ayra, *Taming the Tiger*, Rider, 1995

Ambika, *Ambika's Guide to Healing and Wholeness*, Piatkus, 1993

Ball, Dr. John, *Understanding Disease*, C.W. Daniel, 1993

Barasch, Marc Ian, *The Healing Path*, Arkana/Penguin, 1994

Benson, Herbert, *The Wellness Book*, Simon & Schuster, 1993

Borysenko, Joan, *Minding the Body, Mending the Mind*, Bantam, 1988

Borysenko, Joan, *Guilt is the Teacher, Love is the Lesson*, HarperCollins, 1990

Button, John & Bloom, William, *The Seeker's Guide*, Aquarian, 1992

Chopra, Deepak, *Ageless Body, Timeless Mind*, Rider, 1993

Cooper, Diana, *Transform Your Life*, Piatkus, 1993

Cowmeadow, Oliver, *The Art of Shiatsu*, Element, 1992

Dethlefsen, Thorwald, *The Healing Power of Illness*, Element, 1990

Dossey, Larry, *Healing Breakthroughs*, Piatkus, 1993

Dytchwald, Ken, *Bodymind*, Tarcher/Putnam, 1977

Edwards, Gill, *Stepping Into the Magic*, Piatkus, 1993

Fields, Rick & Editors, *Chop Wood, Carry Water*, Tarcher, 1984

Frawley, David, *Ayurvedic Healing*, Passage Press, 1989

Goldman, Jonathan, *Healing Sounds*, Element, 1992

Graham, Helen, *A Picture of Health*, Piatkus, 1995

Hanh, Thich Nhat, *The Miracle of Mindfulness*, Rider, 1991

Hay, Louise, *You Can Heal Your Life*, Eden Grove, 1984

Hoberman Levine, Barbara, *Your Body Believes Every Word You Say*, Aslan, 1991

Holden, Robert, *Laughter, The Best Medicine*, Thorsons, 1993

Kabat-Zinn, Jon, *Full Catastrophe Living*, Delta, 1990

Kabat-Zinn, Jon, *Mindfulness Meditation*, Piatkus, 1994

Kaptchuk, Ted, *The Web That Has No Weaver*, Rider, 1983

Levine, Stephen, *Healing Into Life and Death*, Gateway, 1989

Levine, Stephen, *Guided Meditations, Explorations and Healings*, Gateway, 1993

Locke, Steven & Colligan, Douglas, *The Healer Within*, Signet 1986

Lowen, Alexander, *Bioenergetics*, Penguin, 1975
MacRitchie, James, *Chgi Kung*, Element, 1993
Montague, Dr. Ashley, *Touching*, Columbia University Press, 1971
Morrison, Judith H., *The Book of Ayurveda*, Gaia, 1995
Ornish, Dean, M.D., *Stress, Diet and Your Heart*, Penguin, 1984
Page, Christine, *Frontiers of Health*, C.W. Daniel, 1992
Pearsall, Paul, *Super Immunity*, Fawcett Gold Medal, 1987
Proto, Louis, *Self-Healing*, Piatkus, 1990
Regan, Georgina & Shapiro, Debbie, *The Healer's Hand Book*, Element, 1988
Saint-Pierre, Gaston & Shapiro, Debbie, *The Metamorphic Technique*, Element, 1982
Shapiro, Debbie, *The Bodymind Workbook*, Element, 1990
Shapiro, Eddie, *Inner Conscious Relaxation*, Element, 1990
Shapiro, Eddie & Debbie, *Out Of Your Mind – The Only Place To Be!*, Element, 1992
Shapiro, Eddie & Debbie, *The Way Ahead*, Element, 1992
Shapiro, Eddie & Debbie, *A Time For Healing*, Piatkus, 1994
Shealy, Norman, *The Self-Healing Workbook*, Element, 1993
Shealy, Norman & Myss, Caroline, *The Creation of Health*, Stillpoint, 1988
Siegel, Bernie, *Peace, Love and Healing*, Harper & Row, 1989
Tillich, Paul, *The Meaning of Health*, North Atlantic Press, 1982
White, Ruth, *Working With Your Chakras*, Piatkus, 1993
Wilber, Ken, *Grace and Grit*, Shambhala, 1991
Williamson, Marianne, *A Return to Love*, HarperCollins, 1992

Debbie & Eddie Shapiro

The relaxation and meditation practices mentioned in this book are available on cassette tape. For a list of tapes and a schedule of workshops with Debbie and Eddie Shapiro, please write to them c/o Piatkus Books, 5 Windmill Street, London W1P 1HF.

INDEX